Sophistication

A Literary and Cultural History

Sophistication

A Literary and Cultural History

FAYE HAMMILL

LIVERPOOL UNIVERSITY PRESS

First published 2010 by
Liverpool University Press
4 Cambridge Street
Liverpool
L69 7ZU

British Library Cataloguing-in-Publication Data
A British Library CIP Record is available

ISBN 978 1 84631 232 8 cased

Typeset in Borges with Museo display by Koinonia, Bury
Printed and bound by Bell and Bain Ltd, Glasgow

Contents

List of illustrations

Acknowledgements

Very particular thanks are due to Anthony Cond of Liverpool University Press. His enthusiasm for my initial idea led me to begin work in earnest on the project, and I have benefited enormously from his encouragement and support throughout. I also found the suggestions in the reader's report on the manuscript extremely astute and constructive. The professionalism and skill of the other staff at Liverpool University Press also deserve acknowledgement, and I am especially grateful to the Production Manager, Andrew Kirk.

Many thanks, also, to my colleagues at the University of Strathclyde, and previously at Cardiff University, for various kinds of assistance and enthusiasm. In particular, the head of department at Strathclyde, Jonathan Hope, was very supportive while I was finishing this book, and Martin Montgomery offered lucid explanations about collocation and semantic prosody. My discussion of nostalgia owes much to the deepened understanding I gained from collaborating with four colleagues at Strathclyde – Sarah Edwards, Kathy Hamilton, Beverly Wagner and Juliette Wilson – on an ESRC seminar series, 'Nostalgia in the 21st Century'.

I am grateful to David Duff for extremely helpful suggestions about my first chapter, and for recommending 'Brummelliana', and to David Francis Taylor, creator of an excellent website on Sheridan, for supplying me with a copy of Hunt's obituary of Sheridan. Also to Andrew McNeillie, Louise Harrington and Rick Rylance for numerous enriching discussions of sophistication, and to Mary Grover and Erica Brown for productive collaborations through the AHRC Middlebrow Network, which have substantially informed my third chapter. I also owe thanks to Sharon Hamilton for stimulating my interest in smart magazines, Rob Gossedge for introducing me to *Zuleika Dobson* and *The Age of*

Acknowledgements

Scandal, Esme Miskimmin for giving me *A Guide to Elegance*, and Patrick Hart for checking my section on *The Leopard*.

I am especially grateful to Will Straw for commenting on a draft of the second chapter, and for his invitation to present a paper at the Media@McGill research centre in Montreal. The audience there provided me with most useful ideas and encouragement (thanks particularly to Allan Hepburn and Robin Feenstra). I also appreciated invitations to present my work on sophistication at the University of Liverpool and at Sheffield Hallam University, where, again, I received valuable feedback.

Jonathan Goldman, Aaron Jaffe and Karen Leick provided most valuable comments on my work on *Vanity Fair*.

Above all, I am grateful to my husband, Jonathan Percy, for endless support and unfailing interest during the writing of this book, for various wise suggestions, and for invaluable assistance with correcting the final manuscript.

Introduction:
Reading sophistication

'If it is the privilege of wisdom,' said M. Verneuil, 'to look beyond happiness, I own I had rather be without it. When we observe the English, their laws, writings, and conversation, and at the same time mark their countenances, manners, and the frequency of suicide among them, we are apt to believe that wisdom and happiness are incompatible. If, on the other hand, we turn to their neighbours, the French, and see their wretched policy, their sparkling, but sophistical discourse, frivolous occupations, and, withal, their gay animated air, we shall be compelled to acknowledge that happiness and folly too often dwell together.'
– Ann Radcliffe, The Romance of the Forest, 1791 (269)

There is nothing smarter than for a finely gowned, handsome woman to become cockeyed at a large formal party. A vulgarian would not be able to get away with it. In such situations, vulgar people go to pieces and scream or hurt somebody. It takes that *je ne sais quoi* which we call sophistication for a woman to be magnificent in a drawing room when her faculties have departed but she herself has not yet gone home. [...] Sophistication might be described as the ability to cope gracefully with a situation involving the presence of a formidable menace to one's poise and prestige.
– 'Answers-to-Hard-Questions Department', The New Yorker, 1930[1]

There is a remarkable distance between sophistication in Ann Radcliffe and sophistication in *The New Yorker*. Disparaged and distrusted in 1791, it is, by 1930, something to aspire to. By what mysterious process did this change occur? Somewhere in the nineteenth century, it appears, the earlier meanings of sophistication – 'falsification', 'specious fallacy', 'disingenuous alteration or perversion', 'adulteration', according to the *Oxford English Dictionary* – were superseded by quite other definitions: 'worldly wisdom or experience, subtlety,

---

1 Vermilye 17–18. 'Wayne Van R. Vermilye' is a pseudonym for James Thurber. *The New Yorker* was largely staff-written in its early years, so many signatures are pseudonyms.

discrimination, refinement'. The *OED* tidily dates this shift to 1850. But the change, of course, was neither sudden nor complete. Indeed, the earlier and the more modern meanings interpenetrate – a closer reading of the quoted passages reveals that 'sophistication' is associated with very similar qualities in the two texts; it is just that Radcliffe rejects those qualities while James Thurber (the author of the 1930 editorial) embraces them.

To begin with, sophistication is connected with Frenchness in both extracts, as indeed it is in many Anglophone literary texts and cultural discourses over the whole period from the eighteenth century to the present. Radcliffe qualifies her rather incendiary remarks about the French – as well she might in the dangerous atmosphere of 1791 – by adding a footnote reminding the reader that this is a historical novel: 'It must be remembered that this was said in the seventeenth century' (269). But Monsieur Verneuil's speech actually expresses a view of the French which was current in late *eighteenth*-century England: he acknowledges the allure of French hedonism and charm (which is also part of the allure of *The Romance of the Forest*) but simultaneously berates them as threats to solid English virtues.[2] The supposed 'vices' of the French, as listed by Radcliffe, are precisely the qualities which *The New Yorker*'s audience was assumed to admire: frivolity, animation and sparkling discourse. Indeed, the founding editor, Harold Ross, wrote in his prospectus for the new magazine: 'Its general tenor will be one of gaiety, wit and satire'.[3] It is therefore unsurprising that *The New Yorker* uses a French phrase, *'je ne sais quoi'*, to convey both the sophistication of the woman described and the indefinability of sophistication itself. 'Sophistication' eludes definition, and yet provocatively invites us to pursue, capture and possess it.

In fact, the editorial in *The New Yorker* is a rare example of an explicit definition, and even this is very tongue-in-cheek, and occurs in the context of an attempt to explain to a rather dim correspondent exactly what makes a good cartoon for *The New Yorker*. Thurber says that he only wants sophisticated cartoons, but there's an air of weariness about his explanation which suggests that anyone who needs to enquire about this will never actually be able to contribute an acceptable drawing. When he quotes an example of a vulgar caption, he says 'If you can't see why that is out, we could never tell you' (Vermilye 18). The exclusionary rhetorical practices of sophistication, which are clearly in operation in the *New Yorker* editorial, are explained by Leland

2   Compare Smollett's *Travels Through France and Italy* (1766), which describes the French as 'a giddy people, engaged in the most frivolous pursuits' and emphasises their 'volatility, prattle, and fondness for bon mots' (57, 45). This is similar to accounts given in other contemporary travel narratives.

3   Harold Ross. Prospectus for *The New Yorker. The New Yorker* Records. 1924, Box 1. Manuscripts and Archives Division. The New York Public Library. Typescript page 1. Quoted in Burstein 238.

Monk in his review of Joseph Litvak's book *Strange Gourmets: Sophistication, Theory and the Novel* (1997):

> What is sophistication? Most of the usual answers to this question invalidate in advance any claim the asker might have to its enjoyment, along the lines of 'if you have to ask, you can't afford it.' If you need the codes spelled out for you, you don't know how the codes work. If you want to know how to do it, you obviously don't understand the meaning of *savoir faire*. Any desire you evince to join the cool club of those-in-the-know automatically disqualifies you from admission. (Monk 257)

Again, a French phrase is used to evoke sophistication, and again, the effect is further mystification. The French words supplement the inadequate English in which sophistication can never quite be described. Since it cannot even be described, it would seem evident – as Monk observes – that it cannot be taught or learned either, and that it can only be recognised by someone who already possesses it. Yet at the same time, and paradoxically, such a person would usually be imagined as educated, culturally aware, fashionable and self-conscious, and all of these things require deliberate effort. This tension is legible in many texts which propose that sophistication is the property of a distinguished elite, and yet covertly offer an education in sophistication: smart magazines furnish prime examples, as do certain kinds of lifestyle guidebooks.

A similar tension appears in some literary texts. It does not seem immediately obvious that a novel could teach sophistication in the way that an issue of *The New Yorker* or *Vanity Fair* might do. But a novel which addresses an ostensibly sophisticated audience – often by means of positioning the reader as much more knowing than the innocent protagonist – may, while dramatising that protagonist's education, also present lessons in manners and models of successful and unsuccessful social behaviour. This happens in, say, Austen's *Northanger Abbey* (1818), in which we may laugh at Catherine's naivety but learn from Henry's stylish methods. Joseph Litvak proposes that readers – especially middle-class readers – turn to fiction 'to learn the sophisticated art of operating, and of operating on, other people's languages' (14). The appeal of Jane Austen, for instance, Litvak suggests, 'has to do, not with some collective longing for a lost gentility, but rather with a persistent, perhaps inexhaustible, middle-class desire for instruction in the hermeneutics of social performance' (15). This desire for instruction becomes comically literal in Daisy Ashford's *The Young Visiters*, written in 1890, in which the low-born Mr Salteena goes to stay in some special 'compartments' in the Crystal Palace, designed for the training of those 'who have got something funny in their family and who want to be less mere' (35, 20). Aristocrats live in Ashford's Crystal Palace at the expense of the *nouveaux riches*, who pay handsomely for the privilege of mixing with those they wish to imitate.

Even though it can be helpful to read literary narratives of sophistication alongside versions presented in other cultural texts, there remains a key difference: magazines and lifestyle guidebooks focus on sophistication in the context of fashion (whether in dresses, etiquette or reading choices), while novels and plays tend to understand sophistication primarily in relation to morality and values. In literary texts, sophistication may take visible form through clothing or manners, but is nearly always revealed, in the end, as a fundamental attitude to life rather than simply a style of self-presentation. It may range from a harmless – indeed, healthy – determination to enjoy life and refuse stifling convention to a dangerous inversion of moral codes and a total self-absorption. In its relation to morality, sophistication is often associated with a degree of hedonism, an unshockable attitude in sexual matters, a distrust of bourgeois values, open-handedness shading into extravagance, and a focus on the pleasure of the moment. It is usually opposed to sexual continence, thrift, productiveness and the work ethic. Its politics are thus potentially subversive, but on the other hand, its association with social aspiration has more conservative connotations, and the characteristic detachment of the sophisticate often appears to empty his or her actions and attitudes of political content.

The reason why any definition of sophistication must remain provisional is explained by Mark Backman:

> At any moment in time, the standards of sophistication can be fixed against the shifting background of social development. Thus, manners and attitudes considered sophisticated fifty years ago appear quaint and precious to us today. Sophistication as a state of being is always at war with sophistication as a process of becoming. (5–6)

Similarly, Jessica Burstein notes: 'Like the dynamic of fashion, sophistication works by relentlessly defining itself against its immediate past, or immediate context' (234). As an example, she cites Dorothy Parker's theatre reviews for *The New Yorker* and *Vanity Fair*, in which she 'distinguishes herself as *uncommon* by ironically parading her tendency to weep. This activity is distinctive precisely because of its context, the urbane and critical milieu of the Algonquin Round Table' (234). Burstein describes this move, which Parker used repeatedly, as 'the ne plus ultra of sophistication by virtue of disdaining it', adding: 'The logic is simple: if everyone else does it, I don't' (235). This concept of sophistication as entirely relational is illuminating and helps explain why sophistication is hard to define and why reading sophistication can lead one into so many intriguing contradictions.

This book is a study of sophistication, literature and modernity. It traces the history of sophistication over the period from the eighteenth century to the present, focusing primarily on the way sophistication has been inscribed into literary texts, but referring also to periodicals, music, film and visual culture. By means of close readings, my book explores a range of aspects of its subject. First, I trace shifts in the meaning of the word 'sophistication' over time, and examine its connections with adjacent and opposite terms. Second, I analyse the politics of sophistication, especially in relation to class, taste and cultural hierarchy, and also in relation to gender and sexuality.[4] A third topic is the tension between nostalgia and modernness in the discourses and imagery of sophistication, and a fourth is the geography of sophistication, particularly in terms of urban/rural dynamics and cosmopolitanism. Lastly, I consider the ways in which narratives and dramas construct and address sophisticated readers and audiences.

The century from the 1860s to the 1960s forms the heart of this study, since this was the period when the definition of 'sophistication' was most contested, and when its newer meaning as a desirable quality was evolved and elaborated. But the discussion also extends backwards to explore the eighteenth-century origins of the modern figure of the sophisticate, and forwards to survey the varieties of sophistication which operate in contemporary culture. The remaining three sections of this introduction examine the development of the word 'sophistication', outline the critical and theoretical contexts for my research, and explain the structure and scope of the book.

The word

I am interested in the changing meanings of the word 'sophistication' and the discursive battles about it which are played out in a variety of literary and cultural texts. My discussion therefore compares references to sophistication occurring in a range of contexts and periods, but this is not the whole of my approach. If it were, many aspects of the history of sophistication would remain submerged, because it is often called by other names, or evident only in the silences of a text. In eighteenth-century texts, the word itself was exclusively pejorative, while the concept which we might now call sophistication began to be elaborated through combinations of other words, and in the gaps between them. 'Refinement', 'subtlety', 'elegance', 'sensibility', 'taste' and 'gusto' are among the terms I pay attention to in my first chapter; all these recur in later periods, in fresh relationships to the increasingly complex notion of sophistication. In the nineteenth century, the moral valency of 'sophistication' was particularly uncertain, as it hovered between the older meaning of disingenuousness or adulteration and the incipient newer sense of worldly wisdom and

---

4   The racial politics of sophistication, which I mention at certain points, would repay detailed further study.

discrimination. It actually occurs, in fiction from this era, much less frequently than 'unsophistication', which can function as a term of (sometimes slightly condescending) praise or, occasionally, as a criticism. In the twentieth century the word 'sophistication' was, with growing frequency, used to convey approbation or admiration. In my Conclusion, I propose possible reasons – derived from my close readings – for this basic shift in meaning.

Both the disparaged and the desirable aspects of sophistication may be traced back to the roots of the term in ancient Greek culture: like 'philosopher', it derives from the words for wisdom and wise, 'sophia' and 'sophos'. 'Sophia' was at first a spiritual quality, a special kind of insight possessed by prophets or poets, but subsequently became associated more with knowledge and learning. From this came the name 'Sophist', describing a set of itinerant Greek educators of the fifth century BCE who gave lectures on rhetoric for a fee, and emphasised individualism and the importance of self-presentation. They did not usually teach philosophy (with occasional exceptions, notably Protagoras), but were nevertheless considered rivals to the centres of education established by Plato and Aristotle who, confusingly, were also referred to by the public as 'sophists', meaning something like 'professors'. Resistance to the itinerant Sophists centred on their preparedness to argue both sides of a question without committing themselves to either, and also on their moral relativism and supposition that the human is the arbiter of his own fate (see Urmson). The resulting term 'sophistry', referring to disingenuous reasoning, has maintained a stable meaning from medieval through to modern English. Part of the anxiety surrounding 'sophistication' derives from its continuing association with 'sophistry'. Even in the twentieth century, traces of the older meanings of 'sophistication' persist in modern usage of the term.

Litvak's statement that 'the *Oxford English Dictionary* lists not a single "positive" definition of the term *sophistication*' (4) is, however, inaccurate. One of the definitions is 'worldly wisdom or experience, subtlety, discrimination, refinement', which should certainly be classed as 'positive'. Even in earlier periods, 'discrimination' and 'refinement' had largely positive connotations, though 'subtlety' has undergone a very similar shift to 'sophistication', moving from 'craftiness, cunning, guile, treachery' towards 'fineness or delicacy of nature' and 'delicate or keen perception of fine distinctions'. It is true, though, that the *OED* does not quite capture the full range of modern meanings of 'sophistication'. All its recent examples and quotations refer to technical and scientific sophistication, or the formal sophistication of modern art. The concept is not pursued into the realm of elegance, style, wit, and detachment, and none of the quotations reveals anything about the orientation of the term in relation to morality or politics.

In 1935, the American critic and historian Dixon Wecter wrote an essay, 'A Brief History of Sophistication'. He proposes that the status of the word 'as an epithet of praise' dates from its use by Gertrude Atherton in her popular novel *Black Oxen* (1923). Following this, 'advertisers were quick to see its appeal for an aspiring and prosperous middle-class; and the bright young people of America, in their myopic search for wisdom, seized upon sophistication instead'.[5] I would not attribute the change to a single author, but my own research confirms Wecter's dating: indeed, 'sophistication' was not generally used as a term of praise until the early 1920s, although it had taken on some of its modern meanings before that point. Wecter presents 'sophistication' as the new name for an ideal which had been referred to as '*ton*' in the eighteenth century, 'elegance' during the Regency, and 'culture' by the Victorians. I would suggest that 'sophistication' is clearly distinct from both elegance and culture, although our modern notion of sophistication includes elements of both. Indeed, part of my aim in this book is to identify the elements of sophistication and explore the different ways in which they may be combined and represented.

In his book on the cultural history of glamour, Stephen Gundle suggests that glamorous subjects are constructed through 'association with a range of qualities including several or all of the following: beauty, sexuality, theatricality, wealth, dynamism, notoriety, movement, and leisure' (6). The listing of associated qualities tends to defer or complicate the meaning of the original term; still, the analysis of glamour as an effect composed of various elements is persuasive. It is more difficult to do the same thing with sophistication, which has an even more involved history and greater diversity of meanings than glamour. Nevertheless, such a list must be drafted, because in many literary texts, sophistication is not directly articulated, but evident only through metonymic resonances with other words, or else through elaboration of its opposite terms. Words used to name elements of what is elsewhere, or later, called 'sophistication' include 'subtlety', 'taste', 'refinement', 'distinction', 'chic', 'elegance', 'cosmopolitanism', 'wit', 'smartness', 'urbanity', 'knowingness', 'irony', 'frivolity' and 'detachment'. The terms against which sophistication defines itself – aside from 'unsophistication' – include 'innocence', 'niceness', 'rusticity' and 'naturalness'. Among the words which have more complex relations with 'sophistication', but still belong to the same lexicon, are 'glamour', 'modernness', 'queer', 'sentiment' and 'sensibility'.

In some contexts, not naming sophistication can be a significant move in itself, since it often provokes embarrassment and disavowal. As Litvak remarks, an interest in sophistication 'somehow always betrays itself as a

---

5   The article appeared in the 20 April 1935 issue of *Southwest Review*, and is quoted in Yagoda 57.

desire: a guilty longing for, or an equally guilty anxiety about, the cultural status that its legitimate possessors or occupants, it would seem, have no need to advertise' (3), and fear of it 'takes the class-conscious form of a nervousness about "elitism"' (5). His point is illuminated by Noël Coward in his 1967 introduction to a collected edition of the works of the Edwardian short-story writer Saki. Coward describes the stories as, 'to use a much abused word, sophisticated' (xiii). Reflecting on Saki's alignment with aestheticism (a very significant phase in the cultural history of sophistication), Coward remarks that the witty, effete young heroes of Saki's fiction belong entirely to the past:

> True, a few prototypes have appeared since but their elegance is more shrill and their quality less subtle. Present-day ideologies are impatient, perhaps rightly, with aestheticism. World democracy provides thin soil for the growing of green carnations, but the green carnations, long since withered, exuded in their brief day a special fragrance, which although it may have made the majority sneeze brought much pleasure to a civilised minority. (xiv)

Coward tries to reclaim sophistication, and to restore the precise meaning it had in the early twentieth century; at the same time, he partially disavows it. His self-consciousness seems to derive from the affiliation between Saki's sophisticated performance and his own, and he wonders what his predecessor would have made of

> that much-maligned period now glibly referred to as 'the Hectic Twenties' when upstart Michael Arlens and Noël Cowards flourished like green bay trees in the frenzied atmosphere of cocktail parties, treasure hunts, Hawes and Curtis dressing gowns, long cigarette holders and enthusiastically publicised decadence. (xiv)

This passage simultaneously enacts and gently satirises the posturing and self-consciousness of sophistication, revealing that it may provoke embarrassment not only because of its elitist strategies, but also because of its frivolity and perceived disconnection from serious current issues.

While 'sophistication' may still be avoided in situations where it could betray elitism or inappropriate detachment, it is actually used with remarkable frequency in other contemporary contexts. I am thinking especially of advertising, in which it is most often invoked to promote fashion items and highly engineered products. The range of reference of 'sophistication' as used in adverts extends from 'elegant' and 'select' (handbags, hotels) to 'advanced' and 'cutting-edge' (cars, mobile phones), but excludes the more ambivalent or pejorative meanings which some literary texts reveal. The frequent repetition of 'sophistication' in advertisements has strongly reinforced the positive semantic prosody of the word, in contrast to its negative semantic prosody in earlier periods. Semantic prosody, a term used in discourse studies, is based on the observation that meaning belongs to whole phrases rather than individual words.[6] Its study involves considering words in relation to their most frequent collocates: that is, the words which most often occur adjacent to, or within the same phrase as, the word in question. Assembling a large number of textual or spoken occurrences of a particular word by means of a corpus reveals typical usages and, as Lynne Flowerdew notes, 'accounts for connotation: the sense that a word carries a meaning in addition to its real meaning. The connotation is usually one of evaluation, that is, the semantic prosody is usually negative or, less frequently, positive' (118).[7] For instance, Michael Stubbs demonstrates that 'cause' is nearly always used with negative collocates (problems, damage, death, disease, concern, pain, trouble), even though the word 'cause' in itself would not, according to a commonsensical perspective, be thought to have any inherent negativity (45–49).

In modern-day English, the ten most significant collocates of 'sophistication' (as generated by the COBUILD corpus), are: 'subtlety', 'technological', 'charm', 'blend', 'continental', 'lack', 'smart', 'taste', 'technical' and 'models'.[8] This list includes several of the keywords of my study (notably 'subtlety', 'continental', 'smart' and 'taste', which have been associated with sophistication over most of the period covered by my research) as well as a number of buzzwords of modern consumerism ('technological', 'technical', 'models'). The collocate 'lack' is supplemented by the next six items on the list: 'level', 'degree', 'increased', 'growing', 'size' and 'greater'. This reveals that sophistication is treated as an attribute with relative quantity: a lack of it, in contemporary usage, is usually to be deplored, while its increase is desirable. In the Corpus of Contemporary American English, in which search results may be categorised according to genre of material, 'sophistication' is found much more often in magazines than in newspapers, which may be due to the greater prevalence in magazines of fashion articles and adverts for luxury goods. Also, the word is infrequent in spoken English, but occurs over three times more often in academic texts. Examples from the corpus suggest that in academic publications, the word is most often used to evaluate theories, designs and so forth ('theoretical sophistication' is a particularly common phrase in academic discourse).[9]

6   The term is drawn from Firthian linguistics, a British branch of structuralism.
7   Flowerdew draws on Hunston (especially 142) in formulating her definition.
8   <http://www.collins.co.uk/Corpus/CorpusSearch.aspx> [accessed 13 January 2009]. The list I give uses the 'Mutual Information Score' rather than the 'T-Score' (known as the Z-Score in other corpuses). 'The Mutual Information Score between any given pair of words [...] compares the probability that the two items occur together as a joint event (i.e. because they belong together) with the probability that they occur individually and that their co-occurrences are simply a result of chance' (McEnery and Wilson 86). The stronger the connection, the higher the score, to a maximum of ten. The scores for the words I have listed range from 9.5 for 'subtlety' to 5 for 'models'.
9   The scores are 7.3 occurrences per million words in academic texts; 6.9 in magazines; 4.5 in

9

The contexts

My research has been informed by a varied body of critical and theoretical texts. To begin with, I have referred to books which trace the history of particular words. Raymond Williams's *Keywords* (1976) provides a particularly valuable model for the analysis of individual words in terms of their historical trajectories and relationships with larger structures of thought and feeling. He writes of his interest in 'words which, beginning in particular specialized contexts, have become quite common in descriptions of wider areas of thought and experience' (14). 'Sophistication' would certainly come into this category, since from the fifteenth to eighteenth centuries it related only to specious reasoning, the adulteration of commodities, and the alteration of a literary text in the course of copying or printing, but subsequently it developed a much broader meaning designating particular attitudes towards culture and forms of personal style. I argue in this book that sophistication is an important affective mode in modern literature, and that it bridges more narrowly conceived epochs such as Romantic, Victorian and modernist. At the same time, it alters over time, responding to (and acting on) dominant structures of feeling in each period: sentimentalism, Romanticism, modernism and so on.

Although 'sophistication' is not one of the keywords Williams explores, he does include numerous terms which are directly or tangentially relevant to it, including 'aesthetic', 'class', 'civilisation', 'criticism', 'culture', 'city', 'educated', 'elite' and 'taste'. His entry on 'sensibility' classes this word with 'taste', 'cultivation' and 'discrimination' because

> [all] describe very general human processes, but in such a way as to specialize them; the negative effects of the actual exclusions that are so often implied can best be picked up in *discrimination*, which has survived both as the process of fine or informed judgment and as the process of treating certain groups unfairly. *Taste* and *cultivation* make little sense unless we are able to contrast their presence with their absence, in ways that depend on generalization and indeed on *consensus*. (281)

The consensus is, of course, difficult to achieve, and the question of what constitutes 'good taste' can be endlessly debated among individuals and groups (and is an issue which recurs at several points in this book). Nevertheless, the idea of 'good taste' does indeed depend on a notion of standards which might, at

---

newspapers; 2.2 in spoken English; and 1.6 in fiction. This corpus extends from 1990 to 2008. See <http://www.americancorpus.org/> [accessed 13 January 2009]. In material from the British National Corpus extending over the 1980s and up to 1993, 'sophistication' occurs more than ten times more often in academic than in spoken discourse (7.1 versus 0.6 words per million). Newspapers and magazines are not separated in the Brigham Young University portal, which I used. See Mark Davies, BYU-BNC: The British National Corpus (2004) at <http://corpus.byu.edu.> [accessed 13 January 2009].

least in some imagined realm, be specified and defined, and it is also predicated on the assumption that most people have bad taste.

The contingency and relativity of terms such as 'taste', 'cultivation' and indeed 'sophistication' takes me on to William Empson's observation about 'the return of the meaning of the word to the speaker' in *The Structure of Complex Words* (1964):

> most judgements about other people, when you make them public, can be felt to raise a question about how you would be judged in your turn. This is particularly so of inherently shifting moral terms like the miserly-thrifty group; when one man calls another thrifty he is a little conscious of what people would call him. To call someone else clever is rather to imply that you are not clever yourself. [...] It has become unusual to talk about anybody being chaste, partly because people do not want to imply either that they themselves are or that they aren't, and it is difficult to use the word without one or the other. [...] Proust gives a neat example, when Morel delights Charlus by calling him 'mon vieux' and thus implies he is as young as Morel; the idea is 'we are both experienced' rather than 'both old', but anyway it can be assumed to be mutual. And on the other hand in calling a man a 'Cad' it is usual to imply no less clearly that you are not a cad yourself. (18)

It could be suggested that, in contemporary terms at least, the recognition of sophistication confers it, so that to use the word about someone else would identify the speaker as sophisticated. But in earlier periods, when the term had a more critical edge, this might not hold true. The question becomes even more interesting in the case of 'unsophistication', because in the eighteenth and nineteenth centuries, the distrust of sophistication was such that 'unsophistication' was a term of praise, and yet to describe someone in this way certainly implies that you are superior in sophistication yourself. (I explore this in Chapter 1.)

Eve Kosofsky Sedgwick makes a related point in *The Epistemology of the Closet* (1990), focusing on two words which are intimately connected to 'sophistication':

> 'Worldly' or 'urbane' is par excellence one of those categories that, appearing to be a flatly descriptive attribution attached to one person, actually describes or creates a chain of perceptual angles: it is the cognitive privilege of the person described over a separate perceived world that is actually attested, and by a speaker who through that attestation lays claim in turn to an even more inclusive angle of cognitive distancing and privilege over both the 'urbane' character and the world. The position of the reader in this chain of privilege is fraught with promise and vulnerability. The ostentatious presumption by the narrator that a reader is similarly entitled – rather than, what in truth she necessarily is, disorientated – sets up relations of flattery, threat, and complicity between reader and narrator that may in turn restructure the perception of the conformation originally associated with the 'worldly'. (97)

One of my primary concerns in this study is to analyse the hierarchies of sophistication which are constructed in literary narratives, and which position reader, narrator and characters in shifting and sometimes perplexing relations to one another. As Sedgwick suggests, notions of flattery, complicity and even coercion emerge from such analyses.

In addition to accounts of the significance and functioning of particular words, a considerable range of critical and theoretical material is potentially relevant to this study. I will here briefly survey the books and articles which I have found most helpful. Only two previous books have actually been devoted to the subject of sophistication. Mark Backman's *Sophistication: Rhetoric and the Rise of Self-Consciousness* (1991) is primarily concerned with philosophy, education and politics. From his professional viewpoint as a communications consultant, he argues that the culture of modernity is governed by a series of principles which first emerged in the era of the Greek Sophists and formed the basis of the art of rhetoric. He describes the attraction of the Sophists, and their legacy in modern times:

> They seemed to overthrow many of the ideas that were at the center of communal life. They preached a reliance on individual initiative, intellect and the mastery of public presentation, all of which were fast becoming the essential ingredients of success in the burgeoning Greek democracies. Any person could gain power over other minds if only they would submit to an education that produced a sophisticated appreciation of language and power.
>
> 'Sophist' is also at the heart of our concept of sophistication, the much sought after quality that distinguishes one person or idea or invention from all others. It values the worldly-wise, the experienced, the tested and the refined. [...]
>
> To sophisticate something, however, also means to deprive it of its simplicity and genuineness. [...] There are no accidental sophisticates, in art or life. Most important of all, sophistication plays on emotion and it relies on the force of an articulate personality although, at times, it is disguised as reasonableness, modesty and even humility. (4–5)

Backman presents sophistication as a damaging element in modern society, despite – or perhaps because of – the fact that it can be used to advantage by canny educators and business people. This reading of sophistication as necessarily dangerous might well be disputed.[10] Indeed, Joseph Litvak's *Strange Gourmets: Sophistication, Theory and the Novel* takes quite an opposite approach, concentrating on the allure and liberating potential of sophistication, though simultaneously exploring the embarrassment generated by a too-evident

---

10 Backman's book is not a typical scholarly work. It does not draw extensively on (or reference) previous work in the field, and it is primarily a polemic about education and business practices. I find the passage quoted here insightful, though the historical accuracy of Backman's account of the Sophists and the development of rhetoric has been challenged by scholars (see for instance Swartz).

desire for it. Litvak's detailed studies of five novelists and theorists (Austen, Thackeray, Proust, Adorno, Barthes) have provided an inspiring model for my own analyses, and his discussions of consumption and its relation to eroticism, language and economics have been especially valuable. His research 'proceeds from a specifically gay academic perspective, and one of its most urgent motives is to provide analytic resources against homophobia and anti-intellectualism' (5). Since *Strange Gourmets* maps this terrain so effectively, I do not myself rehearse arguments about sophistication and homosexuality in detail, although I do discuss camp and effete styles in connection with the work of Beerbohm, Wilde, Saki, Coward and others.

Several other literary critics have explored sophistication, relating it to some of the additional ideas which are central to this book, such as class, snobbery, conspicuous consumption, social performance, deceit, sentiment, glamour, camp, frivolity and cosmopolitanism. John Kucich in *The Power of Lies* (1994) writes that 'in postromantic culture [...] a familiarity with deceit, conventionally understood, must have become indispensable to autonomous selfhood', because '[if] individual freedom involves turning oneself into an intuitively guided moral sophisticate rather than observing moral rules, then subjective standards of truth and falsity necessarily come into conflict with social norms of truth and falsity' (26). His book is a study of Victorian fiction, but insights such as this apply across a broader period. Similarly, Sean Latham's *'Am I a Snob?' Modernism and the Novel* (2003), which concentrates on Thackeray, Wilde, Woolf, Joyce and Sayers, also advances general arguments about snobbery which are illuminating in relation to sophistication:

> The snob eagerly demonstrates the ways in which aesthetic knowledge can be used to generate social prestige and financial reward. To facilitate this commerce in money, access, and social credit marks, the snob commands [...] the ability to manipulate shrewdly the external signs of social and cultural sophistication. He or she must grasp the fact that even the most complex aesthetic artifact is subject to the purely semiotic nature of fashion. (7)

Related issues are explored in Nina Miller's *Making Love Modern: The Intimate Public Worlds of New York's Literary Women* (1999), in which she discusses the politics of sophistication through an analysis of the writing and social performances of members of the Algonquin Round Table. Jessica Burstein's 'A Few Words About Dubuque: Modernism, Sentimentalism, and the Blasé' builds on Miller's account of New York literary sophistication in the 1920s, and these two excellent studies were among the inspirations for my project.

Stephen Gundle's *Glamour: A History* (2008) has also been helpful. It traces the development of the notion of glamour by focusing on a series of nineteenth- and twentieth-century glamorous figures and exploring their representation in contemporary forms of media and publicity. *Glamour* is a follow-up to the book Gundle co-authored with Clino Castelli, *The Glamour System* (2006), which analyses glamour as a language of visual seduction, in the framework of sociology and media studies. These books have helped me to work through the differences between 'sophisticated' and 'glamorous', two words which often occur in the same contexts (particularly in magazine articles on fashion, travel, restaurants and so forth), yet which are in some senses oppositional. Gundle begins his book with a reflection on Gianni Versace, describing him as 'the king of glitz, the man who combined beauty with vulgarity' (1–2), and noting that 'glamour' was the word which recurred most frequently in media comments on Versace, whose style 'catered to those who desired to flaunt their wealth or sex appeal' (2). This is precisely what sophistication is not. Vulgarity and flaunting are just what sophisticates in all eras eschew, and as Clive Scott notes: 'Because of its culturedness, "sophistication" often has a social pedigree which "glamour" can function without' (156).

Nevertheless, sophistication and glamour present similar problems of definition, each raising the question of whether it is innate (a gift) or whether it can be learned (or purchased). As Gundle remarks:

> Glossy magazines featuring spreads on the glamorous homes and glamorous wardrobes of beautiful people who have glamorous jobs and lives conjure up a world that is familiar as fantasy but utterly removed from the daily lives of average people. [...] On the other hand, magazine articles, books, and television programmes continually spell out how every woman can glamorize herself. (3)

In addition, both glamour and sophistication have affinities with camp. Camp's connection with glamour is quite obvious; its affiliation with sophistication goes rather deeper, and is somewhat elusive, as Susan Sontag indicates in the opening passage of her influential essay 'Notes on Camp' (1964):

> Many things in the world have not been named; and many things, even if they have been named, have never been described. One of these is the sensibility – unmistakably modern, a variant of sophistication but hardly identical with it – that goes by the cult name of 'Camp'. (275)

Sontag's account has been challenged by numerous critics (particularly for its elision of the affiliation of homosexuality with camp, or, to put it another way, its attempt to appropriate camp from homosexuals),[11] but it remains one of

11 See Meyer; Miller; Newton for critiques of Sontag. Newton, for instance, sees camp as having an entirely homosexual provenance. Miller identifies Sontag's urbanity as a discursive strategy upholding heterosexual privilege. Commenting on Sontag's objection to her book *AIDS and its Metaphors* (1989) having been reviewed by experts on AIDS rather than as a literary performance, Miller writes: 'The claim for the precession and superiority of form over a content whose main function is to justify the elaboration of artistic or literary devices is of course a familiar one

the most intriguing analyses of the subject. According to her definition: 'the essence of Camp is its love of the unnatural: of artifice and exaggeration' (275). The love of artifice certainly connects camp to sophistication, though sophistication fluctuates between exaggeration and restraint, rather than wholly identifying itself with excess, as camp taste does. As Sontag suggests, camp may be understood as a variant of sophistication: a kind of specialised form which 'converts the serious into the frivolous' (276) and, as Robert F. Kiernan notes in *Frivolity Unbound: Six Masters of the Camp Novel* (1990), frequently plays on 'a contrast between negligible content and elaborate form' (12). These descriptions would apply to some of the texts considered in this book: most obviously to Max Beerbohm's parodic dandy novel, *Zuleika Dobson* (1911), which is mentioned in both Sontag's and Kiernan's accounts, but also, arguably, to Stella Gibbons's *Cold Comfort Farm* (1932) and Vladimir Nabokov's *Lolita* (1955).

Kiernan theorises the relationship between camp and frivolity in ways which also illuminate the potential of literary sophistication. He describes camp as 'a frivolity unbound by conventional considerations of morality', and identifies its propensity for 'interweaving itself with the canonically approved genres' as a 'strategy for accommodating its special audacity' (148). This reminds me of the subversive potential of sophisticates such as Henry Crawford or Sir Clement Willoughby within the otherwise proper moral frameworks endorsed in Austen's *Mansfield Park* (1814) and Burney's *Evelina* (1778). Sophistication repeatedly eschews earnestness and embraces frivolity, but frivolity is not, as Jonathan Goldman observes, 'a totalizing designation', even for authors such as Beerbohm or Ronald Firbank, since '[f]rivolous writing can coincide with satire, irony, parody, camp, and other specificities used to classify these authors'. He adds: 'The extent to which frivolity is shunned by writers and ignored or derided by critics, however, may delineate exactly the threat frivolity poses' to conventional systems of literary representation (292). I have chosen several frivolous, comic, parodic and ironic texts for this project, including several which tend to be 'shunned' by critics, and I have found Kiernan's and Goldman's studies useful in analysing the subversive potential of these texts and also the forms of laughter which they provoke. According to Kiernan, '[camp] invites a sophisticated, amoral mode of laughter' (16), and this argument points to one of the most significant connections between camp and sophistication.

'Nothing in nature can be campy', according to Sontag. 'Rural Camp is still man-made, and most campy objects are urban. (Yet, they often have a

---

[…]. As the case of Wilde best illustrates, however, the argument for the secondariness of content typically surfaces in contexts where the content in question, far from being trivial, enjoys a particular volatility whose ignition would catastrophically overwhelm both personal and public spheres together' (91).

serenity – or a naïveté – which is the equivalent of pastoral. A great deal of Camp suggests Empson's phrase "urban pastoral")' (279). I am not surprised to find Sontag drawing on Empson's *Some Versions of Pastoral* (1935), since it repeatedly turns out to be relevant to camp taste, and much more often to sophistication. Indeed, the whole concept of pastoral is fundamental to sophistication. This may seem counterintuitive, since sophistication is generally associated with the urban, but, of course, pastoral itself depends on a *dynamic* between urban and rural, and so – frequently – does sophistication. Empson's theories of pastoral were derived from a long tradition of thinking on the subject, going back at least to George Puttenham's *The Arte of English Poesie* (1589); subsequently, Empson's ideas were developed by later critics.[12] But I have found *Some Versions of Pastoral* especially relevant to my study, partly because of Empson's focus on the little girl (his discussion of Lewis Carroll is important to my reading of the *Alice* books in Chapter 2) and partly because of his articulation of pastoral's relationship to aristocracy. In his discussion of Shakespeare's sonnet 94, 'They that have power to hurt and will do none', he comments on the 'clash of admiration and contempt [which] seems dependent on a clash of feeling about the classes', adding:

> One might connect it with that curious trick of pastoral which for extreme courtly flattery – perhaps to give self-respect to both poet and patron, to show that the poet is not ignorantly easy to impress, nor the patron to flatter – writes about the poorest people; and with those jazz songs which give an intense effect of luxury and silk underwear by pretending to be about slaves naked in the fields. (83–84)

The sophisticate's complex identification with, and repudiation of, aristocratic privilege recurs frequently in my discussion; and in the texts I consider, it is often played out in direct relation to environment. Semi-rural locations such as gardens take on particular importance as ambivalent spaces of sophistication and sites for the negotiation of social power.

Equally important is the urban context of sophistication. From amongst the enormous range of critical accounts of the city and modernity, I would pick out Georg Simmel's essay 'The Metropolis and Mental Life' (1903), with its account of 'the difficulty of giving one's own personality a certain status within the framework of metropolitan life' (18). He writes of the city dweller's attempt to gain 'the attention of the social world', explaining:

> This leads ultimately to the strangest eccentricities, to specifically metropolitan extravagances of self-distanciation, of caprice, of fastidiousness, the meaning of which is no longer to be found in the content of such activity itself but rather in the form of 'being different' – of making oneself noticeable. (18)

---

12 On successive theorisations of pastoral, see Gifford, especially 22–28.

16

Simmel's essay is helpful in understanding sophistication's emphasis on distinction from context, and I have drawn on it particularly in my discussion of the blasé attitude in early twentieth-century culture (Chapter 3). Other obvious reference points on the subjects of distinction, class, fashion and social performance are Thorstein Veblen's *The Theory of the Leisure Class* (1899) and Pierre Bourdieu's *Distinction: A Social Critique of the Judgement of Taste* (1979); indeed, Bourdieu is often regarded as the direct successor of Simmel and Veblen. Veblen's satirical analysis of the effects of American affluence challenges conventional narratives of progress and civilisation by equating the modern imperative to accumulate, display, decorate and imitate with 'the higher stages of the barbarian culture' (7). His account of the difference between 'exploit and drudgery' – in other words, the privileging of 'prowess' over 'diligence' (14) – is directly relevant to the sophisticate's disdain of productive labour, while his description of the actual effort required in order to display leisure is equally relevant to the learned practice of sophistication:

> under the competitive struggle for proficiency in good manners, it comes about that much pains is taken with the cultivation of habits of decorum; and hence the details of decorum develop into a comprehensive discipline, [...] a laborious drill in deportment and an education in taste and discrimination as to what articles of consumption are decorous and what are the decorous methods of consuming them. (37)

Bourdieu argues along similar lines: 'Aesthetic stances adopted in matters like cosmetics, clothing or home decoration are opportunities to experience or assert one's position in social space, as a rank to be upheld or a distance to be kept' (57). His practice of connecting taste in the sense of choice of clothes, décor, reading material and so forth with tastes for food and drink has been especially helpful to my study; questions of eating, consumption and even cannibalism are explored in many of my readings of literary texts.

Bourdieu's discussion of the operation of pretension is also important to an understanding of sophistication. As he explains, the forms of imitation which lead to the widespread adoption of habits previously associated with a higher social or intellectual class devalue those class markers, and the elite are forced to 'engage in an endless pursuit of new properties through which to assert their rarity' (252). The rejection of tastes which were previously embraced, but which risk becoming too popular, points to an incompatibility between sophistication and mass appeal. Among more recent books which continue Bourdieu's exploration of taste, I would pick out Denise Gigante's *Taste: A Literary History* (2005). Focusing on the Romantic period, Gigante explores 'the creative power of taste as a trope for aesthetic judgment and its essential role in generating our very sense of self' (2), and proposes that '[not] only is taste bound up with the unruly flesh; traditionally, it is associated with *too* intense bodily pleasure and the consequent dangers of excess' (3). Gigante's insights inform my discussion of one of the central dynamics of sophistication, that between excess and restraint.

I have given further accounts of important critical material in the introductory sections to each chapter, in which I discuss topics of particular relevance to one period. For instance, I examine sensibility, celebrity and luxury in Chapter 1; childhood, dandyism and decadence in Chapter 2; middlebrow, modernism and sentiment in Chapter 3; and nostalgia in Chapter 4.

The texts

An enormous range of literary and cultural material might potentially have been included in this study. My final choice is inevitably idiosyncratic, but I hope that my personal enthusiasm for the texts I discuss will give a sense of the possible pleasures of reading sophistication. As to the principles underlying the content and structuring of the book, its chronological scope is perhaps the first consideration. Since my aim is to analyse sophistication in relation to modernity, the later eighteenth century seemed a natural starting point. This was the period just before the word 'sophistication' began its semantic shift from pejorative to affirmative, and therefore my first chapter, on Romantic-era texts, provides a context for the discussion in later chapters of emerging modern meanings. In addition, there were, seemingly, distinct cultural shifts in the eighteenth century which make this an appropriate point of departure. The figure of the dandy, who is important in several sections of my book, first emerged in the British Regency era. Robert Scholes argues in *Paradoxy of Modernism* (2005) that '[in] eighteenth-century Britain the High/Low distinction became a function of a new discourse on Taste, in which the aesthetic and the social are wonderfully mixed' (26), while Susan Sontag begins her outline of camp taste with the eighteenth century 'because of that period's extraordinary feeling for artifice, for surface, for symmetry' (280). These reasons also apply to my study.

Of course, ideas and tastes related to what we would now call sophistication may be found in earlier periods: it would be possible to study its antecedents during the Renaissance or the English Restoration, though a more obvious locus for early modern sophistication would be seventeenth-century France. Georgia J. Cowart, in *The Triumph of Pleasure: Louis XIV and the Politics of Spectacle* (2008), explains that in the early seventeenth century, 'the ancient doctrine of Epicurus was revived by Pierre Gassendi and a loose circle known as the *libertins érudits*', while later in the century, 'the designation *libertin* was applied to a wide variety of individuals who combined in varying degrees a personal hedonism, the idea of sexual freedom, and a dangerous brand of political free thought' (xviii). Cowart suggests, further, that

> [t]hroughout the reign of Louis XIV, the ideal of pleasure was [...] associated with a court aristocracy, for whom the delicate, erotically charged aesthetic of *galanterie* defined a noble identity and way of life. Especially as a young man, Louis XIV shared with this noble elite a propensity for a bold hedonism clothed in a refined sensibility of manners and taste. (xviii–xix)

Joan DeJean, in *The Essence of Style* (2005), more explicitly traces the origin of sophistication back to the court of the Sun King, arguing that the status of the French as arbiters of taste and fashion was established during his reign. Indeed, she subtitles her book – using deliberate anachronisms – 'How the French Invented High Fashion, Fine Food, Chic Cafés, Style, Sophistication, and Glamour', and suggests that '[in] the 1660s, Paris began a reign over luxury living that still endures, three and a half centuries later. This happened because the French understood the importance of marketing' (4). Sophisticated tastes in food, clothing and leisure activities which were previously confined to court and aristocratic circles began to be disseminated to the wider urban population in the later seventeenth century, and this not only encouraged aspiration and imitation, but also led to innovations such as celebrity hairdressers, city nightlife, and haute cuisine. These fashions, DeJean suggests, subsequently spread to England and other European countries.

DeJean collapses glamour and sophistication together, and identifies both as seventeenth-century inventions. Stephen Gundle, by contrast, insists that glamour is 'a quintessentially modern phenomenon' (6) which began in the nineteenth century, because

> [a]lthough monarchs, courts, and aristocrats offered examples of luxurious living and high style, it was the fabrication of these by the emergent men and women of the bourgeois era, by the new rich and commercial establishments and the world of entertainment that was glamorous. (6)

He suggests that 'neither the monarchy nor the aristocracy was the principal originator or social bearer of glamour' (6), and that glamour 'had no prior existence before becoming commodified and commercialized' (7). By contrast, sophistication, I propose, was certainly originated by the upper class, and has always been associated with breeding, elitism and a disdain for the market economy. Certainly, more recently evolved forms of middle-class sophistication can be closely involved with the commercial, yet they almost invariably retain a nostalgia for aristocratic styles. The word 'sophistication' undoubtedly has a much longer and more etymologically complex history than 'glamour';

I would also argue that the idea of sophistication as a desirable quality goes back a little further than the idea of glamour. There are, I think, forms of modern sophistication which are specific to the nineteenth and twentieth centuries, but the connections with eighteenth- and, to some extent, seventeenth-century antecedents are clear.

It would be impossible to provide a full history of the varieties of sophistication represented in modern culture; instead, this book offers a set of samplings. The four chapters cover successive periods in the evolution of sophistication: the Romantic era (Chapter 1), the Victorian and Edwardian periods (Chapter 2), the interwar years (Chapter 3), and the 1950s and 1960s (Chapter 4), while the Conclusion reflects on late-twentieth- and twenty-first-century culture. This arrangement roughly corresponds to conventional literary periodisation because, as noted above, shifts in the meanings of 'sophistication' are related to shifts in other affective modes which determined the labelling of each period in the first place: Romanticism, Victorianism, modernism, postmodernism. Each chapter is divided into five sections. The first part provides literary, cultural and critical contexts for the period, referring to a wide range of authors and texts. The remaining four sections focus each on one literary text (or pair of texts), offering arguments which are deliberately diverse, since my aim is to capture the richness of this subject and the remarkable range of views it invites. Sophistication is not theorised in every single paragraph. At many points, I am principally concerned with tracing – and appreciating – its effects in the particular text under consideration; indeed, this approach is fundamental to my practice of reading sophistication.

I have chosen texts for close reading which may be productively compared with one another, but which, at the same time, represent a mixture of styles and genres. English fiction forms the core of the study, but American, French and Italian novels, together with drama, travel writing, children's literature, journalism and lifestyle guides, are also represented. The 'history' is primarily a literary one, but in venturing at times beyond the range of the strictly literary, the book suggests possible alternative modes for investigating sophistication. For instance, the section on *Vanity Fair* magazine demonstrates the potential of a cultural materialist approach, and while I have not had space to develop this in detail, questions of materiality recur in my later discussion of Genevieve Dariaux's *A Guide to Elegance*, and elsewhere. Similarly, I use examples drawn from visual culture, including eighteenth-century paintings, fashion illustrations, films and advertisements. Many of these images and visual narratives are richly suggestive, and it would not be difficult to imagine a complementary history of sophistication which reversed my own practice and placed the image centrally, with the text as a subsidiary concern.

I discuss roughly equal numbers of male and female authors. This was not, in fact, a conscious choice, and I have not found a clear difference in the ways in which they represent sophistication. Indeed, my research has revealed that questions of class are rather more significant than questions of gender to the formation and evolution of the notion of sophistication. Accordingly, while gender arises fairly frequently in the discussion, since it is often pertinent to the close readings, it does not determine the analytical paradigms. Distrust of the sophisticate extended to men as well as women in the eighteenth century; admiration of the sophisticate likewise encompassed both genders in the twentieth. It is true that innocence was, especially in the Romantic and Victorian eras, more highly prized in girls than in men, which might imply that sophistication was particularly discouraged in girls. Yet by the early twentieth century, the 'sophisticated lady' was quite as much admired as the dandy. Margaret Lawrence, in her book *The School of Femininity* (1936), writes:

> Irony presupposes superiority of mind. You do not spread it before fools. It is, therefore, as it manifests in a woman, essentially part of the equipment of the sophisticate. It is a supersensual appeal which acts downward upon the senses. [...] The sophisticated lady and the sophisticated writer have to be persons of pre-eminent self-control. This, inversely, is highly attractive to men and readers. (301)

Lawrence's book is about women writers, and contains a whole chapter entitled 'Sophisticated Ladies'. In general terms, the large number of women authors, artists, and public figures who have embraced or explored sophistication might suggest that it could be conceived as a regendered form of dandyism, or a form available to both genders. But I would argue that sophistication is a larger and more complex notion than dandyism, and that it is potentially more subversive. Both practices challenge boundaries of gender and also of class, but dandyism is principally concerned with reinventing masculinity and aristocracy. Sophistication, by contrast, deconstructs traditional gender divides, allowing women access to conventionally male realms and roles but also accommodating men who do not conform to traditional models of manhood. Sophistication also deconstructs, rather than merely breaching, class divides, with its complex strategies of aspiration combined with slumming and its validation of certain forms of middle-class taste.

Some of my chosen books have been extensively analysed by previous critics, but sophistication is very rarely the focus of such analyses.[13] My re-readings of canonical writers such as Sheridan, Burney, Austen, James, Fitzgerald and Nabokov are complemented by discussions of authors who have received very

---

13 I have therefore been very selective in my references to secondary material on individual authors, citing only those most relevant to the theme of sophistication.

limited critical attention, such as Daisy Ashford, Max Beerbohm, Françoise Sagan and Winifred Watson. In making these selections, I am not seeking to construct a 'canon of sophistication'; rather, I hope to show how a preoccupation with – or a performance of – sophistication connects unexpected groups of texts together, and can form the basis for a reading practice which transcends categories of genre, nation and language, and crosses boundaries between high and low, literary and commercial, serious and frivolous.

1

Scandal, sentiment and shepherdesses: the emergence of modern sophistication

Sophistication is, seemingly, incompatible with Romanticism. The setting of sophistication is usually thought to be the metropolis; that of Romanticism, the countryside or wilderness. The sophisticate's emphasis on style, wit, urbanity and polish is not easily reconciled either with the idealisation of sentiment and sensibility in the fiction of the later eighteenth century, or with the idealisation of innocence and naturalness in much Romantic poetry. The sentimental or Gothic heroine, the innocent child, and the shepherds and vagrants of Romantic pastoral are alike representative of unsophistication. A good example is Miss Walton in Henry Mackenzie's novel *The Man of Feeling* (1771): 'Her conversation was always cheerful, but rarely witty; and without the smallest affectation of learning, had as much sentiment in it as would have puzzled a Turk, upon his principles of female materialism, to account for' (13). The narrator notes the 'natural tenderness of her heart' (13), a quality which also belongs to the children, rustic people, and idiots celebrated in Blake's *Songs of Innocence* (1789) and Wordsworth and Coleridge's *Lyrical Ballads* (1798).[1] Rustic figures were chosen, according to Wordsworth's Preface to the 1800 *Lyrical Ballads*, because they are 'less under the action of social vanity' than city dwellers, and so 'convey their feelings and notions in simple and unelaborated expressions' (245). Wordsworth's preoccupation with unsophisticated subjects, then, emerges from his emphasis on direct and uncomplicated style, and he objects to poets who whose work exhibits 'false refinement or arbitrary innovation' (246). The Romantic privileging of expressiveness entailed a rejection of artifice and literary sophistication, and was directly related to the

---

1 Dating the *Lyrical Ballads* is complex. The second edition in 1800 reordered the contents and incorporated additional poems and a new preface by Wordsworth. The edition of 1802 contains an extended preface, while that of 1804 shows textual variants.

growing preoccupation with honesty in nineteenth-century English literature: as John Kucich remarks, 'there is always a latent moral exordium beneath the ardors of Wordsworth's "spontaneous overflow"' (13).

Yet while many sentimental and Romantic texts strongly reject sophistication, they simultaneously construct a sophisticated reading position for their audiences. In order to appreciate rural simplicity, childlike unselfconsciousness, or untutored sensibility, the reader must be aware that they themselves have lost – or never possessed – these qualities. In Empson's terms, this is the basis of pastoral: 'a double attitude of the artist to the worker, of the complex man to the simple one ("I am in one way better, in another not so good")' (*Pastoral* 19). The readers of poetry and serious fiction in the late eighteenth century were not themselves unsophisticated people; most were highly literate members of the middle or upper class.[2] Indeed, class itself, with all its associated formations of self-consciousness and competition, is an important preoccupation in both the literature of sentiment and the Gothic novel, and even the Romantic poets could not avoid it. Empson observes: 'One purpose of the Romantics was to break the class barrier that the Augustans had put into literature; they felt that the couplet was too smart and high-class' (*Pastoral* 153). But he concludes: 'This part of the programme seems to have been a complete failure', remarking that Wordsworth's 'description of himself as doing poetic field-work among country people who address him as Sir' seriously compromises his democratic project (153–54). Even the most resolutely pastoral poems and most tear-drenched fictions of the later eighteenth and early nineteenth centuries, then, may be invaded by sophistication in the sense of a conscious superiority of class, intellect or taste, which precludes the kind of immediacy of response that Wordsworth longs for.

In addition, it is an oversimplification to identify Romanticism purely with pastoral primitivism. There is also an urban Romanticism, which was explored in Raymond Williams's *The Country and the City* (1973) and has recently been the subject of critical reassessment. A 2005 essay collection, *Romantic Metropolis: The Urban Scene of British Culture, 1780–1840*, edited by James Chandler and Kevin Gilmartin, connects texts about the city with broader contexts of urban literary culture, spectacle, publicity and cosmopolitanism. Blake's 'London' from *Songs of Experience* (1794) is considered in relation to his engagement

---

2   Literacy rates are hard to determine accurately, but by 1750 approximately 60 per cent of men and 40 per cent of women in Britain could read (Barker-Benfield 163). Only a proportion of these would have had the means and leisure to buy and read new books, although reading was rapidly becoming a more widespread activity. See St Clair's *The Reading Nation in the Romantic Period* for detail on the production, pricing, sales and circulation of books. He notes that the publishing industry 'estimated a fourfold increase in output during the last quarter of the century' (118) and discusses the growth of reading among working-class people (119).

with London radicalism, while Wordsworth's 'Composed Upon Westminster Bridge, Sept. 2 1802' from *Poems in Two Volumes* (1807) is explored in conjunction with his and Coleridge's lectures in London. Indeed, much canonical Romantic writing may be understood in terms of dynamics between urban and rural rather than retreat into the pastoral. In some other contemporary genres of art and literature, pastoralism is abandoned altogether in favour of a focus on the elegant rituals of the social. The silver fork novel of the later 1820s and 1830s, for instance, unashamedly celebrates sophistication. These books, the best known among which are Benjamin Disraeli's *Vivian Grey* (1826–27) and Edward Bulwer-Lytton's *Pelham* (1828), describe the minutiae of upper-class British life, emphasising luxury, leisure and manners, and they attained considerable – though short-lived – popularity among aspirational middle-class readers. In other texts from this era, sophistication is more deliberately – though, as a rule, only partially – recovered. In Sheridan, Goldsmith and Fanny Burney, conflicts between sentiment and sophistication are dramatised; in Byron, the Romantic attack on Augustan poetic language is ironised; in Jane Austen's juvenile fictions, the excesses of sentimental literature are parodied. (Her novella *Love and Freindship*, written about 1790, famously features two heroines who 'fainted alternately on a sofa' [77].) In Gothic fiction, the villain's sophistication often lends him a distinct attractiveness. The Marquis de Montalt in Radcliffe's *The Romance of the Forest* may be libidinous, but he is also 'polite, affable, and attentive: to manners the most easy and elegant, was added the last refinement of polished life. His conversation was lively, amusing, sometimes even witty; and discovered great knowledge of the world' (99). The heroine, Adeline, though appearing to contrast with the Marquis in her 'innocence', 'artless energy' and 'captivating sweetness' (6), is also characterised by 'elegance and [...] refinement' (7). Both heroine and villain, then, are 'refined' and 'elegant', and through these qualities the villains become dangerously appealing to virtuous people of good taste.

In the broader culture of Georgian and Regency Britain, some of the most celebrated public figures were icons of sophistication: most obviously Beau Brummell and Lord Byron, but also Georgiana, Duchess of Devonshire, the Duke of Queensbury, Richard Brinsley Sheridan, and various other aristocrats, dandies, writers and actors.[3] In the public discourses of media and gossip, attitudes towards celebrities were complex. Consider Leigh Hunt's obituary of Sheridan, who died in 1816:

---

3 Celebrity is a current theme of Romantic scholarship. See especially Tom Mole's *Byron's Romantic Celebrity* (2007), which argues that the cultural apparatus of celebrity took shape in response to the expansion and mechanisation of print culture in the Romantic period, and that Byron is 'one of its earliest examples and most astute critics' (xi).

> Mr Sheridan was more painstaking than Mr Fox, and had much less the appearance of it than Mr Burke; and [...] yet his wit and judgement united enabled him to recall a point of artificial perfection superior, we think, to both. [...]
>
> To sum up the character of Mr Sheridan, he was a man of wit, a lively and elegant dramatist, a winning and powerful orator, a sound politician, a lover of real freedom, a careless liver; an Irishman, in short, with much of the worst, and more of the best, of his naturally light-hearted but unfortunate countrymen. (Hunt 434–35)

Hunt's reference to Sheridan's careless living (another paragraph specifies that he was a spendthrift and heavy drinker) correlates with a broader tendency, in this period, to associate sophistication with moral laxity and self-indulgence. The praise of the 'artificial perfection' of the sophisticate, however, is unusual, and contrasts markedly with the more common conviction that sophistication should be distrusted precisely because of its artificiality.

A more deeply ambivalent response to the public display of sophistication can be found in Hazlitt's essay 'Brummelliana', of which two versions exist. In the earlier piece, published in 1820 and possibly co-authored with Leigh Hunt,[4] Hazlitt writes of the dandy Brummell:

> Never was any thing more exquisitely conscious, yet indifferent; extravagant, yet judicious. His superiority in dress gave such importance to his genius, and his genius so divested of insipidity his superiority in dress, that the poet's hyperbole about the lady might be applied to his coat; and
>
> > You might almost say the body thought.
>
> It was a moot point which had the more tact, his gloves or his fingers' ends. He played the balls of wit and folly so rapidly about his head, that they lost their distinctions in one crowning and brilliant halo. (330)[5]

This passage suggests that Brummell's personal qualities are so very literally bodied forth in his clothes and manners, and his thoughts so wholly materialised, that there is no longer any distinction between the inner and the outer man. Hazlitt presents sophistication as spiritually and intellectually void: pure form with no content. Yet he acknowledges its allure, and admits that Brummell is unique in his extreme exquisiteness. This delicate balancing between admiration and contempt is even more striking in the second 'Brummelliana', published in 1828:

> We look upon Beau Brummell as the greatest of small wits. [...] All his bon-mots turn upon a single circumstance, the exaggerating of the merest trifles into matters of importance, or treating everything else with the utmost nonchalance and indifference, as if whatever pretended to pass beyond those limits was a bore, and disturbed

4 On the two 'Brummelliana' essays and their attribution, see Wu 326–29.
5 The line Hazlitt quotes is from Donne's 'Of the Progress of the Soul: The Second Anniversary' (1612).

the serene air of high life. [...] It is impossible for anyone to go beyond him without falling flat into insignificance and insipidity: he has touched the ne plus ultra that divides the dandy from the dunce. But what a fine eye to discriminate: what a sure hand to hit this last and thinnest of all intellectual partitions! (152)

In late eighteenth-century fiction, the dandy or coxcomb is generally a contemptible minor character, though subsequently, in the silver fork novels, he becomes the protagonist and grows more complex and attractive. Vivian Grey is 'a graceful, lively lad, with just enough of dandyism to preserve him from committing gaucheries' (17), and while not the most morally upright character, he is accomplished and charming. Even in these texts, though, there is a continual emphasis on externals; Hazlitt wrote with exasperation that, on dipping into a novel such as *Vivian Grey*, 'you [...] may fancy yourself reading a collection of quack or fashionable advertisements: – Macassar Oil, Eau de Cologne, Hock and Seltzer Water, Otto of Roses, *Pomade Divine* glance through the page in inextricable confusion' ('The Dandy School' 143).

The affectations of the dandy's precursor, the Macaroni of the 1760s and 1770s, were still more viciously caricatured. Macaroni fashion, as Jennifer Craik notes, 'epitomised the desire of aristocrats to distinguish themselves from the growing bourgeoisie and minor gentry through their clothes'. She adds that '[they] drew on images from the French and Italian courts to emphasise that difference' (182); this also demonstrated their well-travelled, cosmopolitan status. Flamboyance and extravagance in male dress could be read as a form of resistance to standardisation and subsequently (particularly in the later nineteenth century) to the cultural emphasis on earnestness. Inevitably, though, such fashions were satirised in anti-aristocratic literature, in which, according to Valerie Steele, '[e]laborate and modish male dress was perceived as symptomatic of corruption, tyranny and foreign attitudes, while plainer male dress was heralded as an emblem of liberty, parliamentary democracy, enterprise, virtue, manliness, and patriotism' (98–99). From the middle-class point of view, the Macaroni and the dandy represented the unacceptable face of sophistication, and yet dandyism was also an available style for a middle-class man seeking distinction. With his perfectly finished social performance, the dandy is an important figure in the history of sophistication, and his extreme yet highly regulated behaviour also raises the question of the potential affinity between sophistication and excess.[6]

In spite of its apparent opposition to the values of Romanticism, then, sophistication was subtly pervasive in British elite society and print culture. If the scope of the enquiry is extended to Europe, a new set of sophisticated texts and public figures come into play, from Mozart's *Così fan Tutte* (1790),

6   For further discussion of dandyism, see Chapter 2.

Figure 1: Elisabeth-Louise Vigée Le Brun, *Marie-Antoinette*

Timken Collection, image courtesy of the Board of Trustees, National Gallery of Art, Washington

'the ultimate comedy of artificiality' (Pack and Lelash 222),[7] to Choderlos de Laclos's complicated novel of seduction and deceit, *Les Liaisons dangereuses* (1782); from Marie Antoinette's performance of pastoral pleasures at the Petit

---

7   The description continues: 'A work of wisdom and sophistication, and of impeccable stylistic grace, *Così fan Tutte* portrays the coming-of-age of four utterly immature young people' (222).

Trianon to the Empress Joséphine's later remodelling and refinement of court and salon society at the Tuileries. I will concentrate here on the pastoral theme, since this is an important strand in the succeeding sections of this chapter. Aristocratic fantasies about the simple life were enacted through very self-aware masquerades, and Marie Antoinette perfectly exemplifies this fashion. Around 1780 she abandoned elaborate clothes and heavy make-up in favour of simple white drawstring muslin gowns, tied at the waist with sashes (Fraser 207). She is shown in this costume, with a wide straw hat, in the famous 1783 portrait by Madame Vigée Le Brun (Figure 1) (though the supposed simplicity and innocence of the outfit was rather compromised, in the eyes of early audiences, by its similarity to underwear).[8] During this period, Marie Antoinette spent an increasing amount of time at Le Petit Trianon, where she had established a model village. She also took part in amateur theatricals there, playing shepherdesses and dairymaids, and Le Petit Trianon offered a highly refreshing contrast to the elaborate rituals and formality of court life (see Fraser 245–46). Her pastoral fantasies were not original: in the seventeenth and earlier eighteenth centuries, many aristocratic women had posed for portraits dressed as milkmaids and shepherdesses, savouring the contrast between the sophistication of women of fashion and the apparent innocence of the country girl. Sir Peter Lely, Gerard Soest, and Charles Jervas were among the artists who worked in this mode.

By the mid-eighteenth century, such pictures were no longer fashionable.[9] Artists such as Thomas Gainsborough and Johann Zoffany continued to deploy garden or countryside backgrounds, but their subjects wore elaborate clothes which would be far more appropriate to a drawing-room. The deliberate incongruity of these conversation-piece portraits echoes highly artificial social practices such as the *fête galante* or *fête champêtre*, forms of outdoor entertainment which simulated rusticity but were always highly contrived. They might involve orchestras concealed behind trees, elaborate feasts, or fancy dress, and required landscaped settings with classical statuary, pavilions and follies. These events were popular throughout the century; in its earlier decades they were represented in paintings by Jean-Antoine Watteau and Nicolas Lancret, whose work then influenced the mid-century genre painting

---

8   See Spooner 25 on the shock value of the chemise dress. The picture exists in several versions; opinions vary as to which are copies. The one reproduced here is at the National Gallery of Art, Washington. Others are at Versailles and the Château de Wolfsgarten.

9   Occasional examples still appeared, such as Sir Thomas Lawrence's *Sophia, Lady Burdett*, painted in the 1790s. The subject sits on a woodland stile, wearing a simple gown, flowers and a straw milkmaid hat. The National Portrait Gallery website comments: 'Lady Burdett's deliberate adoption of this old-fashioned, pastoral style aims to lend her a simple charm, though it is at odds with her spotless white dress, dainty pointed slipper-shoes and the fashionable detailing of her accessories.' <www.npg.org.uk> [accessed 1 November 2008].

of François Boucher and Jean-Siméon Chardin.[10] In his pictures of elegant interiors and women in dishabille, 'Boucher displays decorative disorder and luxurious *ennui*' (Vogtherr 34), and his salons and boudoirs are 'arranged and refined to create a highly sophisticated type of visual seduction, designed to please both the senses and the intellect' (Hedley 68). Chardin's technique for representing human subjects in domestic settings was rather different; in his work, the 'apparent simplicity is misleading and conceals an utmost complexity and maturity' (Vogtherr 28). Subsequently, an artist who studied under both Boucher and Chardin, Jean-Honoré Fragonard, created fantasy worlds of luxury, pleasure and coquetry in paintings such as *The Swing* (1767), which were at once elegant and shocking, delicate in technique but voyeuristic in point-of-view.

Boucher and Chardin and their contemporaries often represented scenes of tea-drinking, an increasingly widespread element of civilised social interaction. As Ann Eatwell notes, tea-ware was often prominently exhibited in dining rooms, and the ritual of preparing the tea took place in front of the guests in order 'to display the expensive equipment' (66). She adds, though, that the increasingly popular habit of tea-drinking was often criticised in print as unaffordable, unpatriotic and time-wasting (67). Critics working in eighteenth-century and Romantic studies have, in recent years, paid increasing attention to food and drink and their relation to the rise of consumerism and to philosophies of taste.[11] Denise Gigante writes in *Taste: A Literary History*:

> Romantic gastronomers, self-proclaimed professors of taste, considered the profoundly physical pleasures of the palate to be the pinnacle of aesthetic appreciation. Various 'committees of taste' established in early nineteenth-century Britain elevated food to the status of the fine arts, adopting the same juridical language and concern with philosophical principles that defined the eighteenth-century discourse of aesthetics. Just as the Enlightenment Man of Taste worked hard to distinguish specific qualities of beauty and to pronounce exact judgements of taste, the Romantic gourmand worked with equal aesthetic imperative to distinguish among different flavors of food. [...] Taste, call it *gustus*, *gusto*, or *goût* (the Continent, after all, got there before the English), was an apt metaphor for a kind of pleasure that does not submit to objective laws. (1-2)

---

10 The hierarchy of types of painting established by the French Royal Academy in the seventeenth century ran: History, Portrait, Genre, Landscape and Still Life. History was privileged because it evoked the noblest events of human life, while genres which did not involve human subject matter were subordinate. Genre paintings took subjects from everyday life, focusing on representative figures or groups in domestic or social settings. In the 1710s, French genre painting assumed greater importance as it was redefined by Watteau's pastoral *galanterie* (see Cowart xii–xiii; 222–52).
11 See for instance Morton's collection *Cultures of Taste/Theories of Appetite: Eating Romanticism* (2004).

The rapid growth of industrial production and the increasing range of consumer goods which became available in the early nineteenth century meant that individuals had to exercise greater discrimination, and could acquire distinction by making tasteful selections. At the same time, rules in such matters could not be firmly laid down, since consumption and taste are ultimately matters of individual choice. This paradox exercised many writers and philosophers of the period, and questions about what constituted good taste, and what relation existed between taste in food and taste in aesthetic matters, were discussed by intellectuals from Kant to Wordsworth, Hazlitt to Byron. In his essay 'On Gusto', Hazlitt writes: 'gusto in painting is where the impression made on one sense excites by affinity those of another', so that the eye may 'acquire a taste or appetite for what it sees' (598). The Romantic idea of gusto, according to Gigante, is located 'at the intersection of the Enlightenment concept of taste and the nineteenth-century genre of gastronomy', and is 'coterminous with, and in many ways emblematic of, the culture of sophistication and social positioning we associate with modern gastronomy' ('Romanticism and Taste' 407). This Romantic strategy anticipates the critical practice of twentieth-century theorists of taste, notably Pierre Bourdieu.

It would be productive to explore sophistication in the literature and culture of the later eighteenth and early nineteenth centuries from a whole variety of perspectives. From among the possibilities, I have chosen to focus in this chapter on questions of consumption and taste, and also on the geography of sophistication in English literature (including pastoral modes, urban/rural contrasts, and transatlantic dynamics). These subjects are, as in the rest of the study, analysed in the framework of class hierarchy and shifting ideas about leisure, wealth and inheritance. As Raymond Williams observes in *The Country and the City*, Georgian England was 'an acquisitive, high bourgeois society at the point of its most evident interlocking with an agrarian capitalism that is itself mediated by inherited titles and by the making of family names'. This produces contradictions, since '[an] openly acquisitive society, which is concerned also with the transmission of wealth, is trying to judge itself at once by an inherited code and by the morality of improvement' (115). Williams' insight bears on the class-based contestation explored in the literature of the period, and directly illuminates the texts discussed in this chapter: Richard Brinsley Sheridan's *The School for Scandal* (1777), Fanny Burney's *Evelina* (1778), Jane Austen's *Mansfield Park* (1814), and Fanny Trollope's *Domestic Manners of the Americans* (1832). These texts are closely connected by their shared engagement with the themes I have just outlined, though they are very diverse in style and genre. Sophistication functions in a subtly different way in each book. In all four, it is a necessary strategy for survival in a complex, evolving, and expanding social world, but when sophistication becomes extreme, or is displayed too overtly, it is rejected or ridiculed. A comparison of the two earlier with the two later texts also reveals certain shifts in the way sophistication was deployed.

The chapter pays attention to the words used in this period to name sophistication, as well as various related or opposite concepts. The word had not yet gained any currency in its modern sense: in the 1799 edition of Johnson's Dictionary (which was originally published in 1755), 'sophistication' is still defined simply as 'adulteration, not genuine' and 'sophistical' as 'fallaciously subtle, logically deceitful' (305). In the literature of the Romantic era, a range of other words refer to qualities which later coalesced under the heading 'sophistication'. Among the most important are the three which the *OED* uses to capture the newer, more desirable conception of sophistication: 'subtlety, discrimination, refinement'. My readings explore the relationships among these terms, and between these and the older idea of sophistry. In the late eighteenth-century context, the highly charged words 'sensibility' and 'sentiment' must also be brought into the frame. Janet Todd writes in *Sensibility: An Introduction* (1986):

> Sensibility is perhaps the key term of the period. Little used before the mid-eighteenth century [...], it came to denote the faculty of feeling, the capacity for extremely refined emotion and a quickness to display compassion for suffering. Its adjectives tell the tale of its rise and fall. It is 'exquisite' in Addison, 'delicate' in Hume, 'sweet' in Cowper, and 'dear' in Sterne. But as it declines from fashion, it becomes 'acute' in Austen, 'trembling' in Hazlitt, 'mawkish' in Coleridge, and 'sickly' in Byron. In the 1760s and 1770s many poems extol sensibility, while in the 1780s and 1790s book titles such as *Excessive Sensibility* become common. [...]
>
> 'Sentimentality' came in as a pejorative term in the 1770s when the idea of sensibility was losing ground. It suggested and still suggests debased and affected feeling, an indulgence in and display of emotion for its own sake beyond the stimulus and beyond propriety. (7–8)

It would be tempting to propose that sophistication underwent an opposite trajectory. During the era when sensibility still retained some purchase, sophistication was not likely to be prized, as it suggested detachment, manipulation, and dissimulation. Thus it is 'cunning' in Ann Radcliffe, 'rank' in Leigh Hunt and 'vain' or 'mere' in other sources, yet in later periods, when sensibility had been rejected, sophistication became 'dazzling', 'poised', 'heady' and 'elegant'. But the situation is actually much more complex, since there is no simple opposition between sophistication and sensibility. Indeed, the *OED* shows the overlap in its definition of sophistication as 'subtlety, discrimination, refinement' and of sensibility as the 'capacity for refined emotion; delicate sensitiveness of taste'.[12] Raymond Williams makes the point even clearer in *Keywords*, noting that during the eighteenth century, 'sensibility' was 'more than *sensitivity*, which can describe a physical or an emotional condition. It was, essentially, a social generalization of certain personal qualities'. He adds: 'It thus belongs in an important formation which includes *taste, cultivation* and *discrimination*, and, at a different level, *criticism* and *culture*' (281).

Characters such as Burney's Evelina and Austen's Fanny Price inhabit this overdetermined space between sophistication and sensibility: they are very much associated with deep feeling, but also with discrimination and refinement. But while sophisticated in some ways themselves, they reject the dangerous sophistication (urbanity, wit, levity) of the rakes and flirts whom they encounter. In Fanny Trollope's writing, refinement is again a key word, and is repeatedly used to elucidate the superiority of European over American culture. References to taste appear frequently in these books, and also in *The School for Scandal*, which abounds in images of mouths and tongues. In all four texts, scenes of eating are important in negotiating sophistication, and each author also dramatises contests among different versions of sophistication. In Burney and Austen, the clash is between middle-class sophistication (as embraced by the heroines) versus a degenerate form of aristocratic sophistication, while in Trollope it takes the form of American posturing and display versus English politeness, comfort and leisure. In Sheridan, the dangerous sophistication of the scandal-mongers is juxtaposed with the gourmandise of the pleasanter gentlemen, and also with the pretentious pastoral fantasies of the upwardly mobile women. Many of these contests are mapped out through contrasts between urban and rural scenes; in Burney and Sheridan, these moral geographies are reasonably straightforward, but Austen complicates them considerably, while Trollope reinvents them in a New World context. These four texts exhibit sophistication in transition: it is no longer a quality to be unhesitatingly rejected, but it has not yet evolved into its modern, attractive form. All the terms which later became elements of the modern concept of sophistication are sites of contestation in the literature of the Romantic era. Discourses of sophistication remain submerged and, to a considerable extent, oppositional.

12 This is one among several definitions for 'sensibility'. See also Empson's chapter on the words 'sense' and 'sensibility' in *The Structure of Complex Words* (250–69).

'To learn a little ingenuity and artifice': *The School for Scandal*

> A School for Scandal! Tell me, I beseech you,
> Needs there a school this modish art to teach you?
> No need of lessons *now*, the knowing think;
> We might as well be taught to eat and drink. (Garrick 5)

In his prologue, David Garrick immediately alerts us to the intense orality of Sheridan's most admired play. Tongues and mouths are its primary metaphors, and *The School for Scandal* is as much about what goes into the mouth (food and wine) as about what comes out (rumour and whispers). As it turns out, 'the knowing' think wrongly: there *is* a need for lessons in scandal, because its prevalence makes the social world treacherous, even for the virtuous. And the fourth line makes their error clear, since fashionable people are, in fact, 'taught to eat and drink': an educated palate has always been a marker of upper-class status.[13] In connecting the practice of eating and drinking with the practice of bad-mouthing, Garrick's prologue (disingenuously) presents both as natural. But 'natural' is among the most loaded words in the text of Sheridan's play. As one of sophistication's main opposite terms, its meaning is, of course, equally open to debate:

LADY SNEERWELL:
> Wounded myself, in the early part of my life by the envenomed tongue of slander I confess I have since known no pleasure equal to the reducing others to the level of my own injured reputation.

SNAKE:
> Nothing can be more natural. (Sheridan, *Scandal* 11)[14]

The implication here is that Lady Sneerwell's suffering makes her reciprocal infliction of pain in some sense 'natural'. Yet her indulgence of it is a highly artificial practice. Snake, comparing Lady Sneerwell with another woman, Mrs Clackitt, who is an inveterate gossip, remarks: 'her colouring is too dark and her outlines often extravagant. She wants that delicacy of hint and mellowness of sneer which distinguishes your ladyship's scandal' (11).

The virtuous Maria says of the vicious gossips she encounters at Lady Sneerwell's: 'nothing could excuse the intemperance of their tongues but a natural and ungovernable bitterness of mind' (46). This unusual image – intemperate tongues – actually makes perfect sense because Sheridan's villainous and deceitful characters all eschew indulgence in food and especially in wine,

---

13 As Bourdieu explains in *Distinction*, economic power asserts itself through the display of freedom from necessity, and this leads to the elaboration of a 'life-style' which 'organizes the most diverse practices – the choice of a vintage or a cheese or the decoration of a holiday home in the country' (56).

14 References to play texts are given using page numbers.

substituting indulgence in scandal. Indeed, the gossiping women (and one man, Sir Benjamin) are dangerously sophisticated because the subjects of their slanderous talk become, on a metaphorical level, their food: 'Lady Stucco is very well with the dessert after dinner;' says Lady Teazle, 'for she's just like the French fruit one cracks for mottoes – made up of paint and proverb' (42). Litvak observes:

> the exercise of sophisticated taste rather horrifyingly involves the consumption of the 'edible bodies', not just of those lesser animals that ordinarily pass for, or end up as food, but – symbolically at least – of other consumers. To be sophisticated, that is […] to outsophisticate the other is to incorporate the other. (9)

Sheridan's cannibal-sophisticates emphasise their own superiority by pointing out their victims' oral failings. Agreeing to the observation that Miss Simper has pretty teeth, Lady Teazle maliciously adds: 'Yes; and on that account, when she is neither speaking nor laughing (which very seldom happens), she never absolutely shuts her mouth, but leaves it always on a jar, as it were' (39). She also describes another acquaintance, Miss Prim, who has lost some front teeth and therefore 'draws her mouth till it positively resembles the aperture of a poor's box and all her words appear to slide out edgewise' (39–40). Almost everyone in *The School for Scandal* is defined at some point in terms of his or her mouth, but these minor figures, Miss Simper and Miss Prim (who do not even appear on stage), have no attribute besides their mouths.

In contrast to Lady Sneerwell's mouthy guests, several of the sincere and likeable characters refrain from scandal but relish good wine and food. Charles Surface, who is a spendthrift and epicure, but far more open-handed and honest than his nasty brother Joseph, considers abstinence from drink unnatural, lamenting:

> 'Fore Heaven, 'tis true – there's the great degeneracy of the age! Many of our acquaintance have taste, spirit, and politeness; but plague on't they won't *drink*. […] Instead of the social spirit of raillery that used to mantle over a glass of bright burgundy, their conversation is become just like the Spa-water they drink, which has all the pertness and flatulence of champagne, without its spirit or flavour. (67–68)

The brothers' rich uncle, Sir Oliver, likes Charles but abuses Joseph's insincerity: 'Oh, plague of his sentiments! If he salutes me with a scrap of morality in his mouth, I shall be sick directly.' He then invites Sir Peter Teazle: 'Well, come, give us a bottle of good wine, and we'll drink the lads' health' (51). A taste for good wine unites Sir Peter, Sir Oliver and Charles, whereas Joseph's mouth contains only scraps and so he provokes intense disgust in his uncle. Bourdieu's comment on distaste is helpful here:

Tastes (i.e. manifested preferences) are the practical affirmation of an inevitable difference. It is no accident that when they have to be justified, they are asserted purely negatively, by the refusal of other tastes. In matters of taste, more than anywhere else, all determination is negation; and tastes are perhaps first and foremost distastes, disgust provoked by horror or visceral intolerance ('sick-making') of the tastes of others. [...] [E]ach taste feels itself to be natural – and so it almost is, being a habitus – which amounts to rejecting others as unnatural and therefore vicious. (56)

The moral question, which has implications for dramatic form, is how entertaining raillery is to be distinguished from damaging gossip, and how the slanderers and hypocrites are to be prevented from becoming attractive through their cleverness and wit.[15] Mark S. Auburn writes: 'in attacking slander and scandal, [Sheridan] had a particular problem: it appears to be witty, intellectual fun. How can he both exploit scandal to provide good comic entertainment and at the same time expose malicious gossip as the lowest of selfish pleasures?' (140). Auburn's argument is that Sheridan solves this problem by carefully sequencing the Scandal School scenes so that the slanderers become progressively less witty, and the objects of their invective progressively less ridiculous. The audience, Auburn suggests, must undergo a 'process of growth', since 'we must see vice and think it attractive [...]; only upon growing familiar with it will we realize its hurtful potential' (144). Indeed, in a self-reflexive moment in the drama, Joseph Surface implicates the audience in the scandal-mongering by remarking: 'To smile at the jest which plants a thorn in another's breast is to become a principal in the mischief' (17).

But there is some doubt as to how seriously we are meant to take this statement, and whether it is in fact possible for the audience to learn not to smile at a cruel jest. After all, though vice becomes less attractive over the course of the play, virtue does not get any more exciting, and the unsophisticated Maria remains dull and tiresome. Joseph's remark, too, may appear rather hard to swallow, since it is in the same style as the many other pompous platitudes he comes out with. They are referred to in the text as 'sentiments', but the whole identity of the 'Man of Sentiment' (13) is actually a disguise, as Lady Sneerwell acknowledges when she describes Joseph as 'artful, selfish, and malicious – in short, a sentimental knave' (13). F. W. Bateson notes in an editorial footnote to this line:

The paradox depends on two conflicting contemporary senses of the word *sentimental* (a term not recorded until the later 1740s): (i) as the English adjective of Fr. *sentiment* (= aphoristic moral generalization of some special moral issue); (ii) as the

---

15 For an interesting discussion of Joseph as the potential hero of the play, see Charles Lamb's 'On the Artificial Comedy of the Last Century' (1822), p. 187.

primarily English shorthand for the *enjoyment* of private emotion for its own sake (primitive form of romanticism), as in parts of Sterne's *Sentimental Journey* (1776). (Sheridan, *School* 13)

The ideological charge of 'sentiment' is unstable in Sheridan's writing, and its meaning is implicitly debated. In *The School for Scandal*, sentimentalism begins to approach the meaning it has in modern critical discourse, which Jessica Burstein identifies as 'a common and commonizing tendency, either reeking of or redolent with the mainstream' (234). Thus, sentimentalism is generally rejected by those who would be sophisticated, though it can also be strategically embraced as a disguise. Among his intimates, Joseph Surface generally discards his sententious platitudes, and when he begins to revert to them, Lady Sneerwell says to him, 'O lud, you are going to be moral and forget that you are among friends'. Joseph replies, 'Egad, that's true. I'll keep that sentiment til I see Sir Peter' (Sheridan, *Scandal* 15). Their sophistication depends on an ability to assume, and put off, sentiment at appropriate moments, and also on their skill in sophistry. In this text, and others from the period, sophistry and sophistication retain a direct connection. Joseph excels in sophistical argument: the most striking example is his scene with Lady Teazle, in which he persuades her that if her husband suspects her of infidelity, 'it becomes you to be frail in compliment to his discernment' (91).

When the middle-aged Sir Peter Teazle takes a young wife, he chooses a girl who appears to be a child of nature: 'I chose with caution – a girl bred wholly in the country, who never knew luxury beyond one silk gown, nor dissipation above the annual gala of a race ball'. But now, he adds, 'she plays her part in all the extravagant fopperies of the fashion and the town, with as ready a grace as if she had never seen a bush nor a grass plat out of Grosvenor Square' (27). When he reprimands her for extravagance, she retorts:

LADY TEAZLE

> For my part, I should think you would like to have your wife thought a woman of taste.

SIR PETER

> Aye! There again! Taste! Zounds, madam, you had no taste when you married me.

LADY TEAZLE

> That's very true, indeed, Sir Peter; and after having married you I should never pretend to taste again, I allow. (34)

The urban sophisticate, Sir Peter, imagines his chosen wife as a semi-pastoral figure, fondly remembering the day 'when I saw you first, sitting at your tambour in a pretty figured linen gown with a bunch of keys by your side, your hair combed smooth over a roll, and your apartment hung round with worsted fruits of your own making' (32). But while he identifies this rural style with the simple and natural, Lady Teazle herself remarks: 'a curious life I led – my daily occupation to inspect the dairy, superintend the poultry, make extracts from the family receipt-book' (32). According to her recently acquired fashionable tastes, this rural life appears 'curious'; to Sir Peter its unsophistication had – paradoxically – the allure of novelty. Crucially, Lady Teazle was not actually a dairymaid or shepherdess but belonged to a socially middling family – 'the daughter of a plain country squire' (32). Hence, she was likely to aspire upwards, and she affirms her raised status by flaunting her spending power. Sir Peter exclaims: ''Slife, to spend as much to furnish your dressing room with flowers in winter as would suffice to turn the Pantheon into a greenhouse and give a *fête champêtre* at Christmas' (31–32). His wife demonstrates her new sophistication by rejecting the natural in favour of the artificial or exotic: out-of-season flowers and a midwinter outdoor feast.

Lady Teazle's pastoral fantasy aligns her with aristocratic style, and forms an interesting comparison with a portrait of Charles Surface's aunt. Charles points to 'my great-aunt Deborah, done by Kneller [...]. There she is, you see, a shepherdess feeding her flock' (81). At this point, Charles is selling off the paintings of his ancestors in order to pay his debts, not knowing that the purchaser is his Uncle Oliver in disguise. Oliver laments in an aside: 'poor Deborah – a woman who set such value on herself!', and adds aloud: 'Five pounds ten – she's mine' (81). Deborah affirms her 'value' as a sophisticated aristocrat through her pose as a rural labourer, and thereby enters an economy of symbolic goods (in terms of both her own class status and the value of her portrait as art). Yet in the transaction between Charles and Oliver, she is reduced to an object of purely economic exchange, and a cheap one at that. This is partly because the sophistication of earlier eras does not always retain its value for later generations. Sophistication can operate through nostalgia (self-conscious reference to the styles of the past), but it cannot be old-fashioned. Therefore, sophisticated nostalgia is much more likely to focus on the unfamiliar glamour of a long-past era than on the merely outdated fashions of recent generations. Great-aunt Deborah's portrait, if painted by Godfrey Kneller (1646–1723), is more than fifty years old, and the vogue for painting English society women as shepherdesses, at its height in the later seventeenth and very early eighteenth centuries, had waned considerably by the time of *The School for Scandal*. It is unsurprising, then, that Lady Teazle does not wish to dress as a milkmaid or shepherdess – not only are these no longer very fashionable poses, but they are uncomfortably close to the activities she carried out in her former home. Instead, her outdoor festivities evoke the more modern and luxurious pastoral fantasies of French rococo style.

In the sale scene, Oliver (who is pretending to be a money-lender called Mr Premium) persists in equating the portraits with the ancestors themselves – ''Odd's life, do you take me for Shylock in the play that you would raise money of me on your own flesh and blood?' (78) – but Charles mocks this notion: 'Well, you see, Master Premium, what a domestic character I am. Here I sit of an evening surrounded by my family' (80). In a complex speech, Charles says that the paintings are

> not like the works of your modern Raphael, who gives you the strongest resemblance, yet contrives to make your own portrait independent of you, so that you may sink the original and not hurt the picture. No, no; the merit of these is the inveterate likeness – all stiff and awkward as the originals, and like nothing in human nature beside. (79)

Charles here offers a startlingly modern insight into the workings of an image-based culture. The pictures of his ancestors ('the Surfaces' [79]) are too realistic to be attractive; their value is purely totemic. By contrast, he sees the modern picture becoming an autonomous aesthetic object, its meaning and value no longer dependent on the significance of the person represented. Indeed, the image may come to substitute for the represented subject, which is 'sunk'.

The picture gallery scene raises questions of reputation, recognition and notoriety, and the most sophisticated characters in the play are those who can most successfully negotiate the culture of surfaces which they inhabit. Ultimately, though, all the characters are subject to the larger, impersonal operations of what, in a modern sense, might be understood as a celebrity system. Then, as now, it was sustained by gossip, but the circulation of scandal and rumour cannot be controlled by any one person, even so powerful a woman as Lady Sneerwell. She comes to grief in the end through the treachery of Snake, who says that though Lady Sneerwell had paid him well for his lies, he has now 'been offered double to speak the truth' (134). He requests, however, that his truth-telling shall not be made public, since 'I live by the badness of my character. I have nothing but my infamy to depend on' (136). The disabling of Lady Sneerwell and her accomplice returns us to the line in the verse preface which reveals that Scandal is ultimately an uncontrollable force: 'Cut Scandal's head off, still the tongue is wagging' (Garrick 6). The central image of the tongue points to all the key themes of the play: scandal, consumption, taste and finally the unnamed yet ever-present theme of sophistication.

'She is quite a little rustic': Fanny Burney, *Evelina*

Fanny Burney's first novel, *Evelina*, develops the popular eighteenth-century theme of the innocent though well-born country girl encountering the perils and sophistications of high society life. Subtitled *The History of a Young Lady's Entrance into the World*, it is an epistolary novel which tells – mainly in her own words – the story of Evelina Anville. Unaware that her name is a fiction, since her real father, Lord Belmont, has refused to own her, Evelina lives contentedly in Dorset with her aged foster-parent, the Reverend Mr Villars. He reluctantly allows her to depart on a visit to his friend Lady Howard and her daughter Mrs Mirvan, who subsequently take her to London. There, she encounters many fashionable people, and unexpectedly meets her vulgar grandmother, Madame Duval, a set of ill-bred cousins, and a mysterious young man called Mr Macartney, who later proves to be her brother. Evelina next travels (for her health) to Bristol Hotwells, accompanied by a rather satirical lady named Mrs Selwyn. They stay at the house of an acquaintance, Mrs Beaumont, and in Bristol Evelina and Mr Macartney are reunited with their repentant father. Everywhere Evelina goes, she is pursued by many suitors and libertines, whose attentions cause frequent misunderstandings between her and her heroic admirer, Lord Orville.

During the earlier phases of the narrative, the heroine is repeatedly described as 'rustic', a term which – in the logic of pastoral – is one of the possible opposites to 'sophisticated'. In the text, 'rustic' is one of several words whose meaning is contested, played on and ironised; among the others are 'quality', 'smart' and 'polite'. These words are inflected by a competition between different conceptions of sophistication, explored through the characters' various attempts to display or, alternatively, to disavow it. In advance of Evelina's visit, Mr Villars writes anxiously to Lady Howard: 'She is quite a little rustic, and knows nothing of the world' (12), but his friend perceives the social capital which this may represent:

> Her character seems truly ingenuous and simple; and, at the same time that nature has blessed her with an excellent understanding, and great quickness of parts, she has a certain air of inexperience and innocency that is extremely interesting. (13)

Evelina's innocence, however, initially evokes contempt. During her first dance with Lord Orville, she is in some alarm: 'how will he be provoked, thought I, when he finds what a simple rustic he has honoured with his choice! one whose ignorance of the world makes her perpetually fear doing something wrong!' (25). Her embarrassment leads Lord Orville to describe her as 'a poor weak girl' (30), and he is bemused by her artless and incredulous laughter at the behaviour of the foppish Mr Lovel. Another gentleman, setting up as

Evelina's champion, says of her response to Lovel: 'Ha! ha! ha! why, there's some *genius* in that, my Lord, though perhaps rather *rustic*' (32). In her letters, Evelina often italicises slippery words which may be used in various senses. Here, the emphasis on 'rustic' indicates the gentleman's patronising tone, as opposed to Mr Villars' cherishing usage of the same term; he clearly wants to appropriate 'genius' to himself, rather than seriously attributing it to her.

Evelina, then, is presented (at least partly) as a pastoral figure, whose virtue and unsophistication cannot be accommodated by fashionable society. She censures the frivolity, cruelty and extravagance of two of Mrs Beaumont's guests, who settle a hundred-pound bet by a race between two old women. Lord Orville, increasingly allured by her innocence, is pleased by this reaction: '"I am charmed," said he, "at the novelty of meeting with one so unhackneyed in the world as not yet to be influenced by custom to forget the use of reason"' (353). In this scene, Evelina seemingly corresponds to Empson's definition in *Some Versions of Pastoral* of the simple person. Empson explains (or voices) 'the tone of humility normal to pastoral' as follows:

'I now abandon my specialized feelings because I am trying to find better ones, so I must balance myself for the moment by imagining the feelings of the simple person. He may be in a better state than I am by luck, freshness, or divine grace; value is outside any scheme for the measurement of value because that too must be valued.' Various paradoxes may be thrown in here; 'I must imagine his way of feeling because the refined thing must be judged by the fundamental thing, because strength must be learnt in weakness and sociability in isolation, because the best manners are learnt in the simple life.' (23)

In his admiration of Evelina, Lord Orville adopts the 'double attitude of [...] the complex man to the simple one ("I am in one way better, in another not so good")' which Empson describes as the basis of both straight and comic pastoral.

Lord Orville is sophisticated not simply because of his taste, discernment and experience, but because he is capable of imaginative sympathy with unsophistication. In his love scene with Evelina, his dual position of subjection and domination is enacted through posture:

'My Lord,' cried I, endeavouring to disengage my hand, 'pray let me go!'

'I will,' cried he, to my inexpressible confusion, dropping on one knee, 'if you wish to leave me!'

'Oh, my Lord,' exclaimed I, 'rise, I beseech you, rise! – such a posture to me! – surely your Lordship is not so cruel as to mock me!'

'Mock you!' repeated he earnestly, 'no, I revere you! I esteem and I admire you above all human beings! you are the friend to whom my soul is attached as its better

41

half! you are the most amiable, the most perfect of women! and you are dearer to me than language has the power of telling.'

    I attempt not to describe my sensations at that moment; I scarce breathed; I doubted if I existed, – the blood forsook my cheeks, and my feet refused to sustain me: Lord Orville, hastily rising, supported me to a chair, upon which I sank, almost lifeless. (416–17)

As befits a pastoral figure, Evelina is here both idealised and (despite Lord Orville's protestations) mocked. She casts herself in a semi-comic role: the deliberately excessive nature of the scene is visible in an extravagant use of exclamation marks, while her claim that she cannot articulate her sensations is followed instantly by her detailed account of them. The comedy becomes more overt when Mrs Selwyn arrives, surprising Lord Orville on his knees, and Evelina is 'overwhelmed' by shame (417). The shame of the simple person is counterpointed by the mirth of the sophisticates: at Mrs Selwyn's sarcastic comments and 'most provoking look', Lord Orville 'could not help laughing' (417). Mrs Selwyn's elaborate wit is far removed from Evelina's spontaneous (yet socially unacceptable) laughter at Mr Lovel. The older woman's sophisticated humour protects her; Evelina's sense of the ridiculous sometimes makes her vulnerable.

Evelina, indeed, is vulnerable in many ways: her timidity, combined with her lack of understanding of urban manners, makes for a series of conflicts, errors and alarms. The sheer violence of some of these incidents results, in part, from the mid-eighteenth-century fictional and dramatic conventions on which Burney draws, but it also images the terrifying and absurd nature of Evelina's new social milieu. She is sixteen, yet is constantly infantilised and referred to as 'my child' (17), 'this child' (54) and 'a little angel' (13). Bewildered by the adult world, she repeatedly gets lost in crowds or is overcome by shyness. Commenting on the development of the pastoral form, Empson describes a shift in feeling which, 'after the middle of the eighteenth century', caused pastoral imagery and structures of thought to become 'silly unless kept for children and young girls' (167), so that serious pastoral was gradually displaced by mock pastoral, and afterwards became invested in the Victorian cult of the child. *Evelina*, then, is chronologically located in the period of transition, and Evelina herself may be read as a transitional figure in relation to both pastoral and sophistication.

Although, as suggested above, she partly conforms to the pastoral conception of the simple person, she does not entirely match it. Apparently socially obscure, she is in fact the daughter of an aristocrat; while her manner can be awkward or 'rustic', she is extremely delicate in her responses. In addition, Evelina exhibits the self-consciousness of the pastoral narrator (or, in

Empson's terms, 'complex man'): she refers, for instance, to the ignorant and easily deceived Mr Brown as 'the simple swain' (242). She also approaches 'complexity' in admiring what she cannot wholly approve, as in her attitude to the rake Sir Clement Willoughby. In his polished manners and intelligent conversation she finds relief from the vulgarity and violence of Madame Duval, the Branghtons, and Captain Mirvan, yet she rightly suspects Sir Clement of immorality and opportunism:

> Sir Clement exerted all his powers of argument and of ridicule to second and strengthen whatever was advanced by the Captain: for he had the sagacity to discover, that he could take no method so effectual for making the master of the house his friend, as to make Madame Duval his enemy [...] He managed the argument so skilfully, at once provoking Madame Duval, and delighting the Captain, that I could not forbear admiring his address, though I condemned his subtlety. (61)

Sir Clement's 'argument' depends on sophistry rather than rational contention; his ability to perform a part marks him as sophisticated and subtle in the dangerous sense. 'Subtlety', like 'sophistication', has evolved from a term of disapproval to one of praise. The *OED* gives usages from 1375 until 1654 under the definition 'An ingenious contrivance; a crafty or cunning device; an artifice; *freq.* in an unfavourable sense, a wily stratagem or trick'. This meaning is marked 'obsolete'. For the definition 'A refinement or nicety of thought, speculation, or argument; a fine distinction; a nice point', the examples begin in 1654 and extend into the twentieth century, while the quotations using 'subtlety' to mean 'fineness or delicacy of nature, character, manner, operation' are all taken from nineteenth-century texts. 'Subtlety', in *Evelina*, appears to retain its earlier pejorative meaning, though the newer sense is beginning to emerge as the heroine acknowledges the intelligence underlying Sir Clement's behaviour.

Evelina's ambivalent positioning in relation to sophistication and to the pastoral is clearly imaged in the scenes set in gardens. The garden, an intermediate space between the pure virtuous air of the country and the dissipation and danger of the city, takes on especial significance during Evelina's stay at Mrs Beaumont's house. On one occasion, she is surprised in the arbour by Sir Clement, who detains her by force and declares his passion; and in the same spot, Sir Clement clashes with Lord Orville over their respective intentions towards Evelina. Yet despite these associations, Lord Orville still chooses the arbour as the fittest place for a romantic discourse. He cannot, though, preserve a pastoral atmosphere; not only is the arbour contaminated by Sir Clement's libertine behaviour, it is also invaded by Mrs Selwyn's acerbic sophistication. Once again, she surprises the couple at a particularly tender moment:

> 'So, my dear,' cried she, 'what, still courting the rural shades! I thought ere now you would have been satiated with this retired seat, and I have been seeking you all over the house. [...] However, don't let me disturb your meditations; you are possibly planning some pastoral dialogue.' (436)

Mrs Selwyn turns the putatively romantic scenes into mock pastoral. In the London and Berry Hill sequences, elements of serious pastoral are often present, as the traditional opposition between country virtue and city vice is upheld. But in the ambiguous and overdetermined space of the garden, the narrative becomes self-conscious about pastoral conventions.

The garden, then, is not a genuine pastoral location. In general terms, it represents an attempted recreation or imitation of a 'natural' setting within the city or, more broadly, within the framework of civilised life (as in a country-house garden). During her stay in London, the most perilous situations in which Evelina finds herself occur in public gardens. At Marybone, she becomes separated from her party and is molested by several men. She mistakenly applies for 'protection' (281) to two prostitutes, whereupon she encounters Lord Orville and fears he will think her degraded to their condition. At Vauxhall, Evelina's vulgar cousins, Bid and Polly Branghton, take her into the dangerous 'dark walks' (230), where all three are seized by men who presume their favours are for sale.

As Janet Todd observes in her study of eighteenth-century fiction, '[in] mid-century literature, London was frequently the place of vice and frivolous pleasure; in later decades it stood also for social malice and economic greed', whereas 'in the country it seemed that man and virtue had not yet parted company' (14). Owing to her country-bred inexperience, Evelina is continually surprised, both pleasantly and unpleasantly, by the sights and social practices of London. This amuses the Branghtons, who believe themselves to be more sophisticated, in the modern sense of worldly and knowledgeable. Yet Evelina's far better taste and education are repeatedly evidenced, especially during the scene at the opera:

> 'What a jabbering they make!' cried Mr Branghton; 'there's no knowing a word they say. Pray, what's the reason they can't as well sing in English? – but I suppose the fine folks would not like it, if they could understand it.'
>
> 'How unnatural their action is,' said the son; 'why now, who ever saw an Englishman put himself in such out-of-the-way postures?'
>
> 'For my part,' said Miss Polly, 'I think it's very pretty, only I don't know what it means.'
>
> 'Lord, what does that signify?' cried her sister; 'mayn't one like a thing without being so very particular? – You may see that Miss likes it, and I don't suppose she knows more of the matter than we do.' (104)

This conversation enacts a series of position-takings in a broader debate on sophistication and high culture. Mr Branghton, preferring vernacular art forms, rather astutely suggests that opera's inaccessibility to mass audiences makes it an effective means for cultured people to display their distinction. His son associates sophisticated cultural products with foreignness and artificiality, while his daughter Polly artlessly confesses her ignorance while also laying claim to some taste in finding the opera 'pretty'. Her elder sister exemplifies pretension: imitating Evelina's attitude to the opera in order to appear discerning, she simultaneously denies her cousin's superiority.

The Branghtons' pretentious acquaintance Mr Smith also attracts Evelina's contempt. When he insists on taking her to a ball, she notes 'the inelegant smartness of his air and deportment', adding: 'his visible struggle against education to put on the fine gentleman, added to his frequent conscious glances at a dress to which he was but little accustomed, very effectually destroyed his aim of *figuring*' (263). Evelina here connects distinction with gentility, implying that it cannot be successfully imitated by lower-class aspirants. She bolsters her own precarious class status by presenting Mr Smith's pretensions to her hand as insulting. Evelina's word 'smartness' is telling: it suggests cheap showiness, and is a word – rather like 'posh' today – which classifies those who use it. Evelina employs it with disdain; Mr Smith, on the other hand, considers 'smartness' desirable. Explaining his previous reluctance to marry, he requests her to 'suppose you had such a large acquaintance of gentlemen as I have, – and that you had always been used to appear a little – a little smart among them', and then asks, 'why now, how should you like to let yourself down all at once into a married man? (270). The meaning of 'smart' is further complicated when Mr Smith uses it to defend himself against Evelina's sophisticated grammar and logic, which he apparently cannot understand. When he forces her to accept the ball ticket, she says: 'If you were determined, Sir [...] in making me this offer, to allow me no choice of refusal or acceptance, I must think myself less obliged to your intention than I was willing to do', and he retorts: 'You're so smart, there is no speaking to you; indeed, you are monstrous smart, Ma'am!' (263). Once again, the label used classifies the classifier: it is in fact Mr Smith who is 'monstrous smart', and indeed, simply monstrous.

While Mr Smith fails to seem sophisticated because he tries too hard, Lord Orville succeeds perfectly by not appearing to try. Lord Orville embodies an ideal which is crucial to Evelina's system of values:

Lord Orville, with a politeness which knows no intermission, and makes no distinction, is as unassuming and modest as if he had never mixed with the great, and was totally ignorant of every qualification he possesses; this other Lord, though lavish of compliments and fine speeches, seems to me an entire stranger to real good-breeding [...] his conscious quality seems to have given him a freedom in his way of speaking to either sex, that is very little short of rudeness. (131)

Lord Orville is distinguished because he 'makes no distinction' – that is, he treats everyone with equal courtesy; and he is great because he does not trade on his acquaintance with greatness. The other Lord is conscious of his 'quality', meaning his upper-class status, but this very consciousness reduces his actual quality (in the evaluative sense) in Evelina's eyes. The comparison between Lord Orville and the other Lord might be understood in the terms suggested by Joseph Litvak, who characterises modern culture as 'a *contest of sophistications*, where victory often redounds to those who best disavow their sophistication' (5). Though he identifies Austen's fiction as the first modern treatment of sophistication (14), it might be argued that Burney's work is in transition from a mid-eighteenth-century to a Regency-era conception of sophistication, and certainly, the idea of the 'contest of sophistications' is directly relevant to *Evelina*.

While Lord Orville delicately disavows sophistication, the determinedly middle-class Captain Mirvan loudly denounces it. He particularly dislikes Frenchified manners, and repeatedly attacks the affected Mr Lovel, who continually uses French phrases, and the English-born expatriate Madame Duval. When she says: 'I shall only just visit a person of quality or two, of my particular acquaintance, and then I shall go back to France', he shouts: 'Ay, do [...] and then go to the devil together, for that's the fittest voyage for the French and the quality' (51). He associates these two groups not with elegance, sophistication and polish (as might be more usual), but with a dangerous challenge to English masculinity – when Madame Duval recommends that he travel to the continent, he responds: 'What, I suppose you'd have me learn to cut capers? – and dress like a monkey? [...] And powder, and daub, and make myself up, like some other folks?' (65). Yet despite his violence and discourtesy, there is, at times, a degree of alignment between Captain Mirvan's opinions and Evelina's. In particular, both are disturbed by challenges to traditional gender boundaries. Evelina says of the witty and unforgiving Mrs Selwyn: 'her understanding, indeed, may be called *masculine*; but, unfortunately, her manners deserve the same epithet; for, in studying to acquire the knowledge of the other sex, she has lost all the softness of her own' (326). Evelina also remarks with surprise that, during her first shopping expedition in London, she was mostly served by men, 'and such men! so finical, so affected!'. She adds: 'they recommended caps and ribbands with an air of so much importance, that I wished to ask them how long they had left off wearing them' (21).

In her representation of both Mrs Selwyn and the shop assistants, Evelina presents sophisticated style as a threat to the 'natural' – that is, heteronormative – order. Litvak writes that sophistication

> by no means lacks detractors, who are quick to point out its various offenses. But, since one of those 'offenses' is its association with intellectuality and homosexuality, both of which are resented as by definition excessive, as self-indulgent and unproductive, it has seemed to me worthwhile to affirm it precisely on the basis of this association. (18)

This comment exactly describes Evelina's resentment of sophistication as manifested in her bluestocking chaperone and the male milliners. Presumably, then, an interpretation of *Evelina* which affirms sophistication must align itself with Mrs Selwyn's, rather than Evelina's, outlook; such a reading would, at first sight, appear a resistant one. Yet the novel actually permits such a reading because Mrs Selwyn, though unmannerly, always demonstrates acuity in her critiques of fashionable society:

> 'O,' cried [Lord Merton], 'never mind Jack Coverley, for he does not know how to drive.'
>
> 'My Lord,' cried Mr Coverley, 'I'll drive against *you* for a thousand pounds.' [...]
>
> 'These enterprises,' said Mrs Selwyn, 'are very proper for men of rank, since 'tis a million to one but both parties will be incapacitated for any better employment.' (342)

Moreover, Mrs Selwyn's remarks are contained by the framing narrative of Evelina's letters: Evelina first describes a piece of folly, then comments on it by quoting her friend's verbal attacks. In her own modest persona, Evelina could not say such harsh things, but she certainly countenances, and even tacitly affirms, Mrs Selwyn's views. As narrator, her self-awareness and penetration move her towards a sophisticated point of view, even though her behaviour as character in the scenes described is often extremely naive.

The argument can be taken still further: Evelina might even be understood as highly sophisticated herself if we distinguish, as Litvak does, among the different versions of sophistication which belong to different classes. 'Playing both sides against the middle – against itself,' he writes in his chapter on *Pride and Prejudice*, 'middle-class sophistication vulgarizes mere (i.e. aristocratic) sophistication and sophisticates mere (i.e. lower-class) vulgarity' (29). He goes on:

> In a culture that tolerates the sophisticated even less than the disgusting – indeed, for which the sophisticated paradoxically represents the disgusting at its most egregious – and that constructs its middle class as the sacred repository of normality itself, the sophisticated middle-class connoisseur of the disgusting commits an offense that includes but is not limited to the sexual. Or rather, her sexual offense *counts* as a social offense, and vice versa. (31)

At first sight, this description, which refers to Elizabeth Bennet, may not seem to apply equally to Evelina. But consider the following passage from Burney's text:

> the conversation turned wholly upon eating, a subject which was discussed with the utmost delight; and had I not known they were men of rank and fashion, I should have imagined that Lord Merton, Mr Lovel, and Mr Coverley had all been professed cooks; for they displayed so much knowledge of sauces and made dishes, and of the various methods of dressing the same things, that I am persuaded they must have given much time, and much study, to make themselves such adepts in this *art*. It would be very difficult to determine whether they were most to be distinguished as *gluttons* or *epicures*; for they were at once dainty and voracious, understood the right and wrong of every dish, and alike emptied the one and the other. I should have been quite sick of their remarks, had I not been entertained by seeing that Lord Orville, who, I am sure, was equally disgusted, not only read my sentiments but, by his countenance, communicated to me his own. (343–44)

Evelina rejects aristocratic sophistication (that is, the finicky taste and superfluous discrimination of the wealthy, bored Lords), covertly associating it with sexual perversity by applying the word 'dainty' to men. At the same time, she distances herself from the vulgarity of excessive appetite and excessive utterance. Entrenching herself further in middle-class attitudes, Evelina disdains the knowledge of food, which she sees as the preserve of servants; her italics indicate that she will not admit cookery to be a legitimate '*art*'.[16] As Gigante says of attitudes to eating and taste in the late eighteenth-century: 'Once middle-class ideals of tasteful moderation governed the ideology of consumption, neither the rich (whose palates were symbolically vitiated by overindulgence) nor the poor (whose objective was merely to eat) contributed representative members to tasteful society' (10).

Evelina's social offence is her refusal of the tastes of her company; her sexual one is the secret communication with Lord Orville. Through her silent interchange with her lover, mutual desire is perversely intensified by mutual disgust. It is worth noting, finally, that the behaviour of the aristocrats at dinner is mimicked by Evelina's disreputable relations – she writes of their supper, eaten in 'a conspicuous place' at Vauxhall: 'Much fault was found with everything that was ordered, though not a morsel of anything was left; and the dearness of the provisions, with conjectures upon what profit was made by them, supplied discourse during the whole meal' (228). This is pseudo-sophistication: instead of discriminating among good and bad dishes, the

16 In my 1903 edition, the novel's preoccupation with consumption and taste is emphasised by a drawing on the contents page of a gentleman at a table, holding a 'Bill of Fare'. This also presents the book itself as something to be consumed.

Branghtons abuse them all in order to appear to have educated tastes, while their preoccupation with cost quite negates the public display of their own lavish consumption. *Evelina*, then, dramatises the contest of sophistications, and the victors are indeed those who avoid seeming to desire sophistication – that is, Evelina and Lord Orville. Despite Evelina's actual aristocratic birth, her version of sophistication is recognisably middle-class. In Jane Austen, a similar kind of sophistication is revealed, and without the protection of an occluded upper-class lineage. Only one of her heroines has a titled parent; the rest range themselves in different strata of the genteel. The heroine with the most ambivalent and precarious social status, Fanny Price, will be the focus of the next section.

'The first ardours of her young, unsophisticated mind': *Mansfield Park*

Concepts of sophistication resonate throughout Jane Austen's work. She explores sophistication in its modern, attractive sense (subtlety, discrimination, refinement), and also in its older form (disingenuousness, amoral worldliness). Yet Austen never once uses the term 'sophisticated' in her fiction. In its newer meaning, of course, it was not yet current, but the word does not occur in its pejorative guise either, and there is only one instance of its opposite. 'Unsophistication' is used in the passage in *Mansfield Park* describing the attachment between Fanny and William Price:

> An affection so amiable was advancing each in the opinion of all who had hearts to value any thing good. Henry Crawford was as much struck with it as any. He honoured the warm hearted, blunt fondness of the young sailor [...] – and saw, with lively admiration, the glow of Fanny's cheek, the brightness of her eye, the deep interest, the absorbed attention, while her brother was describing any of the imminent hazards, or terrific scenes, which such a period, at sea, must supply.
>
> It was a picture which Henry Crawford had moral taste enough to value. Fanny's attractions increased – increased two-fold – for the sensibility which beautified her complexion and illuminated her countenance, was an attraction in itself. He was no longer in doubt of the capabilities of her heart. She had feeling, genuine feeling. It would be something to be loved by such a girl, to excite the first ardours of her young, unsophisticated mind! She interested him more than he had foreseen. (191)

According to the moral logic of *Mansfield Park*, 'unsophistication' is the privileged term in the binary 'sophistication/unsophistication'. But the sentence in which 'unsophisticated' occurs is written in free indirect style: it is, in effect, Henry Crawford's choice of word. And Henry Crawford himself is the epitome of sophistication. Here, he (like Lord Orville in *Evelina*) demonstrates this quality through his ability to recognise and appreciate its opposite. At the same time, he continues to position himself as superior to the Prices – that word 'blunt', also belonging to Crawford's inner discourse, proves it – and therefore continues to privilege sophistication. There is, as so often in Austen, a layering of points of view in this passage. Crawford is more sophisticated than the Prices, and we can share his admiration of the spectacle of unself-conscious fraternal affection. Yet readers are required to be both more and less sophisticated than Crawford. More so, in the sense of worldly wisdom: we must perceive his errors (especially his mistaken assumption that because Fanny is young, she cannot yet have fallen in love) and foresee that his sudden enthusiasm for youthful innocence will not endure in the face of other temptations. Less so, in the sense of morality: the ideal reader addressed by the novel will remain committed to pure-minded Fanny and reject Crawford's unsteady poses.

The episode when Henry Crawford begins to feel interested in Fanny restages an earlier scene, at the very start of the novel, in which the ten-year-old heroine, newly arrived at Mansfield, is befriended by her cousin Edmund:

> Fanny's feelings on the occasion were such as she believed herself incapable of expressing; but her countenance and a few artless words fully conveyed all their gratitude and delight, and her cousin began to find her an interesting object. He talked to her more, and from all that she said, was convinced of her having an affectionate heart, and a strong desire of doing right; and he could perceive her to be farther entitled to attention, by great sensibility of her situation, and great timidity. (21–22)

Fanny is entirely intelligible here – her face expressing her feelings, and her words 'artless'. But she very soon learns the art of concealment, and spends virtually the entire novel successfully hiding the great fact of her life – her love for Edmund – from everyone around her. All the other characters continue to view her expressions, speech and behaviour as transparent, but each of them is deceived, and so Fanny's identification with unsophistication and naivety is gradually undone.

Indeed, this process of undoing begins – ironically – from the moment of Edmund's recognition of Fanny's artlessness. The next paragraph starts: 'From this day Fanny grew more comfortable', and this comfort results from her learning to imitate and to perform: 'she began at least to know their ways, and to catch the best manner of conforming to them. The little rusticities and awkwardnesses which had at first made grievous inroads on the tranquillity of all, and not least of herself, necessarily wore away' (22). The use of 'rusticities' is the same here as in *Evelina*, but as the heroine's trajectory is mapped out differently in terms of geography, the word takes on slightly altered associations in Austen's novel. Fanny might easily fit into the traditional plot (reiterated and refined in *Evelina*) in which the innocent, though emotionally refined, country girl is confronted with the perils of sophisticated city life. But in fact this movement is reversed: Fanny moves from a city (Portsmouth), a place of slatternliness and discourtesy, if not of actual vice, to the country, and there she discovers both the pleasures of the rural *and* the dangers of sophistication.

In her new country home, Fanny gradually learns the love of nature and distaste for city life which Evelina possesses from her infancy. Nevertheless, sophistication exerts its dangerous influence at Mansfield. This is most visible during the invasion of Mary and Henry Crawford, with their London stylishness and lax morality. But Mansfield was, in some senses, ready for the Crawfords. In spite of its country location, it is in no sense a rustic place. On arriving at Mansfield Parsonage to stay with Mrs Grant, Mary has some 'doubts of her sister's style of living and tone of society', but is relieved to find that she is 'without preciseness or rusticity' and that her house is 'commodious and well fitted up' (41). Certainly, both comfort and easy, fashionable manners are requirements of the sophisticate. More importantly, Mansfield Park is prepared for the Crawfords in that three of the Bertram children have already embraced their values. Tom 'had been much in London, and had more liveliness and gallantry than Edmund' (45). Maria and Julia, like the Crawfords, aspire to be social leaders, but are approved in their neighbourhood because they mount a flawless performance of naturalness and modesty: 'Their vanity was in such good order, that they seemed to be quite free from it, and gave themselves no airs' (35). In disavowing their sophistication, they only become more sophisticated. It is unsurprising, then, that both fall in love with Henry Crawford.

The Crawfords are more showy performers than the Miss Bertrams; their conversation has a metropolitan wit and cleverness. They insist explicitly on distinction, in professional, monetary and social terms. Henry says of Edmund's future parsonage at Thornton Lacey:

> By some such improvements as I have suggested [...] you may give it a higher character. You may raise it into a *place*. From being the mere gentleman's residence, it becomes, by judicious improvement, the residence of a man of education, taste, modern manners, good connections. All this may be stamped on it; and that house receive such an air as to make its owner be set down as the grand land-holder of the parish, by every creature travelling the road. (198)

Henry imagines the recreation of Edmund's house as a spectacle of self-conscious sophistication (in the newer sense of educated tastes and elegant manners), to be exhibited to passing travellers. The Crawfords' concept of class and distinction is directly indexed to income and expenditure: Henry suggests that the Thornton Lacey house looks like one which 'a respectable old country family had lived in from generation to generation, through two centuries at least, and were spending from two to three thousand a year in' (197). In estimating so precisely the value and the pedigree of his imagined family, he claims social authority on the basis of his ability to discriminate in these matters. As Bourdieu observes, 'Social subjects, classified by their classifications, distinguish themselves by the distinctions they make' (6).

But the Crawfords's scale of values is not endorsed by the novel: for all their style, they are nevertheless subtly associated with vulgarity because of their obsession with money and status. Edmund and Fanny, by contrast, prefer a more middle-class version of gentility, and hope for domestic tranquillity and comfort rather than riches or high living. When Edmund says that he aspires only to avoid poverty and attain to 'the something between, in the middle state of worldly circumstances', Mary Crawford, disappointed that he intends to take orders instead of entering an exciting military or political career, rejoins: 'I must look down on any thing contented with obscurity when it might rise to distinction' (174). But Edmund and Fanny look down on her in their turn, joining several times in strictures on Miss Crawford's frivolous speeches, materialism and unsteady principles.

The final damning of the excessively sophisticated characters, and of those who are drawn in by them, cannot, however, undo the effect of the rest of the narrative, in which the allure of sophistication has frequently prevailed. The reader, with the benefit of Fanny's insights, can easily unmask the Crawfords, yet the balance of sympathy is often tipped dangerously in their favour. Their charm is abundantly evident, and contrasts strikingly with Fanny's overly earnest discourse with its archaic phrasing and moralising tendency. Even the most sympathetic readers of the novel are likely to find their identification with its heroine intermittent and shaky, and it is hardly surprising that Miss Crawford is 'untouched and inattentive' (170) when Fanny is making such remarks as: 'How beautiful, how welcome, how wonderful the evergreen' (171). Henry Crawford's attractions are demonstrated by their effect even on Fanny, who dislikes him. When he reads aloud from *Henry VIII*, she tries not to listen:

> But taste was too strong in her. She could not abstract her mind five minutes; she was forced to listen; his reading was capital, and her pleasure in good reading extreme. [...] In Mr Crawford's reading there was a variety of excellence beyond what she had ever met with. [...] whether it was dignity or pride, or tenderness or remorse, or whatever were to be expressed, he could do it with equal beauty. It was truly dramatic. His acting had first taught Fanny what pleasure a play might give, and his reading brought all his acting before her again. (270)

It is of course Mr Crawford's facility in *acting* which ultimately repels Fanny, and disinclines her to trust him. At the same time, it is precisely Fanny's taste, the one quality she possesses which aligns her with sophistication, which makes her vulnerable to Crawford's seductions. This point is underlined by the narrator, who remarks in a rare first-person intervention that had Fanny not already been in love, 'I have no inclination to [...] think, that with so much tenderness of disposition, and so much taste as belonged to her, she could have escaped heart-whole from the courtship (though the courtship only of a fortnight) of such a man as Crawford' (188).

Through such complex interactions as these, the novel draws the reader into a subtle exploration of the nature of taste and the possible meanings of sophistication and distinction. As Litvak observes, 'reading any Austen novel means submitting, consciously or not, to a rigorous *aesthetic* discipline, undergoing subtle but incessant schooling in the ever-finer classifications, discriminations, and aversions that maintain Austen's exacting (because never quite explicit) norms of good manners and good taste' (22). The distinction between Fanny Price and Mary Crawford turns out not to be, after all, a distinction between unsophistication and sophistication, but one between different versions of sophistication – taste and discrimination versus worldly wisdom and experience:

> Miss Crawford was very unlike her. She had none of Fanny's delicacy of taste, of mind, of feeling; she saw nature, inanimate nature, with little observation; her attention was all for men and women, her talents for the light and lively. (72)

Throughout the narrative, Fanny is strongly identified with an ability to distinguish. Her taste is developed through Edmund's coaching, but even at the start of the novel, though ignorant of many things, she is – importantly – 'not vulgar' (17). So she offers promising material for Edmund's project of 'assisting the improvement of her mind, and extending its pleasures', to which end 'he recommended the books which charmed her leisure hours, he encouraged her taste, and corrected her judgement' (26). The novel thus presents taste as something which requires both a natural faculty and also guidance from outside. This is not sophistication as artifice, disguise, or performance, but as a natural superiority, cultivated through study and practice. Fanny, the daughter of a coarse working man and a mother who, though of genteel birth, is slatternly and ill-judging, is brought up for ten years in a house of squalor, unmannerliness and noise. Despite these disadvantages, she possesses an innate distinction and delicacy of mind which fit her for the elegant, civilised society into which she is transplanted, and where she blossoms. This developmental narrative is repeated in the story of her sister Susan, whose abilities Fanny, on returning to Portsmouth, immediately recognises and begins to nurture.

In this way, the novel intervenes in the ongoing debate about the relative influence of inheritance and environment on the formation of character and taste. The same theme is explored when Edmund and Fanny attribute the Crawfords' faulty conduct largely to their unfortunate upbringing in the home of their uncle, Admiral Crawford, 'a man of vicious conduct' (40). But while Fanny considers them as irredeemably spoiled, Edmund, and also Mrs Grant, believe that a more wholesome social environment could reform them. The Crawfords' cynical comments on such important subjects as marriage and commitment lead Mrs Grant to express a hope that 'Mansfield shall cure you both' (45). But they are not cured. They remain sensualists to the last, continuing to indulge in 'all the riot of [their] gratifications' (105). Mansfield does not, in fact, possess enough of the redemptive pastoral quality which Mrs Grant attributes to it, nor are Fanny and Edmund powerful enough to counteract all the others. And Edmund, of course, is himself rather vulnerable. In the early part of the novel, he is proud of his own unsophistication: 'there is not the least wit in my nature. I am a very matter of fact, plain spoken being, and may blunder on the borders of a repartee for half an hour together without striking it out' (82). He is suspicious of worldly manners, and reprobates Miss Crawford's lack of respect for religious and familial authority. But he is simultaneously attracted by the Crawfords' wit, charm and easy manners, and his romantic positioning between Mary and Fanny reproduces this split in his attitude.

Edmund's wavering has far-reaching effects; towards the end of the novel, he has even begun to succeed in persuading Fanny to unbend towards Henry Crawford. Mansfield, by this point, has become extremely open to sophistication in its dangerous form, and nothing less than the violent rending of the family caused by Maria's affair with Crawford can restore it to stability. Mansfield is finally converted into the idyllic country home which Sir Thomas has always fondly imagined it to be, but many drastic changes are necessary to achieve this. First, there is the removal of Maria, Julia, Mrs Norris, the Grants and the Crawfords, and the addition of Susan Price. Second, there is the amazing alteration of Tom Bertram, who 'regained his health, without regaining the thoughtlessness and selfishness of his previous habits' (369), and the enlightenment of Sir Thomas, who is '[s]ick of ambitious and mercenary connections, prizing more and more the sterling good of principle and temper, and chiefly anxious to bind by the strongest securities all that remained to him of domestic felicity' (376–77). Third, there is Edmund's eventual realisation that Fanny would make a much more desirable wife than Miss Crawford. Litvak, in a passing reference to *Mansfield Park*, writes that Mary and Henry are 'expelled from the text in a climactic paroxysm of moral revulsion'. He suggests that, rather than endorsing this ending, a resistant reader might choose to celebrate the transgressive possibilities embodied in the Crawfords: 'to cultivate – indeed, to *savor* – whatever perverse reader relations that plot may permit'. This means that, '[instead] of casting the Crawfords out, as one is expected to do, an ill-mannered reader of *Mansfield Park* may try to keep them in, guarding them, perversely, in [...] one's own reading body' (24–25).

Sheila Kaye-Smith and G. B. Stern may not be quite the kind of resistant readers envisaged by Litvak, but their jointly authored book *Talking of Jane Austen* (1944) performs exactly the reincorporation of the Crawfords which he recommends. 'Henry Crawford,' writes Stern in one of her chapters, 'needed only one instant of acknowledgement from his creator, and we would have had him where I truly believe most of us desire him: as the hero of *Mansfield Park*, instead of its attractive villain' (Kaye-Smith and Stern 60). She explains further:

> Why does Jane Austen condemn in Crawford what she condones in Wentworth, flirting with two sisters simultaneously, certain (whatever the motive) that the result must be to make at least one, if not both, unhappy? Why always this extra call for discipline where Crawford was concerned, as though the author herself were in danger and determined not to succumb to his fascination and lack of moral rectitude? (65)

The sophisticated reader cannot help but be fascinated by Henry too, and during the scenes of his visit to Portsmouth, he even begins to seem deserving of Fanny. Indeed, the novel explicitly permits this reading of Henry as potential hero. A remarkable passage in the last chapter runs: 'Would he have persevered, and uprightly, Fanny must have been his reward – and a reward very voluntarily bestowed – within a reasonable period from Edmund's marrying Mary' (373). This possibility of an alternative happy ending is not opened up in any of Austen's other novels. We are left in no doubt that if Marianne had married Willoughby, or Anne been persuaded into accepting Mr Elliot, the result would have been misery. The flirtations between Emma and Frank Churchill, Elizabeth and Wickham are transient, and Catherine is merely annoyed by John Thorpe's attentions. Only in *Mansfield Park* does the 'villain' come so near becoming the hero.

G. B. Stern writes that in the conclusion of the novel, 'we are bidden contemplate, not the triumph of evil, but certainly what is not far removed from it, the failure of goodness: Edmund and Fanny could *not* redeem the Crawfords; not by example, nor the influence of love' (Kaye-Smith and Stern 66). This leads her to suggest that perhaps 'Jane Austen, for some reason unknown to us [...] revised her original intentions with regard to the *Mansfield Park* quartette' (67). She adds: 'in *Mansfield Park* the power of steadfast goodness acting on worldly sophistication might well have been the original theme, deeper and truer than simply showing a good young couple rather tamely consoling one another in the end' (68). Sheila Kaye-Smith, in another chapter of *Talking of Jane Austen*, claims to like Henry Crawford 'much better than his author would allow' (Kaye-Smith and Stern 203), but adds that she cannot agree with Stern that Austen ever intended to end the story by marrying Mary to Edmund and Fanny to Henry, because 'we know that Jane liked Edmund – though not, I think, quite blindly – and disliked Miss Crawford' (203), and therefore would not have wished to punish Edmund with an unhappy marriage.

The debate enacted in *Talking of Jane Austen* proves nothing, of course, with respect to the intentions of Jane Austen, but it does prove the complexity of the novel, and its resistance to straightforward interpretation. The awkward and shifting concept which is at its heart is, I would suggest, sophistication. *Mansfield Park*, like *Evelina*, might be seen as 'a *contest of sophistications*' (Litvak 5). Austen, though, complicates the geography of sophistication: while Burney's Evelina encounters dangerous sophistication primarily in urban and public settings, Fanny finds it invading rural locales and domestic environments.

'The progress of refinement': *Domestic Manners of the Americans*

Fanny Trollope's celebrated travel book, published in 1832, is about the unsophistication of America. Occasional passages praise the progress of some of the eastern cities towards European-style culture, manners and social habits, but the majority of the narrative deplores the failings of the United States in the areas of taste, elegance, delicacy, leisure, and above all refinement. These are the keywords of the text – they name the ideals to which Fanny Trollope clings during her travels, and their repetition is part of her strategy for constructing herself as a sophisticate, in contradistinction to the bluntness and barbarism of the New World.

Trollope was writing at a period when the dominant meaning of 'sophistication' and all etymologically related words was still that of 'specious fallacy'. At one point in her text, she uses the term in this sense. Referring to a lecture by the Scottish social reformer and enthusiast for America Fanny Wright, Trollope remarks that there was 'one passage from which commonsense revolted; it was one wherein she quoted that phrase of mischievous sophistry, "all men are born free and equal"' (58). This, in fact, points to the principal theme of *Domestic Manners of the Americans*: that distinction is inevitable and equality impossible, and that an insistence on equality has the effect of reducing everyone to the lowest level and destroying any prospect of advanced cultural development. Although Trollope did not hold this view on her departure from England (at which period she still idolised Fanny Wright), her eventful and often unpleasant transatlantic trip destroyed her illusions and led her to regard the American rhetoric of equality as sophistical.

There is, though, one other occurrence of the word in Trollope's text, and this time it seems to be used in its more modern sense. Trollope, observing debates in Congress, notes that individual states continually insist on their independence from the federal government and refuse to contribute to national transportation or improvement projects. She writes:

> This strange jealousy is an illustration, *en grand*, of the democratic principle, and if pushed to its utmost perfection, would speedily dislocate every social compact, and leave each individual man as gloriously free as a bear on the unsophisticated shores of Bering's Straits. (191)

'Unsophisticated' is being used in a critical sense, to describe a place from which culture, community and civilisation are absent, and this suggests that 'sophistication' is beginning to acquire the positive meaning which gradually became its dominant one. Significantly, this sentence occurs in one of the footnotes added by the author for the fifth English edition, published in 1839. Fanny Trollope's shift in usage may, then, suggest that the modern conception of 'sophistication' began to acquire a limited currency towards the later 1830s. It seems very unlikely that it dates back any earlier: my searches through e-text versions of numerous novels of the 1820s reveals that 'sophistical' and 'sophistry' occur with some frequency, but that 'sophisticated' is never used as a term of approbation. A similar search on novels of the 1830s reveals 'unsophistication' being more widely applied as a term of praise for innocence or unpretentiousness (Disraeli, Peacock, Bulwer-Lytton), but also some instances of 'unsophistication' used, as in Trollope, to criticise naivety or lack of culture (Dickens in 1836 and 1839, and Frederick Marryat in 1836).[17]

In any case, during the period when Trollope was writing, the dominant sense of 'sophistication' remained pejorative, and she uses 'refinement' to designate what we might now call 'sophistication'. She insists that America's greatest difference from England is its 'want of refinement' (39), continuing:

> I will not pretend to decide whether man is better or worse off for requiring refinement in the manners and customs of the society that surrounds him, and for being incapable of enjoyment without them; but in America, that polish which removes the coarser and rougher parts of our nature, is unknown and undreamed of. (39)

---

17 Among the books searched were Scott's *The Abbot* (1820) and *Count Robert of Paris* (1831), Hogg's *The Private Memoirs and Confessions of a Justified Sinner* (1824), Disraeli's *Vivian Grey* (1826–27) and *Venetia* (1837), Bulwer-Lytton's *Paul Clifford* (1830) and *Last Days of Pompeii* (1834), Peacock's *Crotchet Castle* (1831), Richardson's *Wacousta* (1832), Carlyle's *Sartor Resartus* (1833–34), Edgeworth's *Helen* (1834), Marryat's *Mr Midshipman Easy* (1836) and Dickens's *Pickwick Papers* (1836–37) and *Nicholas Nickleby* (1838–39). For further comments on Dickens's usage, see the next chapter.

The refined person may appreciate simple pleasures, but certainly not coarse ones. This idea is elaborated by later authors: the sophisticate is revealed as one who can pursue specialised tastes and enjoyments even to excess, but who never takes pleasure indiscriminately. (Nabokov's Humbert Humbert or Giuseppe de Lampedusa's Prince of Salina are among the examples considered in subsequent chapters of this study.) In Trollope's narrative, though, refined pleasures are not generally compatible with excess.[18]

Trollope defines her literary persona as sophisticated in a variety of ways. To begin with, she displays her familiarity with Continental languages and cultures, referring to the sights of Paris and using untranslated French or Italian phrases and quotations. These strategies construct the narrator as cosmopolitan, emphasising that she has the breadth of experience and ability to understand and compare different cultures which would qualify her as a travel writer. However, none of this appealed to readers in the United States. The *American Quarterly Review* said that Fanny Trollope made many mistakes in her book, a failing it attributed to her 'education, which appears to have been French and flippant'.[19]

Trollope further emphasises her sophistication through scenes of urban cultural consumption, in which she demonstrates substantial knowledge about theatre, the visual arts, bookshops and periodical publishing, and criticises the backward state of the American arts. In a related move, she expresses admiration for cities in which there are avenues for people of fashion to promenade in, and other spaces for the display of leisure. But the sophisticate must also be able to appreciate rural pleasures, and Trollope's persona goes into raptures over scenery: Niagara reduces her to 'trembling' and tears (336). Knowledge of the picturesque was a desirable accomplishment among the upper classes of Europe,[20] but Trollope finds no evidence of it among Americans. During her stay at Niagara, she recounts:

> Now and then a first-rate dandy shot in among us, like a falling star.
>
> On one occasion, when we were in the beautiful gallery, at the back of the hotel, which overlooks the horse-shoe fall, we saw the booted leg of one of this graceful race protruded from the window which commands the view, while his person was thrown back in his chair, and his head enveloped in a cloud of tobacco smoke.
>
> I have repeatedly remarked, when it has happened to me to meet any ultra-fine men among the wilder and more imposing scenes of our own land, that they throw

18 Except, perhaps, the extreme emotion felt by the narrator when contemplating sublime scenery (discussed below).

19 This review is reprinted in *American Criticisms on Mrs Trollope's Domestic Manners of the Americans* published in London by O. Rich in 1833, and quoted in Mullen xxii.

20 For discussion, see Bohls. She ends her study in 1818, but most of her comments on 'amateur aesthetic activity' (2) would still apply in the 1820s and 1830s.

off, in a great degree, their airs, and their 'townliness', as some one [sic] cleverly calls these *simagrées*[21] [...], and more than once on these occasions I have been surprised to find how much intellect lurked behind the inane mask of fashion. But in America the effect of fine scenery upon this class of person is different; for it is exactly when amongst it that the most strenuous efforts at elegant *nonchalance* are perceptible amongst the young exquisites of the western world. It is true that they have little leisure for the display of grace in the daily routine of commercial activity in which their lives are passed, and this certainly offers a satisfactory explanation. (342–43)

The English dandy appears truly sophisticated since – like Mrs Trollope herself – he belongs primarily to the cultured, city scene, yet he can adapt to a rural location because he has an educated appreciation for the picturesque. The American dandy, by contrast, strains too hard for effect by adopting the trappings of urban high style (smoking, lounging, fashionable clothes) in an inappropriate setting. Indeed, adaptability to environment is one of the main qualifications of the modern sophisticate, as later fictional characters such as Max Beerbohm's Duke of Dorset or Stella Gibbons's Flora Poste amply demonstrate. By contrast, the ineptly exquisite young men at Niagara are pseudosophisticates.

Although Trollope insistently displays her persona's aesthetic accomplishments, she lightens the effect with self-mockery. Describing her first walk in an American forest with her children, she remarks 'we felt rather sublime and poetical' (5). She later laments her own naivety in having hoped for a pleasant stroll in one of the wilder forests of Ohio: 'we were bit, we were stung, we were scratched; [...] it was painful to tread, it was painful to breathe' (81). In reference to Fanny Wright's experiment in community living in a Tennessee forest, Trollope remarks that it must have been some feeling akin to religious enthusiasm which enabled her friend, 'accustomed to all the comfort and refinement of Europe, to imagine not only that she herself could exist in this wilderness, but that her European friends could enter there, and not feel dismayed' (24). It is characteristic of Romantic and early Victorian writers to construct the wilderness of the New World in terms of the absence of European forms of civilisation; what is more distinctive is Trollope's repeated association of refinement with bodily ease, rather than simply with delicacy and elegant manners. For her contemporaries, such as the Canadian John Richardson, whose novel *Wacousta* also appeared in 1832, the wilderness of North America is fascinating yet illegible, harbouring unknown threats and inconceivable terrors. For Fanny Trollope, by contrast, wilderness is unthinkable simply because it is so extraordinarily uncomfortable.

---

21 *Simagrées*: affected manners designed to attract attention.

In fact, Trollope is not interested in real wilderness: her admiration of landscape is strongly determined by cultural frameworks, and she enjoys it only in the context of civilised and social pleasures. For instance, when witnessing the sublime scenery of the Great Falls of the Potomac River in Maryland, she longs for some companions to share her appreciation in the proper manner:

> A look, or the silent pressure of the arm, is all the interchange of feeling that such a scene allows, and in the midst of my terror and my pleasure, I wished for the arm and the eye of some few from the other side of the Atlantic. (202)

The scene concludes with her return to the house of her hostess:

> and then the entering the cool and moonlit portico, the well-iced sangaree, or still more refreshing coffee, that awaits you, is all delightful; and if to this be added the happiness of an easy sofa, and a friend like my charming Mrs S—, to soothe you with an hour of Mozart, the most fastidious European might allow that such a day was worth waking for. (202)

Fastidiousness, in this passage, encompasses taste in scenery, music and refreshments, and a civilised lifestyle requires comfortable rooms, access to the arts, and pleasing conversation. Mrs Trollope rarely finds any house in America to be sufficient in all these respects; Mrs S— is an exception because she is an emigrant from England.

But while Trollope insists on comfort, she carefully avoids any hint of sensuality or over-indulgence. The sangaree (sangria) is merely the final touch of pleasure after the far more significant experience of viewing of the falls. The Americans, by contrast, are often accused of privileging oral gratification far above intellectual or spiritual satisfaction, and of being unable to appreciate the glories of their own landscape:

> To sit beside this miniature cascade, and read, or dream away a day, was one of our greatest pleasures. [...] A row upon the Ohio was another of our favourite amusements; but in this, I believe, we were also very singular, for often, when enjoying it, we were shouted at, by the young free-borns on the banks, as if we had been so many monsters.
> The only rural amusement in which we ever saw any of the natives engaged was eating strawberries and cream in a pretty garden about three miles from the town. (147)

Mrs Trollope is unimpressed by the strawberry party she attends herself, and it is difficult to read this episode without thinking of the vulgar Mrs Elton's attempted performance of rural pleasures in Jane Austen's *Emma* (1816): 'I shall wear a large bonnet and bring one of my little baskets hanging on my arm [...] We are to walk about your gardens, and gather the strawberries ourselves [...]. Every thing as natural and simple as possible'. Mr Knightley replies: 'The nature and the simplicity of ladies and gentlemen, with their servants and furniture, I think is best observed by meals within doors' (281). Like Austen, Fanny Trollope interrogates the 'natural' and 'simple'. She sometimes points out that ideas of naturalness are culturally relative, though, at the same time, she frequently attempts to erect European customs into a universal norm by contrasting them with the 'strange' habits of Americans.

Fanny Trollope reflects much more extensively than Austen on the pastoral attitude – that is, the idealisation of the simple man or simple life – and she finds it untenable:

> I have read much of the 'few and simple wants of rational man', and I used to give a sort of dreamy acquiescence to the reasoning that went to prove each added want an added woe. Those who reason in a comfortable London drawing-room know little about the matter. Were the aliments which sustain life all that we wanted, the faculties of the hog might suffice us; but if we analyse an hour of enjoyment, we shall find that it is made up of agreeable sensations occasioned by a thousand delicate impressions on almost as many nerves; where these nerves are sluggish from never having been awakened, external objects are less important, for they are less perceived; but where the whole machine of the human frame is in full activity, [...] then every object that meets the senses is important as a vehicle of happiness or misery. But let no frames so tempered visit the United States [...].
>
> The 'simple' manner of living in Western America was more distasteful to me from its levelling effects on the manners of the people, than from the personal privations that it rendered necessary; and yet, till I was without them, I was in no degree aware of the many pleasurable sensations derived from the little elegances and refinements enjoyed by the middle classes in Europe. [...] It requires an abler pen than mine to trace the connection which I am persuaded exists between these deficiencies and the minds and manners of the people. [...] I very seldom, during my whole stay in the country, heard a sentence elegantly turned, and correctly pronounced, from the lips of an American. There is always something either in the expression or the accent that jars the feelings and shocks the taste. (36–38)

Trollope's vocabulary here is not directly suggestive of gourmandise, and certainly not of eroticism, yet her emphasis is firmly on the sensual dimension of taste. The passage might be aligned with other texts which speak more explicitly of the importance of sophisticated consumption. Joseph Litvak remarks, 'In talking about sophistication, one needs to keep all these terms – the culinary, the erotic, the linguistic, the economic – in play' (8), and indeed all these may be discerned in Trollope's narrative. In the quoted passage, speech itself becomes sensual – the sentence is 'turned' and the lips are focused on. The economic dimension of sophistication is also very evident here: Trollope is speaking of comforts which must be paid for, objects which must be bought, and she is clear that these are available only to the middle classes.

61

As to the culinary, *Domestic Manners* comments repeatedly on the Americans' attitudes to dining, deploring their combination of gluttony and unsociability: 'they eat with the greatest possible rapidity and in total silence' (40). At their 'supremely dull' evening parties, 'to eat inconceivable quantities of cake, ice, and pickled oysters – and to show half their revenue in silks and satins, seem to be the chief objects' (256). Fanny Trollope's own ideal is an 'elaborate repast' which, though 'more deeply relished than the sages might approve, […] is redeemed from sensuality by the presence of elegance and beauty' (40). Such sophisticated dining belongs to 'the hours of recreation' (40) – that is, eating is not merely functional; rather, it is presented as a form of culture and an occasion for social interaction. This returns us to one of the central ideas of the book: that of leisure.

In her description of Washington, which she is convinced must be 'a more agreeable abode than any other city in the Union', Trollope writes:

> The total absence of all sights, sounds, or smells of commerce, adds greatly to the charm. Instead of drays you see handsome carriages; and instead of the busy bustling hustle of men, shuffling on to a sale of 'dry goods' or 'prime bread stuffs', you see very well-dressed personages lounging leisurely up and down Pennsylvania Avenue. (182–83)

Trollope repeatedly longs to inhabit a sphere in which work and commerce are invisible and inaudible. This remained the realm of the sophisticate in later eras, even though relationships between public and private spaces, and between labour and leisure, were so extensively redefined during the nineteenth and twentieth centuries. The quoted passage continues: 'Mr Pishey Thompson, the English bookseller, with his pretty collection of all sorts of pretty literature fresh from London, and Mr Somebody the jeweller, with his brilliant shop full of trinkets, are the principal points of attraction' (183). Although the repetition of 'pretty' lends a slightly patronising tone, Trollope is nevertheless clearly delighted to find one place in America where people care enough about beauty and culture to support bookshops and jewellers among them. A modern reader might object that these are, in fact, sites of commerce, even though they generate no noise or smells, but while Mr Thompson and Mr Somebody are certainly engaged in business, the well-dressed personages who are the focus of the scene are engaged only in exhibiting their leisure, wealth and taste. They declare their exemption from the imperatives of profit-making. The bookshop is particularly important because reading, far from being understood as a form of effort, is a sign that the reader commands a certain level of education, income and leisure time. In many later texts, sophisticated characters spend much time reading, and while they may be lavish with money, they conceal or ignore the sordid (or merely tedious) processes by which the money was obtained.

Poor Mrs Trollope would be a prime target of Veblen's satire in *The Theory of the Leisure Class*. He writes:

> It is felt by all persons of refined taste that a spiritual contamination is insepa-rable from certain offices that are conventionally required of servants. [...] Vulgar surroundings [...] and vulgarly productive occupations are unhesitatingly condemned and avoided. They are incompatible with life on a satisfactory spiritual plane – [...] a degree of leisure and of exemption from such industrial processes as serve the immediate everyday purposes of human life has ever been recognised by thoughtful men as a prerequisite to a worthy or beautiful, or even a blameless, human life. (29)

Like many of her contemporaries, Trollope quite seriously espouses this view. But she also condemns working-class Americans for disliking to be employed as servants, arguing that their economic and social status disqualifies them from sharing her refined tastes: 'the man possessed of dollars does command the services of the man possessed of no dollars; but these services are given grudgingly [...], with no appearance of cheerful good-will on the one side, or of kindly interest on the other' (154).

This line of thinking becomes particularly problematic when Trollope relates it to the institution of slavery. In the 1832 text, she recounts that she felt more comfortable when travelling in slave states because, even though she held that slavery was 'essentially wrong', she considered its influence 'far less injurious to the manners and morals of the people than the fallacious ideas of equality, which are so fondly cherished by the working classes of the white population in America' (154). In the 1839 edition, she adds a footnote pointing out that this passage was written before she had seen anything of slavery beyond the domestic slaves in 'one or two well-ordered families', and that her 'detestation of slavery' rapidly increased as she learned more. Even so, she remains mainly preoccupied with its effects on the white population, and suggests that the resentful tone of white American servants is a result of slavery, which 'renders the idea of domestic service shameful' (154). Her argument culminates with a return to the pre-eminence of leisure: 'Were the sinful and unnatural spectacle of a race degraded by legalized tyranny removed, the gradation of ranks INEVITABLE in the progress of all society would take place naturally, [...] leaving tranquillity and leisure for the progress of refinement' (154). Elsewhere in the text, capital letters are used only when the narrator quotes the text of notices or newspaper headlines. This rare use of capitals for emphasis announces the importance of this point in Trollope's narrative. Although appearing in a footnote, it in fact clarifies the argument of large sections of the main text, which reiterate the idea that only a hierarchical social structure can enable leisure, and therefore culture, refinement, elegance, and taste. These are the keywords of the books discussed in this chapter, and they are the elements of what would soon afterwards begin to be called 'sophistication'.

2

Childhood, consumption and decadence: Victorian and Edwardian sophistication

'Taking sides is the beginning of sincerity and earnestness follows shortly afterwards, and the human being becomes a bore' (105) says Lord Illingworth in Oscar Wilde's *A Woman of No Importance* (1893).[1] Earnestness is one of the central ideas which historians and critics use to explain the distinctiveness of nineteenth-century Britain; as John Kucich notes, 'a momentous inflation of the cultural cachet of honesty took place in Victorian England' (6). In this context, sophistication – with its connotations of performance, polish, even deceit – might seem even more incongruous than it had done in the era of Romanticism. But Kucich argues that sophistication became increasingly important to the Victorians precisely because of their excessive investment in truth-telling:

> The power of lies derives, paradoxically, from the centrality of truth-telling in Victorian culture and from the consequent seepage of honesty/dishonesty distinctions into all corners of the symbolic grid formed by Victorian social and sexual oppositions. Such power depends ultimately, however, on the reversibility of these ethical distinctions – which is what I have termed 'transgression'. Validating the lie, or idealizing conduct that hybridizes honesty and dishonesty, gave novelists (among others) the opportunity to construct potent new kinds of moral sophistication. Such sophistication, in turn, justified writers in rearranging the symbolic social and sexual oppositions that the discourse of truth-telling had seemed so securely to order. (3–4)

Victorian novels, he suggests, 'could be seen as a kind of conduct literature defining exactly how one might achieve an aura of sophistication through deceit': that is, through imitating privileged groups and exploiting the blurred

---

1   The dates given for Wilde's plays refer to dates of first performance. In most instances, the plays were first published a year or two later.

or uncertain areas between clear truth and clear falsehood (34). Writing on the same subject, Joseph Litvak comments: 'An ambitious and intricate pedagogy of sophistication, Victorian fiction teaches its readers *how to act* by dramatizing the considerable power and prestige to be gained through a sophisticated manipulation of cultural codes' (14). Litvak explores this thesis through an analysis of Thackeray, and Kucich through readings of Anthony Trollope, Thomas Hardy, Mrs Henry Wood, Wilkie Collins, Elizabeth Gaskell and Sarah Grand. Sean Latham, developing a similar theme in his discussion of Thackeray's *The Book of Snobs* (1848),[2] comments:

> Yet in so cleverly scrutinizing the essentially semiotic nature of social and cultural distinction, Thackeray also produces a new image of the snob as a master of taste and an able counterfeiter of symbolic capital, able to translate his accomplished pose of sophistication into fortune and fame. In the midst of his own analysis, he uncovers the power of the pose. (28)

All three of these insightful accounts have informed my own discussion, and I have pursued the theme of imitation in detail. Using a quite different selection of texts from those chosen by Latham, Litvak and Kucich, this chapter examines a diverse range of points of view on sophistication from the later nineteenth and very early twentieth centuries.

My chapter focuses not only on the obviously sophisticated figures of the era – the cosmopolitan dilettante in Henry James's *Daisy Miller* (1878) and the dandy in Max Beerbohm's *Zuleika Dobson* (1911)[3] – but also on the child. I explore the Victorian child's relationship to innocence and sophistication through readings of Lewis Carroll's *Alice's Adventures in Wonderland* (1865), its sequel *Through the Looking-Glass* (1872), and Daisy Ashford's *The Young Visiters*, written in 1890 when the author was nine and published in 1919. Imitation is learned in childhood, and the strategies of child's play may, in adult life, be applied to the projects of upward mobility described by Litvak and Kucich.[4] The child also introduces questions of forbidden knowledge: indeed, anxieties about how much a young girl, in particular, may be allowed to know emerge repeatedly in Victorian fiction. A second key topic of my chapter is the particularly dangerous – indeed, often fatal – nature of sophistication as it is

2 This book was originally a series of articles in *Punch* in 1847. I have not chosen a Thackeray text for close reading since both Litvak and Latham devote chapters to him.

3 Edward VII died in 1910. However, conventional historical periodisation extends the Edwardian age until either the start or the end of World War I, since the war effectively ended the Edwardian way of life. Several recent books have used the label 'Edwardian' to extend well beyond the official nine-year period: for instance, Helen C. Long's *The Edwardian House: The Middle-Class Home in Britain, 1880–1914* (1993).

4 Kucich does not discuss the child in this connection. Litvak has a section on toys and mass culture in his chapter on Barthes and Adorno, but does not engage with this topic in his account of Victorian fiction.

represented in literary texts. Perhaps because it is more strikingly opposed to consensual public morality in this than in any other period, and yet more fundamental to the maintenance of social and moral structures, sophistication often proves particularly disastrous in Victorian and Edwardian fiction. It can have very physical effects because it is intimately connected with illness and death, on the one hand, and with eating and consumption, on the other. The important subject of consumption, continued from Chapter 1, takes on new resonances in the Victorian context, becoming more closely connected with sexual desire and the maturing body. Death, desire and eating also become subjects for humour in many texts dealing with sophistication, and allow for comic ripostes to Victorian earnestness. Before introducing my chosen literary texts in more detail, I will discuss several important contexts for this chapter – dandyism and aestheticism, degeneration, cosmopolitanism, and nineteenth-century conceptions of childhood. I will also comment on the evolution of the word 'sophistication' in this period.

The contest in *Zuleika Dobson* between the Duke of Dorset, aristocratic, brilliant and entirely self-controlled, and Zuleika, middle-class, unintelligent and self-indulgent, represents the hostility between the dandy and the bourgeoisie. As Ellen Moers argues in *The Dandy: Brummell to Beerbohm* (1960), dandyism consciously distanced itself from the middle classes and allied itself with the aristocracy. But this was a complicated move. In her account of the dandy's style, Catherine Spooner explains that

> the dandies of the nineteenth century sought to reject the horrors of bourgeois vulgarity through the foundation of a new, aesthetically motivated mode of existence. Naturally this [...] confused clear social divisions by encouraging men from a wide range of backgrounds to cultivate the outward appearance of aristocracy. (9)

Indeed, dandyism gradually became a popular phenomenon, as lower-middle-class 'gents' dressed in imitation of the 'swells' who were their superiors. Even their role models were of distinctly middling social origin: Brummell and Wilde are prime examples. They may have mixed with aristocrats, but they advocated a social elite which was based on abilities, genius or style, rather than on birth.

The politics of dandyism – like the politics of sophistication itself – are therefore hard to define. James Eli Adams writes in *Dandies and Desert Saints* (1995):

> Under the conjoint authority of Evangelical faith and Romantic subjectivity, early and mid-Victorian norms of manhood construct an ideal of essential selfhood that repudiates self-consciousness as a mark of theatricality. In attacks on the dandy or 'swell', for example, a theatricality readily accommodated in earlier constructions

of aristocratic manhood is disavowed as the sign of a socially mediated identity, which betrays both religious integrity and the social autonomy fundamental to manhood. (10)

According to Moers, 'throughout the nineteenth century the rising majority called for equality, responsibility, energy; the dandy stood for superiority, irresponsibility, inactivity' (13). Refusing action, 'the dandy's achievement is simply to be himself' (Moers 18) – and this form of selfhood is not the 'ideal of essential selfhood' referred to by Adams; rather, it is a performed individuality which places the dandy in opposition to the community. This is not necessarily a politically progressive stance, though. As Regenia Gagnier says of dandies: 'Politically they appealed, at different times and in different countries, to both the reactionary and the revolutionary: to the reactionary through their refinement and to the revolutionary through their independence' (68). Her comment might equally apply to sophistication, which has elements of both nostalgia and modernness, and may operate through individualism or through imitation.

This conception of the dandy-sophisticate as at once a survival from an earlier, more polished age, and also a harbinger of a new social order, is especially evident in Baudelaire's essay 'The Painter of Modern Life' (1863):

> Dandyism appears above all in periods of transition, when democracy is not yet all-powerful, and aristocracy is only just beginning to totter and fall. In the disorder of these times, certain men who are socially, politically and financially ill at ease, but are all rich in native energy, may conceive the idea of establishing a new kind of aristocracy, all the more difficult to shatter as it will be based on the most precious, the most enduring faculties, and on the divine gifts which work and money are unable to bestow. Dandyism is the last spark of heroism amid decadence. (500)

Baudelaire presents the dandy as in some ways forward-looking, committed to building a new form of meritocratic elite which will prove durable. At the same time, his conception of his own era as decadent suggests a nostalgia for a lost aristocratic golden age. In 'The Painter of Modern Life', as in his decadent poetry, Baudelaire envisages possibilities of beauty in the context of decline: 'Dandyism is a sunset; like the declining daystar, it is glorious, without heat and full of melancholy' (500). The sunset must have been a very lingering one, since the dandy was thriving from the Regency until the Edwardian period, but he certainly achieved an especial prominence at the turn of both the eighteenth and the nineteenth centuries.[5] The ominous sense of approaching change was

---

5   He certainly did not disappear from fiction or from the social scene in the interim. Dandies feature in mid-nineteenth-century novels by Stendhal, Eugène Sue, Dickens, Thackeray and James, amongst others.

present in both periods, in contrast to the more stable High Victorian era which came between.

In the 1890s and the early years of the twentieth century, *fin-de-siècle* anxieties were inflected by theories of degeneration. In *Faces of Degeneration: A European Disorder, c. 1848–1918* (1993), Daniel Pick maps out 'various conceptions of atavism, regression, relapse, transgression and decline within a European context so often identified as the quintessential age of evolution, progress, optimism, reform or improvement' (2). Literary decadence emerged amidst the proliferation of scientific discourses of degeneration which Pick explores, and it undermined Victorian narratives of progress. In the work of Wilde, Aubrey Beardsley, J. K. Huysmans, and a little later Saki, Beerbohm and Ronald Firbank, the dandy is connected with a kind of extreme cultural sophistication which – rather than being progressive – presages decay.

The Edwardian writer Saki (H. H. Munro) provides an interesting example. The protagonists of his short story collections *Reginald* (1904) and *The Chronicles of Clovis* (1911) certainly have the manners, wit and detachment of the dandy, and make all the appropriate gestures: 'Reginald closed his eyes with the elaborate weariness of one who has rather nice eyelashes and thinks it useless to conceal the fact' (Saki 28); 'Clovis wiped the trace of Turkish coffee and the beginnings of a smile from his lips, and slowly lowered his dexter eyelid' (Saki 108). But though Saki's dandies partly inspired Noël Coward's sophisticated characters, Coward's description of his predecessor's work is strangely inaccurate:

> His stories and novels appear as delightful and, to use a much abused word, sophisticated as they did when he first published them. They are dated only by the fact that they evoke an atmosphere and describe a society which vanished in the baleful summer of 1914. The Edwardian era, in spite of its political idiocies and a sinister sense of foreboding which, to intelligent observers, underlay the latter part of it, must have been, socially at least, very charming. It is this evanescent charm that Saki so effortlessly evoked. (Introduction to *The Penguin Complete Saki* xiii)

Sophisticated, yes. But charming? Reginald and Clovis, though highly amusing, are also distinctly vicious characters. 'We've lost Baby', screams Clovis's hostess. '"Do you mean that it's dead or stampeded, or that you staked it at cards and lost it that way?" asked Clovis lazily' (Saki 148). Sandie Byrne remarks in *The Unbearable Saki*: 'Charm is not a word that leaps to mind in relation to Saki's descriptions of country-house life, where animals may mock, gore, or eat the guests, and the guests are worse, with less excuse' (15). Indeed, nearly all the stories involve violence, and animal scenes and images are especially prevalent. Numerous stories feature animals killing people (the stoat in 'Sredni Vashtar', the hyaena in 'Esmé', the elephant in 'Tobermory'); and a great many more describe unfortunate, if not actually fatal, encounters with animals which invade the domestic sphere: an elk haunts the park of a country house, a mouse inserts itself into a gentleman's suit, an ox walks into a living room. The werewolf in 'Gabriel-Ernest' who eats a small child is an especially disturbing figure, but he is only the most overt manifestation of the intense preoccupation with the border between human and animal which runs throughout Saki's fiction. When Reginald is asked whether he believes that 'we are all merely an improved form of primeval ape', he replies: 'I think it decidedly premature; in most people I know the process is far from complete' (Saki 1). Reginald and Clovis are apparently more 'improved' – that is, refined, polished and intellectually developed – than the other characters in the stories, whose obtuseness and conventionality they often mock and take advantage of. Yet in the context of the remarkable horrors which surround Saki's dandies, their pose of sophisticated detachment comes to seem actually inhuman.

From another point of view, this extreme detachment could be interpreted as camp. According to Sontag, '[the] hallmark of camp is the spirit of extravagance' (283), and Clovis and Reginald are indeed (and paradoxically) excessive in their self-control and unemotionalism. In the context of the sentimental and rather ordinary (even though upper-class) people who surround them, Reginald and Clovis appear distinct, specialised, even corrupt. 'Detachment is the prerogative of an elite', suggests Sontag, adding that 'the dandy is the 19th century's surrogate for the aristocrat in matters of culture' (288). The dandy attempts to establish a new social elite based on specialised forms of merit, and the dandiacal identity developed in the context of larger shifts in taste. Following her account of the great period of Camp, which she traces from Congreve through rococo churches to Mozart, Sontag continues:

> But in the 19th century, what had been distributed throughout all of high culture now becomes a special taste; it takes on overtones of the acute, the esoteric, the perverse. Confining the story to England alone, we see Camp continuing wanly through 19th-century aestheticism (Burne-Jones, Pater, Ruskin, Tennyson), emerging full-blown with the Art Nouveau movement in the visual and decorative arts, and finding its conscious ideologists in such 'wits' as Wilde and Firbank. (280–81)

Wilde's dandies, though, are not quite so detached as Saki's. Amanda Anderson argues in *The Powers of Distance: Cosmopolitanism and the Cultivation of Detachment* (2001) that 'Wilde repeatedly grappled with the ethical limits of cultivated detachment, despite his many programmatic utterances to the contrary', and that his 'deeper investments' are legible in his portrayal of dandified men and – especially – women (23). Considering Mrs Allonby and Lord Illingworth in *A Woman of No Importance*, Mrs Erlynne in *Lady Windermere's Fan* (1892), and

Lord Goring in *An Ideal Husband* (1895) as prime examples, Anderson writes: 'the dandy is a significant and charismatic social critic, challenging moral pieties, disrupting the smooth surface of unthinking custom, inducing reflective distance and the heightened self-consciousness that it engenders' (64). Sophistication in Victorian and Edwardian literature, then, is not to be simply equated with amorality, but seems to consist primarily in the ability to cope with – indeed, revel in – paradox and contradiction; an intense self-awareness; an emphasis on individualism and choice; and a tendency towards extravagance.

The shared language of excess connects late nineteenth-century and Edwardian writers such as Wilde, Beerbohm and Saki, as well as the authors of fantastical or satirical texts from earlier in the century, with the commercial culture of the age. In *Shopping with Freud* (1993), her influential study of the consumer subject in literary and psychological texts, Rachel Bowlby quotes from *The Picture of Dorian Gray* (1891), 'A cigarette is the perfect type of a perfect pleasure. It is exquisite, and it leaves one unsatisfied' (Wilde, *Picture* 79). She comments that these words 'may well strike the late-twentieth-century reader as rather strong', because

> [in] representing the cigarette not only as a pleasure, but as the very quintessence of pleasure, they make the kind of exorbitant claim associated not so much with the refinement of aestheticism as with the advertisement's 'unique selling point'. (Bowlby 5)

While '[it] might seem natural to draw a distinction between aestheticism and advertising, identifying the latter with all the vulgarity rejected by the defenders of "art for art's sake"', on the contrary, Bowlby suggests, '[the] aesthete, far from being different from the new consumer of the period, turns out to be none other than his or her "perfect type"' (5). She adds that the cigarette is a case in point, since it was one of the most widely advertised commodities of the era, but is repeatedly celebrated by arbiters of taste and critics of vulgarity such as Wilde. In *Dorian Gray*, 'the utterances of the most tasteful characters [...] are punctuated throughout by reference to their sophisticated modes of lighting up' (5). (It must be added, though, that cigarettes were often promoted using the word 'satisfying', which suggests that Lord Henry's comment in *Dorian Gray* does not quite correspond with the relatively simple texts of tobacco adverts.) Consumption and excess relate in complex ways to sophistication, and are among the principal themes of my discussion in this chapter. In the texts I have chosen, they emerge mostly in relation to food and sexual desire, rather than smoking or shopping; nevertheless, I have discovered a dynamic between exorbitance and fastidiousness which is similar to the pattern Bowlby finds in Wilde's novel.

The popularity of Oscar Wilde in America reveals the transatlantic appeal of the spectacle of aestheticism and dandyism. In 1881, a new Gilbert and Sullivan operetta, *Patience*, opened in London and, a few months later, in the US. It lampooned the aesthetic movement, and featured a character named Bunthorne, who bore resemblances to Wilde. The producer, Richard D'Oyly Carte, invited Wilde to go on a lecture tour in America in order to provide an example of what the highly successful show was satirising. Although this may not have sounded a very attractive prospect, Wilde turned it into an opportunity to enhance his reputation. His extremely enthusiastic reception may have related to his status as a socially obscure gentleman who had so effectively won over high society that he was able to access aristocratic circles (even though he retained the critical detachment of an outsider) and make a living primarily through his personality. According to Sean Latham: 'Having successfully invested his cultural capital in a pose of sophistication designed to reap substantial social and economic profits, Oscar Wilde completes the nineteenth century's transformation of the snob from a vulgar pretender into an arrogant master of tasteful refinement' (32–33). Americans were fascinated by the European leisure class because they were trying to reinvent its structures in a New World context; this, of course, is the main subject of the American cultural critic Thorstein Veblen's *Theory of the Leisure Class*. As Richard Bushman observes, the rich social leaders of post-Civil War America, with 'their mansions, their airs, their pretensions were the natural outgrowth of the aristocratic genteel culture that the American middle class had appropriated from its former rulers' (402). The leisure and wealth of this class was displayed in ways which would attain maximum visibility, both on the social stage and also in newspapers and magazines. Journalists, indeed, were much more important purveyors of leisure-class prestige in nineteenth-century New York than they were in at the same period in the UK (see Montgomery 9), and their extraordinary attention to Wilde far exceeded anything he had experienced in London. Sophistication was important to Americans who aspired to the social elite, since cultural knowledge, refinement and urbanity could be used to demonstrate not only their separation from the burgeoning middle classes but also their equality with the European upper crust.

In America, then, as among the dandies of Britain, an elite was emerging which was not based on birth, but which collaborated with myths of aristocratic superiority in order to gain entry to the upper-class world.[6] This world was increasingly internationalised, as leisure travel became more available and as writers and artists, in particular, sought contact with other cultures.

6   Several recent books offer detailed studies of New York high society in the 'gilded age'; see especially Homberger; Montgomery. See also my section on Wharton in Chapter 3.

In *Modernist Fiction, Cosmopolitanism and the Politics of Community* (2001), Jessica Berman discusses the founding of *Cosmopolitan* magazine in 1886, noting that its masthead slogan, 'The world is my country and all mankind are my countrymen!', clearly 'exemplified an America newly enamored of worldly perspectives' (28).[7] Europeans, too, were seeking points of view which would enable comparison; Wilde, for instance, in 'The Critic as Artist' (1890),[8] constructs nationality as dependent on knowledge of foreign cultures, while Henry James's cosmopolitanism 'rests upon deep encounters with each culture that is met' (Berman 47). Characters in James's fiction who are incapable of such deep encounter are at risk when they travel. In Italy, Daisy Miller, an innocent who is only just beyond childhood, is stranded in a dangerously cosmopolitan and sophisticated world.

The Victorian conception of adulthood as a degenerate falling-away from the idyllic, innocent realm of the child represents another important context for this chapter. Victorian fiction and visual art are full of child characters, some of them ludicrously idealised; and narratives of childhood and of maturation abound. Lewis C. Roberts notes that the nineteenth-century 'focus on childhood is often traced to eighteenth-century concerns over education and the accompanying recognition of childhood as an ideally separate and unique phase of human life' (354). He explains that the Victorians began with two separate notions of childhood: first, the Romantic idea of the child derived from the educational philosophies of John Locke and Jean-Jacques Rousseau, which proposed that all children were born innocent, and could either develop 'into rational, enlightened human beings through a nurturing system of education' (355) or else be corrupted by ill-conceived social institutions; and second, the view espoused by evangelical revivalists, who believed that infants were born into original sin, and 'insisted that childhood was centrally important as a site for redeeming individual souls and reforming society' (355). The extended debates on this subject intensified an existing anxiety about the possible effects of reading on children's development, a question which had taken on new urgency in this era of expanding literacy. The genre of children's literature developed rapidly over the nineteenth century, but most of the books remained (like their eighteenth-century precursors) extremely didactic.

7   Richard Ohmann notes that travel and society features in turn-of-the-century American magazines such as *Cosmopolitan* and *Munsey's* offered 'a vicarious reconstruction of the Grand Tour for those not entitled to it by birth and wealth' (231).
8   When it first appeared in the July and September 1890 issues of *The Nineteenth Century*, this essay was titled 'The True Function and Value of Criticism; with Some Remarks on the Importance of Doing Nothing: A Dialogue'. This title announced Wilde's dialogue with Matthew Arnold, whose essay 'The Function of Criticism at the Present Time' appeared in *The National Review* in 1864 (see Anderson 50–51).

This tendency is parodied by Lewis Carroll, whose books are, in both moral and narrative terms, far more sophisticated than most other texts for children in this period. Another perspective on the same issue comes, indirectly, from attention to Daisy Ashford's work, which clearly reveals that – though only nine – Ashford must have had access to numerous adult novels of a romantic stamp. Roberts remarks on the Victorians' 'desire to protect children from potentially corrupting fictions', adding that 'such corruption was seen in terms of a too-early awareness of adulthood' (356). Ashford's *The Young Visiters*, like Carroll's books and also, though less obviously, *Daisy Miller*, raises the possibility – so alarming to Victorians – of the child becoming sophisticated.

As in Chapter 1, the close readings presented here are especially attentive to the words used to name what we might now call sophistication. All four texts are, in common with much other fiction from the period, very much concerned with the ideas and social practices which 'sophistication' designates, but none of them uses the exact word: 'unsophistication' occurs once in *Daisy Miller*, and 'sophistries' once in *Zuleika Dobson*, but that is all. In fact, though the term 'sophistication' becomes a little more widespread in *fin-de-siècle* and Edwardian writing, it rarely appears in fiction of the High Victorian era. Litvak suggests that it is important in Thackeray:

> The anxiety and ambiguity informing Thackeray's sophisticated practice characterize his use of the word *sophistication* itself. Not only does Thackerayan *sophistication* hover between an older construction of the term, as meaning 'corruption', and a newer one, as meaning something like 'worldly refinement': the mode of its circulation in his text anticipates what I would call the double discourse of sophistication, an ideological incoherence (or ruse) everywhere discernible in, for instance, late twentieth-century mass culture. In *Vanity Fair*, for example, while describing the vulgarly opportunistic interest of the Osborne sisters in the rich mulatta, Miss Swartz, Thackeray snidely refers to the former as 'dear unsophisticated girls'. On the one hand, 'sophistication' is thematically disowned (the Osborne sisters are ironically ridiculed for *being* sophisticated, i.e., materialistic, socially ambitious, insincere); on the other hand, it is rhetorically performed (the irony with which the sisters are ridiculed is itself a sophisticated device). (57)

This is a very important argument, but it is worth pointing out that the word 'sophistication' does not actually circulate in *Vanity Fair* at all, since it is not used even once, while 'unsophistication' occurs on only two occasions. Neither word appears in *The Book of Snobs*. The negative term, indeed, is far more widely used than the positive one in nineteenth-century fiction, which suggests that there was still considerable uncertainty about the precise meaning of 'sophistication', and also about whether it was something to be admired. 'Unsophistication' was nearly always a term of praise, suggesting that 'sophistication' retained a meaning related to sophistry, disingenuousness or perversion.

A comparison of Dickens's usage in *Nicholas Nickleby* (1838–39) and James's in *The Portrait of a Lady* (1881) shows that nothing much changed over forty-odd years. When Dickens's Nicholas does not know the meaning of the word 'reception' in the sense of the applause given to a well-known actor when he first arrives on stage, Mr Folair admonishes: 'what an unsophisticated shepherd you are' (456). Here, 'unsophisticated' is used as a criticism, but in the remainder of their dialogue, Mr Folair fails to understand Nicholas's irony, suggesting that, in fact, it is he who is unsophisticated. In the other occurrence of the word in this text, Nicholas's snobbish mother becomes worked up over whether she will receive a calling card from the kindly but not very stylish Mr and Mrs Browdie, whereupon Nicholas says: 'I don't suppose such unsophisticated people as these ever had a card of their own, or ever will have' (673). Clearly, these are very worthy people and 'unsophisticated' is a term of praise from Nicholas. Both examples show the multivalency of the term, and its different meanings in different moral contexts. In *The Portrait of a Lady*, 'sophistication' is, if anything, more obviously undesirable. Edward Rosier thinks affectionately of the innocent and demure Pansy Osmond as 'this unsophisticated creature' (401), while Henrietta Stackpole tells Ralph Touchett severely: 'You're not at all like Caliban, because you're sophisticated, and Caliban was not' (127). She goes on to explain that Isabel Archer's American innocence is becoming damaged by her encounter with 'these fell Europeans', amongst whom she includes Ralph, and thus it is clear that she does not mean to praise him for being sophisticated. Isabel herself, aware that the democratic Henrietta does not wish to be drawn into the unjust European system of upper-class leisure and privilege, is amused by her friend's intimacy with Mr Bantling, an English gentleman of independent means and aristocratic connections. 'It was to be feared,' remarks the narrator, 'that she was indeed drifting toward those abysses of sophistication as to which Isabel, wishing for a good-humoured retort, had warned her'.

The earliest instance cited by the *Oxford English Dictionary* of 'sophistication' used in the sense of 'worldly wisdom or experience; subtlety, discrimination, refinement' is actually rather misleading. The quotation, dated 1850, comes from the chapter on 'Italian Manners' in Leigh Hunt's autobiography, and is extracted from the following passage: 'You doubly pity the corruptions of a people who, besides their natural genius, preserve in the very midst of their sophistication a frankness distinct from it, and an entire freedom from affectation' (151). The *OED*'s interpretation of Hunt's usage must here be dependent on the older meaning of subtlety as something like 'craftiness', since Hunt clearly associates sophistication with corruption. Only one further pre-twentieth-century quotation is given under this heading, an 1884 text from the *St James's Gazette* which runs: 'No more simple and guileless folk can well be found, in these days of sophistication'.[9] The dictionary moves on to 1934 before it finds an example of a usage which entirely escapes pejorative implication. Indeed, my own research confirms that that 'sophistication' is rarely used in its most modern, positive sense until the twentieth century.

This chapter includes an example of classic realist fiction, the dominant genre of the era, but also considers the marginal and (arguably) oppositional perspectives of fantasy, satire and texts written for and by children. I begin with Lewis Carroll's *Alice* books, in which the rapidly maturing heroine is by turns innocent and canny, submissive and transgressive, and Wonderland is at once fantastic and oddly conventional. My second text, *Daisy Miller*, is also deeply preoccupied with innocence; the effect of sophistication in the novella is to make truth relative or contingent. The inclusion of James also permits development of the theme of transatlantic sophistication, which was initiated with the account of Fanny Trollope in Chapter 1 and will be pursued in the later chapters in readings of Edith Wharton, Scott Fitzgerald and Vladimir Nabokov. The third text, *The Young Visiters*, presents a unique blend of sophistication and naivety. Ashford's narrator is very witty and keenly aware of social discriminations and the finer points of etiquette, but the text betrays a complete ignorance on certain other topics, especially marriage and reproduction. *The Young Visiters* is especially interesting in that it dramatises the imitative practices of two socially aspirational lower-middle-class characters with much greater frankness than an adult Victorian author would have permitted herself. Moving into the early years of the twentieth century, Max Beerbohm's parodic dandy novel *Zuleika Dobson* (1911), which is included in Susan Sontag's sampling of 'the canon of camp' (277), centres on a female magician, whose highly exaggerated erotic promise proves as illusory as her inept conjuring tricks. Yet Zuleika successfully allures the master-dandy, the Duke of Dorset, and causes a lapse in his sophistication.

Consistency, Beerbohm suggests, is crucial to sophistication, and in his novel, as in *Daisy Miller*, the only character to retain perfect sophistication throughout is the narrator. Indeed, all four texts are interesting in terms of how the quality of sophistication is assigned and reassigned among characters and narrator, and also how the reader is positioned in the hierarchy of sophistication. In these Victorian and Edwardian texts, sophistication is both more desirable and more perilous than it was in the Romantic era. In *Daisy Miller*, as in *Mansfield Park*, the unsophisticated young girl is admired while the worldly-wise gentleman gets into a nasty tangle, but Daisy cannot be

9   The reference is given as *St James's Gazette* 6.2 (9 September 1884).

allowed to triumph as Fanny Price did, because she lives in a more dangerous world. In the *Alice* books and in *The Young Visiters*, the young girl's increasing sophistication helps ensure her success, although Carroll infuses a nostalgia for disappearing innocence which Ashford's text, unsurprisingly, is entirely without. In *Zuleika Dobson*, the innocent girl has been quite abolished, and a provocative, yet perversely respectable, young woman takes her place as the focus of male desire.

'Eat me!': *Alice's Adventures in Wonderland* and *Through the Looking-Glass*

'I'm sure I didn't mean – ' Alice was beginning, but the Red Queen interrupted her impatiently.

'That's just what I complain of! You *should* have meant! What do you suppose is the use of a child without any meaning? Even a joke should have some meaning – and a child's more important than a joke, I hope. You couldn't deny that, even if you tried with both hands.'

'I don't deny things with my *hands*,' Alice objected.

'Nobody said you did,' said the Red Queen. 'I said you couldn't if you tried.'

'She's in that state of mind,' said the White Queen, 'that she wants to deny *something* – only she doesn't know what to deny!'

'A nasty, vicious temper,' the Red Queen remarked; and then there was an uncomfortable silence for a minute or two. (Carroll, *Looking-Glass* 225)

This passage is from the 'Queen Alice' chapter near the end of *Through the Looking-Glass and What Alice Found There*. It does explicitly what the preceding text and the earlier book have done covertly: that is, it lures the reader into searching for the meaning of the child and for the meaning of Carroll's jokes. At the same time, Alice's conversation with the Queens makes a mockery of readers' efforts at interpretation by entangling them in sophistical logic and an excessively literal use of words. The reader is forced into Alice's own position: her usual response is first to object, that is, to participate in the nonsensical (yet, in a formal sense, logical) arguments, and subsequently to lapse into a puzzled silence. She also, however, frequently laughs at the scenes around her, and so encompasses the range of possible readerly responses in herself. Alice, then, is both reader and heroine, and to some extent, she is also the author of the fantasy. She frequently begins 'fancying the sort of thing that would happen' (Carroll, *Alice* 32) in certain improbable situations, such as if her cat Dinah began sending her on errands, or if she was so tall that she had to send Christmas presents to her own feet in the post. In these passages, as in the closing scenes of each book, which reveal that the adventures were all part of Alice's dreams, it becomes clear that her own imagination has generated the stories.

An unending stream of critics have joined in the game of analysing Alice, and the results range from masterly interpretations such as Empson's chapter on Carroll in *Some Versions of Pastoral* through recondite exchanges in *Notes and Queries* to lengthy, often pedantic or fanciful footnotes in editions of the text. Several accounts have focused on what it is which Alice denies, taking their impetus from the rather obvious Freudian symbolism of the story.[10] The entry into sexuality, though, is only one element of the theme of growing up which is explored in the *Alice* stories and in the critical discussions they have generated. For the purposes of this book, the child/adult dynamic may be considered in relation to Carroll's play with sophistication and sophistry and, on the other hand, innocence and naturalness. Alice is both innocent and knowing, both an unsophisticated child in a bewildering 'adult' world and a civilised, rational, well-mannered person surrounded by insanity, rudeness and monstrosity. Thus the *Alice* books reproduce some of the patterns seen in *Evelina* and *Mansfield Park*, but Alice's character does not seem to achieve the coherence which, at least at the end of the novel, marks the classic realist heroine. Her divisions are all too visible.

In *Through the Looking-Glass* Alice starts out as a pawn, standing in for baby Lily, a white chess piece who is too young to play, and ends up in the eighth square as a Queen. But while this suggests a simple process of maturation, the text allows for no such straightforward reading. In the 'Queen Alice' chapter, she is first admonished and examined by her elders (the Red and White Queens), then obliged to conceal her own much greater knowledge in order to avoid 'hurting the poor Queen's feelings' (229), and finally placed in the position of mother as her two companions request lullabies and fall asleep in her lap. She subsequently undergoes the ritual of hosting her first dinner party, something which a young Victorian woman would normally do soon after her marriage. Yet, despite her formal and correct behaviour, Alice's party retains childlike dimensions: it is held in the afternoon,[11] and the child's extensively animated world is represented in the talking pudding, flying bottles and walking soup ladle.

Before and during the meal, the Queens continually advise her as to etiquette, insisting that she issue invitations, make conversation, and 'return thanks in a neat speech' (236), but their advice always conflicts with what Alice

---

10 Among more recent examples, see Carpenter; Dimock. Numerous other articles read the *Alice* books in the context of philosophy or language studies.

11 Dinner in the Georgian and Regency periods tended to be eaten in the late afternoon, but Victorian dinner parties were held in the evening. By the end of the nineteenth century, five o'clock was the normal time for tea (see Jameson), and dinner would be several hours later. Children, though, would most likely have their main meal at tea-time in the nursery.

has already learned about adult social behaviour. The passage quoted at the start of this section continues:

> The Red Queen broke the silence by saying to the White Queen, 'I invite you to Alice's dinner-party this afternoon.'
>
> The White Queen smiled feebly, and said 'And I invite *you*.'
>
> 'I didn't know I was to have a party at all,' said Alice; 'but, if there *is* to be one, I think *I* ought to invite the guests.'
>
> 'We gave you the opportunity of doing it,' the Red Queen remarked: 'but I daresay you've not had many lessons in manners yet?'
>
> 'Manners are not taught in lessons,' said Alice. 'Lessons teach you to do sums, and things of that sort.' (225–26)

Alice knows that adult behaviour cannot be inculcated via direct instruction, but must be absorbed through observation and imitation. The more advanced aspects of manners cannot even be spoken of, because they conceal a whole realm of knowledge about power, class and sexuality to which the child is not supposed to have access. Litvak remarks on 'just how titillatingly taboo a subject like manners can seem, especially when *manners* no longer means just officially certified good manners but the whole repertoire of sociality's unwritten rules' (15). Alice's practice of attempting to deduce unwritten rules from what she sees around her enables her to copy the grown-up manners she has witnessed in her ordinary life, and she upholds them in opposition to the peculiar notions of the Queens, who do not propose that their guests shall have any food:

> 'You look a little shy: let me introduce you to that leg of mutton,' said the Red Queen. 'Alice – Mutton: Mutton – Alice'. The leg of mutton got up in the dish and made a little bow to Alice; and Alice returned the bow, not knowing whether to be frightened or amused.
>
> 'May I give you a slice?' she said, taking up the knife and fork, and looking from one Queen to another.
>
> 'Certainly not,' the Red Queen said, very decidedly: 'it isn't etiquette to cut any one you've been introduced to. Remove the joint!' And the waiters carried it off, and brought a large plum-pudding in its place.
>
> 'I wo'n't be introduced to the pudding, please,' Alice said rather hastily, 'or we shall get no dinner at all. May I give you some?' [...] She conquered her shyness by a great effort, and cut a slice and handed it to the Red Queen.
>
> 'What impertinence!' said the Pudding. 'I wonder how you'd like it, if I were to cut a slice out of *you*, you creature!' (234–35)

The punning use of 'cut' (as in 'ignore') is one of the many instances in Carroll of a play between the literal and figurative meanings of a commonly used phrase. Also here, as so often in the *Alice* books, a reversal of roles occurs: the normally inanimate object assumes the moral advantage, forcing the girl to sympathise with its position and feel herself to be monstrous. To quote Litvak again: 'Insisting on a certain literalization of the object, at once killing it and keeping it alive, incorporation is a fantasy not only of eating one's cake and having it but also of *becoming* one's cake, of *identifying* oneself with it' (25). Alice returns the greeting offered by the joint, apparently acknowledging its personhood, yet asserts her newfound sophistication by incorporation, that is, by insisting on redefining the joint and pudding as foodstuffs rather than companions. In this way, Carroll's text offers a variation on the theme (discussed above in relation to *The School for Scandal*) of incorporation as a way of outsophisticating the other.

Alice's attempt to maintain the usual distinctions between eater and eaten is almost impossible in the chaotic space of the dinner party.[12] Turning to her neighbour, she finds that

> instead of the Queen, there was the leg of mutton in the chair. 'Here I am!' cried a voice from the soup-tureen, and Alice turned again, just in time to see the Queen's broad good-natured face grinning at her for a moment over the edge of the tureen, before she disappeared into the soup. (237)

In passages such as this, the rituals of sophisticated life appear – from the point of view of a child – quite ridiculous. Empson compares the scene to the High Table at Christ Church, where 'the crawling self-stultifying machine of luxury has taken on a hideous life of its own' (*Pastoral* 233). Yet Alice's naive outlook gradually alters as she acquires elements of adult sophistication; indeed, she almost seems to pose as a gourmet, and 'always took a great interest in questions of eating and drinking' (*Alice* 65). She proclaims that she has 'often seen' whiting at dinner (*Alice* 91), and is undismayed by the Mad Hatter's offer of wine, only objecting to the fact that there isn't actually any available. Alice, therefore, stages a sophisticated relationship to food, even though her actual tastes remain firmly childlike. When she tries the liquid in the bottle marked 'DRINK ME', she finds it 'very nice (it had, in fact, a sort of mixed flavour of cherry-tart, custard, pine-apple, roast turkey, toffy, and hot buttered toast)' (*Alice* 14). These are all foods which most children like, but the mixture would offend adult taste.[13] The indiscriminate mingling of favourite foods clashes with the broader conception of taste as a mode of

12 Compare the episode earlier in *Through the Looking-Glass* in which Alice buys an egg, which then turns into Humpty Dumpty, who introduces himself to her, again blurring the boundaries between acquaintances and comestibles.

13 Kevin Sweeney, however, in his article 'Alice's Discriminating Palate', suggests ('with a smile') that this actually 'sounds like a fairly accurate evaluative description of a distinctive style of white wine – a high-extract, large-format Chardonnay, probably a Grand Cru white Burgundy such as a Corton-Charlemagne' (17).

restrained, skilful selection and combination, whether of ingredients, clothes, or furniture.

The *Alice* books also contain many references to disgusting foods: in the first book, there is the Duchess's over-peppered soup and the raw eggs which the pigeon accuses Alice of seeking; in the second, the pudding invented by the White Knight and made of blotting paper, gunpowder and sealing wax and also the glasses filled with 'treacle and ink' mentioned in the song which announces the dinner party (*Looking-Glass* 233). These references are more difficult to read in relation to sophistication. On the one hand, disgust is an important method of asserting tastes (to return to Bourdieu's insight, 'tastes are perhaps first and foremost distastes' [56]), and therefore Alice is positioned as more sophisticated than the Duchess or the White Knight. Yet, on the other hand, Carroll's insistence on horrible and improbable foods evokes the child's faddiness and preference for sweet or bland tastes (the nasty dishes, I suggest, stand for items which appeal to a mature palate, such as olives, anchovies, coffee, wine, game dishes and so on). Disgust and delicacy are intriguingly combined in the episode of the treacle well. According to the Dormouse's story at the Mad Hatter's tea-party, the three little girls who live in the well eat only treacle, and though this may be a delicious item in small quantities, as a staple food it constitutes a revolting diet which – as Alice rightly deduces – makes the sisters very ill. At the same time, they might be read, as Empson proposes, as 'a pathetic example of a martyrdom to the conventions; the little girls did not mind *how* ill they were made by living on treacle because it was their rule'. He adds: 'There is an obscure connexion here with the belief of the period that a really nice girl is "delicate"' (*Pastoral* 222).[14] This class implication is reinforced in the passage about the Bread-and-butter-fly, which has reached such a pitch of refinement that it can only live on weak tea with cream, and since it rarely finds any, it never lives long. Too much sophistication is sickening or even fatal. But the *Alice* books contain many more examples of excessive consumption than of enforced fasting. These, too, have class associations: the Hatter and the March Hare are permanently at the tea-table (afternoon tea being one of the rituals of the leisure class), while the Walrus and the Carpenter consume an enormous number of oysters. Sophistication may take the form of gluttonous consumption of luxury items or of overfastidiousness; either way, it appears unhealthy and unnatural.

Like many of the other texts considered in this study, the *Alice* books are preoccupied with what is natural. The word first appears in the opening chapter of the first book, when Alice suddenly sees a white rabbit with pink eyes run past:

14 Compare his account of the word 'delicate' in *Complex Words* (76–79).

81

There was nothing so *very* remarkable in that; nor did Alice think it so *very* much out of the way to hear the Rabbit say to itself 'Oh dear! Oh dear! I shall be too late' (when she thought it over afterwards, it occurred to her that she ought to have wondered at this, but at the time it all seemed quite natural); but, when the Rabbit actually *took a watch out of its waistcoat pocket*, and looked at it, and then hurried on, Alice started to her feet, for it flashed across her mind that she had never before seen a rabbit with either a waistcoat-pocket, or a watch to take out of it. (*Alice* 9–10)

Talking animals are quite usual in the child world, which may account for Alice's sleepy inattention to the rabbit's speech, but a stylish animal, possessed of the accoutrements of the Victorian gentleman, is sufficiently astonishing. This is one of several passages in which the phrase 'seemed quite natural' is used to distinguish between Alice's immediate reaction to events and her later reflections on them. To finding herself dancing with Tweedledum and Tweedlee 'seemed quite natural (she remembered afterwards), and she was not even surprised to hear music playing: it seemed to come from the tree' (*Looking-Glass* 161). When remembering her dreams, Alice insists more vehemently on the distinction between natural and 'queer' (the term she generally uses for anything fantastic or bizarre) than she does when they are actually happening. During the dream-adventures, she is – like the White Queen – willing to believe in impossible things, or at least to consider other possible worlds and to measure them against the one she knows. She even learns to operate successfully according to the conventions of Wonderland:

'You'll see me there,' said the Cat, and vanished

Alice was not much surprised at this, she was getting so well used to queer things happening. While she was still looking at the place where it had been, it suddenly appeared again.

'By-the-bye, what became of the baby?' said the Cat. 'I'd nearly forgotten to ask.'

'It turned into a pig,' Alice answered very quietly, just as if the Cat had come back in a natural way. (*Alice* 58)

At the end of each book, however, the natural is reasserted, the queer world is relegated to dream or imagination, and its logic is once again sophistical rather than persuasive.

Empson also chooses the word 'queer' to describe Carroll's form of pastoral. He concludes his account of the gradual shift in English literature from pastoral through mock-pastoral to child-cult with the sentence: 'The next development of a queer sort of pastoral, already strong in Wordsworth, triumphant in Lewis Carroll, has accepted this decision that it can be used only on the child' (167). There is, indeed, a queerness about Carroll's pastoral. The traditional elements are present: the garden (in both books), the wood (in *Through the Looking-Glass*), and the simple person who can critique the absurdly elaborate conventions of the sophisticated world. 'I wish *I* could manage to be glad!' says the White Queen to Alice. 'Only I never can remember the rule. You must be very happy, living in this wood, and being glad whenever you like!' (*Looking-Glass* 177) The reference to the rule undermines the vision of the woodland lifestyle as natural and joyous. As Empson says of this passage: 'Perhaps chiefly a comment on the complacence of the fashion of slumming, the remark seems to spread out into the whole beauty and pathos of the ideas of pastoral; by its very universality her vague sympathy becomes an obscure self-indulgence' (231). The pastoral landscape in the Alice books often becomes suddenly threatening and distorted, or imposes itself where it does not belong. The second wood Alice enters is 'much darker', making her feel 'a *little* timid about going into it' (*Looking-Glass* 155), and it is a place where everything loses its name; later, when she is in the little dark shop, she finds 'trees growing' and 'a little brook', and suddenly discovers that 'everything turned into a tree the moment she came up to it' (184).

As trees invade indoor spaces and threaten the identity of people and objects, the image of the wood or thicket begins to suggest a confusion of meaning, and Alice's passage through it comes to represent her negotiation of difficult or contradictory ideas. In his study of sophistication and rhetoric, Mark Backman comments: 'A person's sophistication is signalled by the ability to invent shortcuts through the thicket of conflicting words and actions' (10), and this seems particularly applicable to *Through the Looking-Glass*. Backman analyses the relationship between child's play and sophisticated adult behaviour:

> *Pretending* and *imitating* are the most essential kinds of child's play. Adults employ these skills with greater subtlety and precision borne [sic] of self-conscious intent. Pretense and imitation are powerful capacities of the mature mind. They allow us to stand beside ourselves, to seem to be something or someone else. They are the basic instruments of all great actors, the essential components of irony and the basis of a well-developed sense of humor. (9)

This, too, has a special applicability to Alice, since she pretends and imitates a good deal, and also literally stands beside herself:

> 'Come, there's no use in crying like that!' said Alice to herself rather sharply. 'I advise you to leave off this minute!' She generally gave herself very good advice (though she very seldom followed it), and sometimes she scolded herself so severely as to bring tears into her eyes; and once she remembered trying to box her own ears for having cheated herself in a game of croquet she was playing against herself, for this curious child was very fond of pretending to be two people. (*Alice* 15)

This is all part of Alice's process of maturation; she enacts the part of her mother or governess, and so rebukes the childish parts of herself. In Wonderland and the looking-glass world, she acts out a wider range of roles, including those of a queen, a maid, a baby nurse, and a hostess.

Owing to this multiplicity of roles, Alice's status in relation to others is extremely unstable. In 'real life', she has a definite age (seven and a half in the second book). In the fantasy worlds, however, the creatures continually ask her how old she is: it seems that this cannot be deduced from her appearance. She is sometimes admonished as if she were very small – 'So young a child,' says an illogical gentleman in the train carriage, 'ought to know which way she's going, even if she doesn't know her own name!' (150) – and at other times, allowed to participate in adult social occasions such as the Queen of Hearts' croquet-match or the dinner party. Once again, Empson's comments are illuminating:

> talking animals in children's books had been turned to didactic purposes ever since Aesop; the schoolmastering tone in which the animals talk nonsense to Alice is partly a parody of this – they are really childish but try not to look it. On the other hand, this tone is so supported by the way they can order her about, the firm and surprising way their minds work, the abstract topics they work on, the useless rules they accept with so much conviction, that we take them as real grown-ups contrasted with unsophisticated childhood. (*Pastoral* 212–13)

Certainly, some of the animals and other fantasy characters appear more grown-up than others. The supremely sophisticated caterpillar with his hookah is perhaps the most unambiguously adult character: smoking has always been reserved for adults, and the image of a child smoking would be shocking in any context. The Cheshire Cat also has a noticeably worldly air and is skilled in repartee. The King of Hearts, on the other hand, is particularly juvenile, and even resorts to hiding behind Alice at one point, while the Hatter and the Hare demand to be told stories, upset milk jugs and try to stuff the dormouse into the teapot. (Victorian children sometimes kept dormice as pets and they could be housed in old teapots filled with nesting material.) In response to these encounters, Alice's own behaviour ranges from timid politeness with the Caterpillar and Cheshire Cat to determination and confidence at the Hatter's tea-party.

Alice, then, oscillates between child and adult roles, and her class status is similarly ambiguous. Again, in her ordinary life, she has a clear identity as upper-middle-class: this is evident from her own reactions, from her education and from the kind of room she is playing in before climbing through the mirror. During her dream-adventures, she is, on the whole, rather aspirational and not very democratic. She has no sympathy with the mob-like daisies in the Garden of Live Flowers, and sides entirely with the regal Tiger-Lily, helping it to silence the daisies by whispering viciously 'If you don't hold your tongues,

I'll pick you!' (*Looking-Glass* 139). A moment later, she abandons her conversation with the flowers on seeing the Red Queen approach, because 'it would be far grander to have a talk with a real Queen' (141). But in terms of the way she is treated, Alice moves dizzyingly up and down the social scale. In some episodes, she is approached with respect, as if she is of a high social class: the playing-card gardeners, for instance, bow low on her approach, address her as 'Miss' and later run to her 'for protection' (*Alice* 72). Yet the White Rabbit mistakes her for his housemaid, while the White Queen offers her twopence a week to act as her lady's maid. Though Alice laughs out loud at the idea that she might go into domestic service, she is equally conscious that she does not belong to the aristocracy: '"When *I'm* a Duchess," she said to herself (not in a very hopeful tone, though), "I wo'n't have any pepper in my kitchen"' (*Alice* 79). The question of what someone as grand as a Duchess is doing sitting in the kitchen, nursing her own baby and allowing her cook to throw pans at her, does not seem to occur to Alice, but this is relevant since it is all part of the narrative's temporary destabilising of class hierarchies: in the world of make-believe, Alice can ultimately become a Queen, while a Duchess may be subject to her violent cook.

And yet, it is not these things which define the *Alice* books as children's literature. In many classic (adult) Victorian novels, fantasies of class mobility are dramatically fulfilled; numerous others focus on growing up and trace the maturation of the central character. In fact, the question of what makes *Alice's Adventures in Wonderland* a children's book, or whether it is, in fact, primarily a children's book, has been debated at length. Carroll himself referred to 'the little ones for whom it was written',[15] but numerous critics have argued that the book should be understood as part of classic English fiction, rather than categorised as children's fiction.[16] Virginia Woolf said of Carroll:

> Since childhood remained in him entire, he could do what no one else has ever been able to do – he could return to that world, he could recreate it, so that we too become children again. It is for this reason that the two *Alices* are not books for children; they are only books in which we become children. (83)

This comment does offer some insight into what Roger Lancelyn Green calls 'the secret of Lewis Carroll – the circumstances which made him able to write the greatest of all children's books' (xxii). And yet, contrary to Woolf's uggestion, it might be argued that we unavoidably, and perhaps consciously, read the *Alice* books as adults. Undoubtedly, this is a highly sophisticated narrative, much more complex than most writing for children. The puns,

15 Preface to the six-shilling edition of *Alice* (Christmas 1896). Reprinted in Carroll, *Alice* 6.
16 The various critical points of view are referenced in Roger Lancelyn Green's introduction to the Oxford World's Classics edition of the *Alice* books.

double entendres, jokes about death, and play with language, logic and abstraction may well be appreciated more fully by a mature reader (although a child might grasp a good proportion of them). The sexual imagery which has so fascinated critics is also, of course, often cited in support of the argument that this is an adult text. Indeed, the sheer amount of critical debate and interpretive commentary which the *Alice* books have generated reinforces claims for their adult status.

The important point in relation to the present discussion is that, whether or not these are books for children, they are certainly books *about* childhood, and they are also, I suggest, books about the child's relationship to sophistication. A text which is at all concerned with sophistication must itself possess sophistication, but it can still be a book for children; it can even, as I propose later in this chapter in my discussion of Daisy Ashford, be written by a child. Indeed, one of the most interesting questions raised by both Ashford's *The Young Visiters* and the *Alice* books is the question of how much the child (whether author or protagonist) knows, or can be allowed to know. Alice is always looking for 'an opportunity to show off a little of her knowledge' (*Alice* 54), though much of it turns out to be rather inaccurate. In fact, much of her charm results from her lack of knowledge: 'Alice had not the slightest idea what Latitude was, or Longitude either, but she thought they were nice grand words to say' (*Alice* 11). When she evinces too much knowledge, she temporarily loses her innocent air and offends people:

> '*The King has promised me – with his very own mouth* – to – to – '
> 'To send all his horses and all his men,' Alice interrupted, rather unwisely.
> 'Now I declare that's too bad!' Humpty Dumpty cried, breaking into a sudden passion. 'You've been listening at doors – and behind trees – and down chimneys – or you couldn't have known it!'
> 'I haven't, indeed!' Alice said very gently. 'It's in a book.' (*Looking-Glass* 187)

Alice's innocence is upheld: she has not been covertly gaining illicit knowledge, but only reading nursery rhymes. (In contrast, Daisy Ashford could not have written her book without a good deal of surreptitious watching of adults, and secret reading of romantic fiction.) During the trial of the Knave of Hearts, Alice's innocence is again asserted: when asked what she knows about the business, she replies 'Nothing whatever' (*Alice* 104). Empson speculates that Carroll felt it important 'that Alice should be innocent of all knowledge of what the Knave of Hearts (a flashy-looking lady's man in the picture) is likely to have been doing, and also important that she should not be told she is innocent' (*Pastoral* 214–15). It *is* important, of course, in terms of the Victorian idealisation of the child as sexless; despite her attempted performance of sophistication in relation to meals and manners, Alice must not approach sexual sophistication. Thus the child reader is provided with an 'innocent' reading position, in which she or he identifies with Alice, while the adult reader must inevitably know more.

'I am not so innocent': *Daisy Miller*

In *Daisy Miller*, sophistication is fatal. Daisy, a young American girl whose extreme innocence, though continually questioned by those around her, is very evident to the reader, dies as a direct result of her encounter with European sophistication. In *The American Scene* (1907), Henry James observes that the American girl 'had been grown in an air in which a hundred of the "European" complications and dangers didn't exist, and in which [...] she could develop her "powers" in a medium from which criticism was consistently absent'. Arriving 'full-blown, on the general scene', he continues, 'her situation may affect the critic as one of the most touching on record; he may merely note his perception that she was to have been after all but the sport of fate' (348). This is the central theme of *Daisy Miller*, and the opening scene of the novella immediately evokes an environment appropriate to the subject: 'At the little town of Vevey, in Switzerland, there is a particularly comfortable hotel [...] distinguished from many of its upstart neighbours by an air both of luxury and of maturity' (James, *Daisy* 7). Hotels, of course, are often associated with qualities such as cosmopolitanism, indulgence and style, and they are also spaces apart from everyday life, and therefore invite excess, deviations from the usual, and sudden, intense encounters. The hotel, then, is the ultimate setting for sophistication. In addition, the 'maturity' of the hotel where the Millers and Winterbourne stay gestures towards the comparison between the older, more complex and possibly decadent cultures of Europe and the forward-looking American scene. Daisy, who is making her first trip abroad, observes that she has 'never seen so many hotels in my life as since I came to Europe' (18). The hotel initially stands as a sign for European sophistication, in contrast to American innocence, as represented by young and fresh Daisy, though this contrast is interrogated in the course of the narrative.

At Vevey, Daisy meets the Europeanised American dilettante Frederick Winterbourne, who thinks of himself as 'a man of imagination and, as our ancestors used to say, of sensibility' (39), and 'a lover of the picturesque' (81). Winterbourne tries to combine this role of the belated Romantic with the image of a modern sophisticate, priding himself on his detachment, worldliness and experience. But he does not quite manage to be either, because he is weighed down by the atavistic conventions of the expatriate American society: 'you are too stiff' (68), says Daisy. Winterbourne's perspective is also distorted by his cosmopolitanism. In 'Occasional Paris', published the same year as *Daisy Miller*, James wrote: 'To be a cosmopolite is not, I think, an ideal; the ideal should be to be a concentrated patriot. Being a cosmopolite is an accident, but one must make the best of it' (James, *Collected* 721).[17] Jessica Berman comments: 'Accidental cosmopolitanism arrives through a constant need to compare and a concomitant unwillingness to choose sides' (45). This is certainly one of Winterbourne's failings. The fault-lines in his view of himself, and consequently of the world, lead to all the supposed contradictions and ambiguities of this much-debated story. Winterbourne is charmed by Daisy, yet their potential romance is derailed by his continual judging of her in relation to the sophisticated social framework he understands. Her frankness disconcerts him, and he repeatedly wonders whether her apparent innocence conceals a subtle manipulativeness: 'Was she simply a pretty girl from New York State – were they all like that [...]? Or was she also a designing, an audacious, an unscrupulous young person?' (19). Some months after their encounter at Vevey, Winterbourne travels to Rome, where he knows Daisy is spending the winter, but on arriving, finds that she has made friends with a handsome but penniless Italian, Mr Giovanelli, described by the narrator as 'the subtle Roman' (87). Jealous and suspicious, Winterbourne repeatedly misunderstands Daisy when she indicates her affection for him, and rejects her with particular brusqueness on encountering her in the moonlit Colosseum, where Giovanelli has incautiously taken her. Immediately afterwards, he advises her to go home and take some medicine because she has spent the whole evening in a notoriously malarial site. Daisy says, 'in a strange little tone' (85), that she doesn't care if she has caught a fever or not; the implication is that she is so upset that she does not take the pills, since within two weeks she is dead.

But though the effects of sophistication are so disastrous, there is no escape from it in the text. The reader, though invited to pass judgement on Winterbourne and distrust his warped point of view, is not able to access the innocent perspective of Daisy; indeed, the whole text (like all of James's work) is a construct of extreme narrative sophistication. The narrator, though he demonstrates the wrong-headedness of Winterbourne's sophistication, is himself far more sophisticated, as is evident from the moment when he introduces his protagonist:

> He was some seven-and-twenty years of age; when his friends spoke of him they usually said that he was at Geneva, 'studying'. When his enemies spoke of him they

17 This piece was originally titled 'Paris Revisited' when it appeared in *The Galaxy* (January 1878). In later decades, James's view changed. Berman writes that James's 1890s stories depict a 'purposeful version' of cosmopolitanism, and that by then he has 'proposed it as a mode of living made possible by the attainment of a certain honesty of tone' (45).

said – but, after all, he had no enemies; he was an extremely amiable fellow, and universally liked. What I should say is, simply, that when certain persons spoke of him they affirmed that the reason of his spending so much time at Geneva was that he was extremely devoted to a lady who lived there – a foreign lady – a person older than himself. Very few Americans – indeed I think none – had ever seen this lady, about whom there were some singular stories. (8–9)

This prevarication alerts us to the contingency of all the judgements and assessments offered in the text, and yet the narrator retains his own authority precisely by withholding any definite pronouncement. The lady mentioned may, or may not, exist – she never appears in the story – but the rumour about an older, foreign, possibly married lover exactly suits the sophisticated image which Winterbourne wishes to project. His association with her appears to confirm his separation from bourgeois American ideals of marriage and family. On another level, as Robert Weisbuch observes, she represents 'Winterbourne's unseen life […] his pornographic, musty self', and therefore must be hidden. For this reason, 'he cannot believe in Daisy's appearance of innocence, because his own appearance is so unnaturally fashioned to disguise what resides in Geneva and in himself' (Weisbuch 78).

In contrast to the lady from Geneva, Daisy Miller is young, inexperienced and American: suitable material for a wife, according to the conventions of the era. But Winterbourne cannot recognise this. He feels that he has been away so long that he has become 'dishabituated to the American tone' (19), and therefore is unable to make up his mind about Daisy. He wonders if she is a coquette:

> He had known, here in Europe, two or three women – persons older than Miss Daisy Miller, and provided, for respectability's sake, with husbands – who were great coquettes – dangerous, terrible women, with whom one's relations were liable to take a serious turn. But this young girl was not a coquette in that sense; she was very unsophisticated; she was only a pretty American flirt. Winterbourne was almost grateful for having found the formula that applied to Miss Daisy Miller. (19–20)

'Sophisticated' is here invested with a meaning relating to sexuality and cunning: Winterbourne sees Daisy as unsophisticated because she is not trying to draw him into an intrigue. At the same time, 'unsophisticated' contains a hint of the other word which he repeatedly uses to describe her: 'uncultivated' (27, 63, 77).

Winterbourne has not, of course, really 'found the formula' for Daisy; indeed, the rest of the story consists largely of his further speculation about her. He is excited by her apparent wildness: 'it was probable that anything might be expected of her. Winterbourne was impatient to see her again' (28). For him, she represents modernness and novelty: he notes that she sometimes speaks 'smartly' (39) – this word, at the time, certainly belonged to the same lexicon as 'sophisticated'. She also identifies herself with the new (and with the New World) by her repeated references to the sites of European heritage as 'old' – she uses this term in the Colosseum (82), and talks of the Château Chillon at Vevey as 'that old castle' (20). But it is in her defiance of social convention that Daisy is most strikingly modern, and most opposite to Winterbourne who, despite his worldly poses, ultimately obeys the rules of his expatriate community. When Mrs Walker, a respectable lady living in Rome, tries to protect Daisy's reputation by inducing her to abandon her walk with Mr Giovanelli and join her in her carriage, Daisy is affronted. She asks Winterbourne if he thinks she should comply, and he decides that '[the] finest gallantry, here, was simply to tell her the truth'. The narrator adds: 'the truth, for Winterbourne, as the few indications I have been able to give have made him known to the reader, was that Daisy Miller should take Mrs Walker's advice' (61). The 'truth' here is not a moral dictum, it is a question of strategy. For the sophisticated characters in this story, 'truth' is always relative, subjective, contingent (as it was for the Greek Sophists), whereas for Daisy it is simple and stable. Therefore, while the sophisticates can circumnavigate restrictive social norms, Daisy must openly (and unsuccessfully) defy them.

Sophistication seems here to be revealed as conservative: that is, complicit with the repressive social norms of the late nineteenth-century leisure class. It is tempting to counter this idea with the suggestion that, in fact, the balance of sophistication has shifted from Winterbourne to Daisy. Certainly, she is the one who is able to perceive the absurdity of social convention. But this argument does not hold up, though it directs us to one of the central paradoxes of sophistication, which is that although it rejects bourgeois morality, it does not usually reject the complex structures of class, power and reputation which define fashionable manners. The sophisticate accepts the need for precisely orchestrated social performances, a careful negotiation of public spaces, and an evasion of the policing function of gossip. Indeed, he or she is highly adept at these practices, and therefore can do what is forbidden by conventional morality (usually some form of sensual indulgence), but without incurring punishment. The logic of traditional literary forms generally requires eventual punishment, but just consider for how long Madame de Merteuil, Lady Sneerwell, Henry Crawford, Becky Sharp, or even Humbert Humbert actually get away with it. The un-strategic Daisy, by contrast, can get away with nothing. Even walking along in a public square in broad daylight with a gentleman exposes her to hostile comment, whereas other women in the expatriate community have full-blown affairs and yet retain their position in society by maintaining a respectable façade.

Owing to Daisy's ambiguous status in Winterbourne's eyes, the novella has generated a good deal of debate, beginning on its first publication and continuing into recent critical analyses. In 1879, William Dean Howells wrote to James Russell Lowell: 'Henry James waked up all the women with his *Daisy Miller*', adding, 'And there has been a vast discussion in which [...] society almost divided itself into Daisy Millerites and anti-Daisy Millerites' (Howells 230–31). These readers, then, judged Daisy by the standards used by the other characters in the story, and thus got caught up in the very debate – as to whether she was really innocent – which the novella proves to be futile. Indeed, as James notes in the preface to the 1907 New York edition of *Daisy Miller*, the story was regarded by the conservative magazine editor to whom he first submitted it as 'an outrage on American girlhood'.[18] Howells himself felt that the controversy about Daisy's character, however foolish, would at least bring James the attention he had long deserved: 'I hoped that in making James so thoroughly known, it would call attention to the beautiful work he had been doing for very few readers' (Howells 231). This comment implies that the novella could be understood on two levels: that it addresses itself at once to rather unpractised readers, who will become absorbed in the mystery of Daisy which the protagonist himself is trying to solve, and also to sophisti-cated readers, who will realise that it is a story about the divisions in Winter-bourne's mind, and not really about Daisy Miller at all.

Daisy's character is not genuinely undecidable. Her words appear in profu-sion in the text in the form of direct speech, and may be considered apart from Winterbourne's varying and misguided assessments of them. It is clear that, while she is unaware of the conventions of the Anglophone society in Vevey and Rome, and therefore continually violates them, Daisy also has a native grace and a trusting, open character. As Robert Weisbuch remarks: 'The terrible ambiguity, the vexing mystery of her status as innocent or vixen, have nothing to do with her inherent quality'; rather, 'they are all evoked by Winterbourne's misshapen assessment' (66). The contradictions result from Winterbourne's impossible stance as a sophisticate trying to appreciate an unsophisticated girl, and always on his own terms rather than hers. Indeed, the problem the novel revolves around is not whether Daisy is innocent but, to borrow a phrase from Barbara Everett, 'the whole difficulty of maintaining innocence at this late point in human history' (255). Everett was talking about the 1920s, and about another novel concerning an American girl in Europe, Anita Loos's

---

18 To give a fuller quotation – James remarks that the editor of *Lippincott's*, a Philadelphia magazine which had previously published his work, returned his story without comment. This puzzled him until a friend 'declared that it could only have passed with the Philadelphian critic for "an outrage on American girlhood"' (41).

Gentlemen Prefer Blondes. Loos's protagonist Lorelei actually is the kind of girl Winterbourne suspects Daisy of being: that is, an unscrupulous yet charming flirt with an eye for the main chance, whose childlike demeanour conceals a deeper game. But Everett's remark still applies to *Daisy Miller* – in 1878, American travellers were already beginning to view Europe as an exhausted, degenerate culture, in contrast to the more progressive United States. In this context, it is perhaps unsurprising that innocence is embodied in a young American girl, and that she is unable to survive outside her native country.

The word 'innocent' (one of the possible opposites of 'sophistication') gradually becomes complicated over the course of the text, as the characters endlessly redefine it in relation to other terms. For instance, Winterbourne says of the Millers, 'They are very ignorant – very innocent only. Depend upon it they are not bad' (46). When he asserts to Mrs Walker, a respectable lady in Rome, that Daisy is 'very innocent', she retorts: 'She's very crazy' (58). Daisy's innocence is recast as craziness because it leads her to actions which are disallowed by the rules of the expatriate society (just as Alice is continually exposed to suspicion and accusation in Wonderland because its rules diverge so far from those she has been used to). Reading Daisy's behaviour in a framework to which she herself makes no reference, Winterbourne finds it incomprehensible. For instance, when Daisy becomes jealous of Winterbourne's supposed mistress in Geneva, he misses the implication of her attachment to him, and instead finds in her remarks 'an extraordinary mixture of innocence and crudity' (43). He is unable to understand her as simply innocent, and always suspects some admixture, later describing her as 'an inscrutable combination of audacity and innocence' (58). On this occasion, it is because she sees nothing wrong in arranging to meet Mr Giovanelli in a public place, yet does not seem to want to be alone with him and is pleased that Winterbourne remains with them. Winterbourne almost wishes that she had tried to shake him off: 'That she should seem to wish to get rid of him would help him to think more lightly of her, and [this ...] would make her much less perplexing' (58). He wants to be able to dismiss Daisy as someone not worthy of respect, so that he will no longer be troubled by her puzzling manners. But the key to the puzzle is all along visible to the attentive reader: it is that she is in love with Winterbourne. In some senses, indeed, it is he who is the innocent, as his aunt, Mrs Costello, astutely observes:

> 'I really think you had better not meddle with little American girls that are uncultivated, as you call them. You have lived too long out of the country. You will be sure to make some great mistake. You are too innocent.'
>
> 'My dear aunt, I am not so innocent', said Winterbourne, smiling and curling his moustache. (27)

Winterbourne means, of course, that he is not sexually innocent (whereas Daisy is), but he *is* innocent in his naive assumptions and his unawareness of Daisy's feelings.

Mrs Costello consolidates her own social position purely through being 'very exclusive' (25) and refusing to associate with any but the most socially elite Americans. She is dismayed by the fact that new money can purchase the appearance of style, saying of Miss Miller: 'she dresses in perfection – no, you don't know how well she dresses. I can't think where they get their taste' (25). But Daisy's family, she observes, reveal their low origins by their failure to distinguish between actual and imitation gentility: 'They treat the courier like a familiar friend [...] Very likely they have never seen a man with such good manners, such fine clothes, so like a gentleman' (26). Winterbourne tries to accept his aunt's judgement of Daisy, but cannot quite manage it: '"Common" she was, as Mrs Costello had pronounced her; yet it was a wonder to Winterbourne that, with her commonness, she had a singularly delicate grace' (32). On a boat trip with her, he 'took much satisfaction in his companion's distinguished air' (40). Distinction is incompatible with commonness, and this throws Winterbourne into further perplexity: 'He had assented to the idea that she was "common"; but was she so, after all, or was he simply getting used to her commonness?' (40). His underlying fear is that he will somehow be contaminated by this supposed commonness, or that in being attracted by her, he is guilty of a lapse of taste.

Winterbourne attempts to prove his taste and sophistication through his judgements on others. For instance, he suspects Mr Giovanelli of being – like the courier – an imitation gentleman:

> Winterbourne flattered himself that he had taken his measure. 'He is not a gentleman,' said the young American; 'he is only a clever imitation of one. He is a music-master, or a penny-a-liner, or a third-rate artist. Damn his good looks!' [...] It was true that if he was an imitation the imitation was very skilful. 'Nevertheless,' Winterbourne said to himself, 'a nice girl ought to know!' And then he came back to the question whether this was in a fact a nice girl. (57)

Mr Giovanelli, his rival wishes to believe, has simply assumed the outward trappings of sophistication: 'Winterbourne perceived at some distance a little man standing with folded arms, nursing his cane. He had a handsome face, an artfully poised hat, a glass in one eye, and a nosegay in his button-hole' (55). Winterbourne wants to believe that Giovanelli is not quite the thing, so that he can despise Daisy for admiring him, yet the Italian's dandified image is uncomfortably similar to Winterbourne's own.

Towards the last pages of the novel, when Winterbourne has become aware of the amount of time Daisy spends with Giovanelli, he almost gives her up:

'holding oneself to a belief in Daisy's "innocence" came to seem to Winter-bourne more and more a matter of fine-spun gallantry' (77). This is the first time that the word 'innocence' has appeared in inverted commas: he seems to have arrived at an ironic distance from it, and from Daisy herself. In the night-time scene in the Colosseum, he finally decides she has gone too far, and when she appears hurt by his ignoring her, he thinks, 'how smartly she played an injured innocence' (82–83). As this Colosseum episode opens, Daisy is sitting with Giovanelli in the shadows, and Winterbourne appears, brightly lit by the moon, and stares at them. Not immediately recognising him, Daisy says: 'Well, he looks at us as one of the old lions and tigers may have looked at the Chris-tian martyrs!'. Her companion replies: 'Let us hope he is not very hungry [...] He will have to take me first; you will serve for dessert!' (82). This returns us to Litvak's argument that the exercise of sophisticated taste involves the consumption of others: 'to outsophisticate the other is to incorporate the other' (9). Winterbourne certainly hopes to outsophisticate Giovanelli and also Daisy (since he doesn't grasp her complete unsophistication). The image of his eating her horrifyingly prefigures her actual death as a direct result of the scene then unfolding.

Yet at the very end of the narrative, innocence, having almost lost its meaning, is suddenly restored as a stable value, when Giovanelli describes Daisy, now dead, as 'the most innocent' young lady he has ever known (87). Giovanelli recognised and appreciated what Winterbourne did not – Daisy's purity – and hence he is the more sophisticated of the two. In *Daisy Miller*, James's enduring theme of American innocence versus European sophistication (with all its possible variations and reversals) is partly worked out through the obvious device of Daisy's encounter with the dangerously elaborate expatriate social scene in Rome and Vevey. But the international theme is developed in more complex ways through Winterbourne, who turns out not to be the European-ised sophisticate but the American innocent, inferior in many ways to the truly sophisticated Italian Giovanelli. Even Giovanelli, though, cannot approach the dizzying sophistication of the narrator, who fully realises the ambition which Henry James famously stated in an 1888 letter to his brother William: 'I aspire to write in such a way that it wd. be impossible to an outsider to say whether I am an American writing about England or an Englishman writing about America (dealing as I do with both countries,) & so far from being ashamed of such an ambiguity I should be exceedingly proud of it, for it would be highly civilized' (James, *Henry James* 213).

'Other good dodges of a rich nature': *The Young Visiters*

Daisy Ashford's novella *The Young Visiters; or, Mr Salteena's Plan* was written in 1890 when the author was nine, and in 1919 it was published, complete with its idiosyncratic spelling and a preface by J. M. Barrie. *The Young Visiters* is about becoming a gentleman. It is also intensely preoccupied with taste, consumption and even sex. Its lower-middle-class protagonists are seventeen-year-old Ethel and her middle-aged admirer, Mr Salteena, who admits: 'I am not quite a gentleman but you would hardly notice it but cant be helped anyhow' (2). They seek social advancement by visiting a genteel acquaintance, Bernard Clark, to whom Mr Salteena appeals: 'I am quite alright as they say but I would like to be the real thing' (14). Bernard sends him off to 'grow more seemly' (14) by mixing with some aristocrats he knows in London, and in his absence, ensures Ethel is kept entertained.

The astonishing sophistication of this child's text, in terms of its acute and witty observation of the late Victorian manners, desires, and class distinctions, is combined with an utter ignorance of certain adult social taboos, particularly those concerning the relations between the sexes. Ashford allows Ethel to go and stay by herself in the house of a bachelor, and then to venture alone with another man to a London hotel. She even arrives at her wedding in the same carriage with her husband-to-be. As J. M. Barrie remarks in his preface to the first edition, 'Chaperon seems to be one of the very few good words of which our authoress had never heard' (64). Ethel and Bernard subsequently return from a six weeks' honeymoon with 'a son and hair' (46). But these misapprehensions are countered by Ashford's remarkable insight into pretension and aspiration, and a developed irony which functions at the expense of all the characters. This unique blend of sophistication and naivety makes the narrative point of view of *The Young Visiters* both fascinating and awkward to define.

The narrator herself can define exactly, in material, linguistic and behavioural terms, the difference between gentlefolk and the shopkeeping class. The well-bred Bernard has such accoutrements as 'a portly butler' (8), 'a weary smile' (10), 'a lot of ancesters' (11), and a 'sumpshous' bathroom (13). Mr Salteena, the son of a butcher, is continually getting bashful, 'jellous' (25) and 'flustered with his forks' (11), while the still less respectable – though far more charming – Ethel 'did not really know at all how to go on at a visit' (8). Mr Salteena's idioms ('We had better collect our traps said Mr Salteena' [7]) are clearly distinguished, on the one hand, from the casual fluency of the higher classes ('Then Bernard said shall I show you over my domain' [11]), and on the other, from the precise formality of their servants ('Very good sir said the noble footman if you will alight I will see to your luggage there is a convayance awaiting you' [7]). The narrator, however, has a varying prose style, which shifts between colloquialism – 'he soon got dog tired and suggested lunch by the mossy bank' (39) – and literariness: 'He puffed at his pipe for some moments while the larks gaily caroled in the blue sky. Then he edged a trifle closer to Ethels form' (39).

This inconsistent tone reflects the unfixed social positioning of the narrator. There is an unnerving combination of sympathy and contempt in her attitude towards the upstarts Ethel and Mr Salteena, which is comparable to Thackeray's ambivalence towards Becky Sharp. The narrator frequently points out Ethel's and Mr Salteena's social indiscretions, greed, venality, and lack of poise, yet she nevertheless rewards them both: Ethel is married to the attractive and wealthy Bernard, while Mr Salteena receives a title and a position at court. The entry of these two characters into the upper class only makes plain something which is emphasised throughout the text: the fluidity and performativity of class identities, and their dependence on material display. From the child's point of view, ritualistic costumes such as court dress appear highly theatrical:

> Procurio got very intelligent and advised Mr Salteena to wear his black evening suit and role up his trousers. He also lent him a pair of white silk stockings which he fastined tightly round his knees with red rosettes. Then he quickly cut out a star in silver paper and pinned [it] to his chest and also added a strip of red ribbon across his shirt front. Then Mr Salteena survayed himself in the glass. Is it a fancy dress party he asked. (24)

Mr Salteena's attempt to demonstrate his gentility is largely unconvincing: in terms of dress, he appears as a kind of cut-price gentleman with his rolled-up trousers and, on another occasion, his evening suit adorned with 'some ruby studs he had got at a sale' (10). He also tries to seem educated, but this turns out to be pointless. During the drive to Bernard's house, he makes a (rather feeble) show of interest in the picturesque: 'Now my dear what do you think of the sceenery' he asks. 'Very nice said Ethel gazing at the rich fur rug on her knees' (8). Ethel's instinct is the correct one, and both she and her escort eventually gain advancement entirely by means of appearing rich, rather than through acquiring cultural knowledge. They both observe that all the genuine upper-class, aristocratic and even regal characters in the book possess 'costly' items of dress and furnishing; this word recurs through the text, signalling – far more directly than more traditional Victorian novels usually do – the conspicuous consumption which underpins nineteenth-century social hierarchies. The text takes a material interpretation of class to its logical limits. When Mr Salteena travels in the second-class rail carriage, he attracts the contempt of Bernard's 'exalted footman' Horace (7), but later, taking a first-class ticket and with the footman in attendance, Mr Salteena evokes quite a different reaction: 'The other pasengers looked full of envy at the curly white wig and green plush uniform of Horace. Mr Salteena crossed his legs in a lordly way and flung a fur rug over his knees though he was hot enough in all conscience' (16).

Mr Salteena repeatedly overheats, and always at moments when he is admitting to his deficiencies ('To tell you the truth my Lord I am not anyone of import and I am not a gentleman as they say he ended getting very red and hot' [19]), or when he is attempting to act out a social role to which he has no legitimate claim. At the Prince of Wales's levee, Mr Salteena's new acquaintance, the Earl of Clincham, introduces him as Lord Hyssops. On arrival: 'The earl twiddled his mustache and slapped his leg with his white glove as calmly as could be. Mr Salteena purspired rarther hard and gave a hitch to his garters to make sure' (26). Mr Salteena's body is itself classed, and repeatedly lets him down, revealing his shameful unsophistication. As in much eighteenth- and earlier nineteenth-century fiction, blushing can be a sign of unsophistication, but its meaning has changed with the shift in the meaning of sophistication itself. In young girls of earlier generations, it signified a pleasing innocence and reticence; in Mr Salteena, it indicates a failure of style and poise. Ethel, too, is unmasked, in class terms, by her red cheeks. She insists on 'plenty of ruge' (75), and wears such bright clothes and make-up that even Mr Salteena remarks, 'You look rarther rash my dear your colors dont quite match your face' (5). But whilst this suggests a touch of vulgarity, it also confers a certain modernness: at one point Ethel, 'with some red roses in her hat and the dainty red ruge in her cheeks looked quite the thing' (38), and in another scene, 'Ethel had on her blue velvet get up and a sweet new hat and plenty of ruge on her face and looked quite a seemly counterpart for Bernard' (31).

Ethel's blushes are not always artificial. On first being introduced to Bernard, who has 'very nice long legs fairish hair and blue eyes' (9), she is rather overcome: 'Oh yes gasped Ethel blushing through her red ruge'. In response, Bernard 'looked at her keenly and turned a dark red' (9). Ethel's behaviour usually matches Bernard's, whereas Mr Salteena's always contrasts with the behaviour of those around him. Ethel confidently imitates genteel behaviour with her 'small lady like steps' (32), 'dainty smile' (9), and polite remarks, and she even faints when Bernard proposes marriage. Nevertheless, her desires are all too clear. Ethel's emotions, like Mr Salteena's, are often legible on her body, but the difference is that it is her appetites, and not her fears, which appear. These appetites, it might be argued, actually qualify her for membership of the sophisticated upper class, since sophistication may be understood as intimately connected to consumption and excess. Bourdieu writes in *Distinction* of the opposition 'between the taste of necessity, which favours the most "filling" and most economical foods, and the taste of liberty – or luxury – which shifts the emphasis to the manner (of presenting, serving, eating etc.)' (6). He argues that 'the science of taste and of cultural consumption' must perform a 'barbarous reintegration of aesthetic consumption into the world of ordinary consumption' (6). Taking his cue from Bourdieu, Litvak notes that sophistication's 'bodily implication' actually – and rather perversely – 'betokens its "aristocratic" affiliation' (6). He continues: 'sophistication offends not only in its artificiality but in its excessiveness: the sophisticate enjoys (himself or herself) too much, which is to say at the expense of others' (7).

In each of their scenes together, Ethel and Bernard revel in consuming large amounts of food. On this first meeting: 'A glorious tea then came in on a gold tray two kinds of bread and butter a lovly jam role and lots of sugar cakes. Ethels eyes began to sparkle and she made several remarks during the meal' (9). During the scene when the couple are rowing on the river, Bernard suggests stopping for a picnic:

> Oh yes said Ethel quickly opening the sparkling champaigne.
>
> Dont spill any cred Bernard as he carved some chicken.
>
> They eat and drank deeply of the charming viands ending up with merangs and choclates.
>
> Let us now bask under the spreading trees said Bernard in a passinate tone. (39)

Bernard then proposes to Ethel, whereupon she, 'breathing rarther hard', closes her eyes and submits to being 'seiezed' and kissed 'violently' (92). Their wedding feast is also dwelt on in detail:

> They had countless cakes besides also ices jelly merangs jam tarts with plenty of jam on each some cold tongue some ham with salid and a pigs head done up in a wondrous manner. Ethel could hardly contain herself as she gazed at the sumpshious repast and Bernard gave her a glass of rich wine while he imbibed some whisky before going to bed. Ethel got speedilly into her bed [...] and began to plan about how many children she would have. (97)

In all three scenes, Ethel and Bernard's mutual desire is imaged in their excessive consumption of food and drink, but their greed is the greed of the gourmet, since each meal is clearly coded in terms of a luxurious, conspicuously wealthy lifestyle. The confectionery, cakes and champagne represent indulgence rather than nourishment.

In *The Young Visiters*, Ethel's excessive appetites are connected to a certain excessiveness in her speech – she refers to bodily matters which, in polite society, she ought to be silent about: 'Oh Hurrah shouted Ethel I shall soon be ready as I had my bath last night so wont wash very much now' (89). This, in fact, corresponds to the tendency of the book as a whole to make explicit things which no adult woman writer would have been likely to refer to:

> Then Mr Salteena got into a mauve dressing goun with yellow tassles and siezing his soap he wandered off to the bath room which was most sumpshous. It had a lovly white shiny bath and sparkleng taps and several towels arrayed in readiness by thourghtful Horace. It also had a step for climbing up the bath and other good dodges of a rich nature. Mr Salteena washed himself well and felt very much better. (13)

This unusually intimate enquiry into the daily practices of hygiene is part of Ashford's method for classifying her protagonist, whose fascination with the appointments of the bathroom betrays his humble origins. His pursuit of status and sophistication is continually derailed by his unseemly excitement over, and gratitude for, things which a gentleman should take for granted. 'Oh this is most kind said Mr Salteena' (15), on receiving some sandwiches for his journey from the butler. 'Minnit closed his eyes with a tired smile. Not kind sir he muttered quite usual' (16).

As in so many novels of manners, it is dealings with servants which expose the false position of lower-middle-class characters, and Daisy Ashford's early tea episode surely provides the most entertaining example of this in Victorian fiction:

> Mr Salteena woke up rather early next day and was supprised and delighted to find Horace the footman entering with a cup of tea. Oh thankyou my man said Mr Salteena rolling over in the costly bed.
>
> Mr Clark is nearly out of the bath sir anounced Horace I will have great plesure in turning it on for you if such is your desire. Well yes you might said Mr Salteena seeing it was the idear and Horace gave a profound bow.
>
> Ethel are you getting up shouted Mr Salteena.
>
> Very nearly replied Ethel faintly from the next room.
>
> I say said Mr Salteena excitedly I have had some tea in bed. (13)

Mr Salteena's process of social education is, in fact, carried on primarily by servants, who repeatedly instruct him in what is and is not 'the idea'. In fact, the disruption of class distinctions is taken to such extremes in this text that the protagonist actually imitates the servants in his attempt to masquerade as a gentleman. On first encountering Edward Procurio, 'the Groom of the Chambers' (18), Mr Salteena sees him as 'a very superier gentleman in full evening dress' with a 'noble voice' (17), and feels 'very towzld compared to this grand fellow' (23). Procurio advises him on dressing, and even lends him items of clothing, so that eventually Mr Salteena is transformed into an approximate copy of his manservant. As lower-class characters in an upper-class milieu, Mr Salteena and Ethel are in a position analogous to that of a child in a bewildering adult world, and so it is rather appropriate that their behaviour is often reminiscent of the playground. Mr Salteena tells Ethel that she will look very silly in the outfit she plans for the journey to Bernard's, and 'so will you said Ethel in a snappy tone and she ran out of the room with a very superier run' (5). In another of their quarrels, when Ethel 'in a peevish tone' asks him how he comes to be at the Earl of Clincham's, he tells her: 'I am stopping with his Lordship [...] and have a set of compartments in the basement so there' (35).

Since *The Young Visiters* remained unpublished until the twentieth century, we cannot, of course, know how a Victorian audience would have responded to it. In 1919 it was already a period piece. And yet, though it represented a society dating back thirty years, the child's perspective and vocabulary actually lend a curious modernness. Ashford ignores the proprieties of Victorian fiction, uses up-to-the-minute words such as 'piffle' (19), which the OED dates to 1890, the very year in which *The Young Visiters* was written, and even refers to divorce, which was by no means common or socially acceptable at the time.[19] As J. M. Barrie noted:

> The manuscript [...] has lain, in lavender as it were, in the dumpy note book, waiting for a publisher to ride that way and rescue it; and here he is at last, not a bit afraid that to this age it may appear 'Victorian.' Indeed if its pictures of High Life are accurate (as we cannot doubt, the authoress seems always so sure of her facts) they had a way of going on in those times which is really surprising. Even the grand historical figures were free and easy, such as King Edward, of whom we have perhaps the most human picture ever penned, as he appears at a levée 'rather sumshiously', in a 'small but costly crown', and afterwards slips away to tuck into ices. It would seem in particular that we are oddly wrong in our idea of the young Victorian lady as a person more shy and shrinking than the girl of to-day. The Ethel of this story is a fascinating creature who would have a good time wherever there were a few males. (63)

In 1919, the story did not, it seems, have the nostalgic appeal of a book which has 'lain in lavender'; rather, it appeared to be about a modern good-time girl. Its appeal, for early twentieth-century sophisticates, was comparable to that of a book such as Anita Loos's *Gentlemen Prefer Blondes* (1925), or Gertrude Stein's *Autobiography of Alice B. Toklas* (1931). Both of these are written in a child-like idiom, but the difference, of course, is that there is no ironic gap between narrator and author in *The Young Visiters*, whereas in Loos or Stein, the child-like voice is clearly separated from the adult implied author.[20]

Some critics have even suggested that Ashford's narrative has affinities with modernist styles. Jeffrey Mather comments: 'unrestrained and often irreverent,

19 In 1890, 223,028 marriages were contracted in Britain, 644 petitions for divorce were made, and around 70 per cent of these were granted.
20 See Wyndham Lewis's chapter 'Miss Loos and Miss Stein' in his *Time and Western Man*. Lewis thought Loos's work an inferior imitation of Stein; for counter-arguments that both were participants in the modernist project, see Everett; Hegeman; Hammill, *Women, Celebrity* 65–74.

Daisy Ashford's writing resembles modernist techniques'. He adds that her 'disregard for spelling, grammar, and punctuation resembles the fluid stream-of-consciousness style that Joyce and Woolf developed to emphasize internal thoughts over exterior reality' (xiv). Mather compares passages from *The Young Visiters* with extracts from *Ulysses* and Mansfield's story 'The Little Girl', and suggests that while Ashford, unlike Joyce and Mansfield, 'could not have been aware of her own "modern" perspective on the world; nonetheless, society's post-war desire for something new and innovative may partially account for the popularity of *The Young Visiters* during the 1920s' (xv). Taking his cue from a review in *The New York Times Review of Books* ('A Child's Humorous Venture') which speculates that Ashford's book may be the first Cubist novel, Mather goes on to compare it to the 'child-like manner [...] bold strokes and bright colours' of Picasso's paintings, concluding: 'The result, for both Ashford and Picasso, is a less inhibited, more abstract, and sometimes distorted view of the world' (xv). The faked unsophistication of modernism (which, of course, is really a form of sophistication) brings it into relationship with a child's text. This provides an interesting context for the debate about the authorship and authenticity of *The Young Visiters*.

Ashford came upon her manuscript as an adult, and sent it to a friend who was ill, to cheer her up. The friend passed it to Frank Swinnerton, who was a reader for Chatto and Windus, and he suggested that it should be published. It was an instant success, going through 19 printings within the first few months. In 1920, stage versions were produced in London and New York, and by the end of the following year, 230,000 copies had been sold.[21] But in spite of the eccentric spelling and child-like phrasing (such as when Mr Salteena 'got down' from the table instead of getting up [2]), many readers were unable to believe that the story had been written by a nine-year-old, and a rumour began that Barrie was the real author. The resulting publicity, which extended across the Atlantic, further stimulated sales. One offended reader wrote to the *Saturday Review* that the proposal scene 'is a take-off of the Penny novel style, and too nastily precocious for any child' (S. D.). A sophisticated child was clearly an alarming object for this audience. Another contributor to the controversy on the letters page of the *Saturday Review* even denied that such a child could exist: 'we have never known a child horrid enough to write "The Young Visiters"'.[22] In her essay on the epistemology of the child writer, Juliet McMaster comments on this outraged response: 'The focus for the sceptics is

21 For sales figures see Sawallis 255; Swinnerton 89. On the story of the book's publication, see the account which Ashford's grandson, Terry Rose, posted on the Amazon page for *The Young Visiters* in 2003: <http://www.amazon.co.uk/> [accessed 31 January 2008] and reproduced on <http://www.literaturefestival.co.uk/2005/visiters.html> [accessed 31 January 2008].
22 Unsigned letter, *Saturday Review* (16 August 1919): 150.

not the child's artistry', but rather 'how much she *knows*. They want to push her back firmly into Edenic innocence and ignorance' ('What Daisy Knew' 55). Assessments of the book repeatedly evince confusion about how much the narrator knows: phrases such as 'naively sophisticated', 'quaintly pretentious', 'accidental double entendre', and 'unconscious naïveté' recur.[23] In some of the most comic scenes, the narrator attributes ignorance to her characters instead of admitting to her own uncertainty, and the result is an effect of knowingness. Bernard says, in reference to the portrait of one of his ancestors:

> He was really the sinister son of Queen Victoria.
> Not really cried Ethel in excited tones but what does that mean?
> Well I dont quite know said Bernard Clark it puzzles me very much but ancesters do turn quear at times.
> Perhaps it means god son said Mr Salteena in an intelligent voice.
> Well I dont think so said Bernard. (12)

As the editors of the annotated edition of *The Young Visiters* remark in a footnote: 'The combination of *bend-sinister*, the heraldic sign of bastardy, with the chastest of England's monarchs is one of DA's most inspired comic flights.' They add that 'godson' was indeed sometimes used euphemistically to mean 'illegitimate son', particularly in reference to Catholic priests, who were supposedly celibate (Ashford 53). Could the nine-year-old Ashford really have known this, or does the full comedy of this scene emerge only for an adult reader?

The author's own comments do little to clarify the question of how much the child author actually knew. In 1920, a second published volume of her juvenilia appeared under the title *Daisy Ashford: Her Book*, and in her preface, Ashford wrote of the curious feeling of being 'able to laugh at what one wrote in such solemn seriousness' (vii). Difficult though it is to believe that the book was written by a nine-year-old, I find it still harder to believe that it was composed with completely serious intent. It appears that Ashford, even at that young age, had quite a well-developed sense of comedy, and that she was also very well read. The editors of the annotated *Young Visiters* speculate that Ouida, Trollope and Charlotte M. Yonge may have been influences on Ashford, since her style in some scenes is reminiscent of theirs (Ashford 60). As Katherine Mansfield observed in her appreciative review, 'There is evidence that she thoroughly enjoyed the run of her parents' library', as well as 'exceptional opportunities for looking through keyholes, peeping through half-open doors, gazing over the banisters' (Mansfield 400). Juliet McMaster remarks that some of the 'sexually laden material' in the story 'sounds too racy for any fiction allowed

---

23 Mather xvi; unsigned review of *The Young Visiters*, *Dial: A Fortnightly* (23 August 1919): 74; review of the opening night of the stage version in Ramsgate in 1920, quoted in Malcomson 107; unsigned review of *The Young Visiters*, *Outlook* (1 October 1919): 191.

in respectable middle-class families like the Ashfords. The vocabulary and the rhythms in the dialogue suggest that the sources of much of the material must be oral, from overheard conversations of her elders' ('Virginal' 304). What is clear, at any rate, is that Ashford had somehow acquired a sophistication beyond her years, and that this alarmed many Edwardian readers. Remarkably, she even managed to dramatise the process of attempting to acquire sophistication from the point of view of one who has already attained it.

While the concept of sophistication which the *The Young Visiters* purveys may have had a particular resonance in the 1920s, the novella has retained its appeal, going through numerous later editions, some of them illustrated and one annotated, and also being turned into a musical (1968), filmed (1984), adapted for BBC television (2003) and freshly staged in Durham, England (2005). The manuscript, in pencil, in the Berg Collection in the New York Public Library certainly looks like the work of quite a young child, and modern readers, less easily shocked, are perhaps better able to appreciate that 'the combination of innocence and knowingness in *The Young Visiters* was precisely the source of its irresistible appeal' (McMaster, 'What Daisy Knew' 53).

'Well, this is rather queer!': *Zuleika Dobson*

In the first edition of *Zuleika Dobson*, Heinemann included an advertisement for other 'new 6s novels' opposite the title page. It featured such incongruous titles as Frances Hodgson Burnett's *The Secret Garden*, John Galsworthy's *The Patrician*, *Laura* by Caroline Grosvenor, and a book called *Essence of Honeymoon* by one 'H. Perry Johnson, author of "Of Distinguished Animals"'. In the personal copy of *Zuleika Dobson* which he illustrated by hand, Beerbohm drew a cartoon of himself pointing to this list, and saying: 'But perhaps you would rather read one of these?' [24] These books represent the sentimental, the popular, the conventional; all readers who might choose them are excluded from the sophisticated elite addressed by *Zuleika Dobson*. The cartoon implicitly defines Beerbohm's novel in the opposite terms from the others on the list: that is, as modern(ist), eccentric and anti-sentimental.

Beerbohm wrote in a letter about *Zuleika Dobson*: 'If the binders and papermakers don't play me false, the book will *look* nice: not like a beastly *novel*, more like a book of essays, self-respecting and sober and ample' (qtd in Hall). This is, of course, ironic, since the book is as far as possible from being sober and ample, and it isn't really very 'nice', since this term suggests something

---

24 A selection of Beerbohm's illustrations appeared in the 1966 Folio edition of the novel; all are included in *The Illustrated Zuleika Dobson* (2002). The advertisement with the cartoon appears on an unnumbered page in the front matter.

quite opposite from sophisticated.[25] It is, though, strikingly distinct from the average novel, and certainly from the novels advertised in its pages by Heinemann. It is unusual in its excess, whimsicality and excursions into the surreal, and also in its dense literary allusiveness and complex meditations on fiction, modernity and the philosophy of history.[26] The story concerns a remarkably attractive young woman who performs on stage as a conjuror, and garners universal adulation from men. Arriving in Oxford, she receives the homage of all the students, with one (apparent) exception – the dandi-acal and highly distinguished Duke of Dorset, who is so heroic that he seems scarcely mortal. Realising that she could only love a man who did not prostrate himself before her, Zuleika is initially allured by the Duke's feigned indifference. But when she discovers that he has, in fact, fallen in love like the rest, her interest in him ends. The Duke declares that he will die for her, but before he can do so, he realises that Zuleika is worthless, and proceeds with his suicide only because he hears of the arrival of the black owls which always appear at his ancestral home when the present Duke is to die. This unfortu-nately precipitates the suicides of all the other undergraduates, who follow his lead and die for love. Zuleika, feeling temporarily contrite, considers taking the veil, but changes her mind and orders a private train to convey her to Cambridge.

In this novel, sophistication takes an unusually austere form, and is discon-nected from the excessive pleasure and indulgence which are often associated with it. It is true that the Duke is a gourmet: 'I have a third chef, who makes only soufflés, and an Italian pastry-cook; to say nothing of a Spaniard for salads, an Englishwoman for roasts, and an Abyssinian for coffee' (62). But this is part of the demonstration of immaculate taste and open-handedness which he sees as a necessary part of the public role of an aristocrat; he says nothing about his actual enjoyment of food. When at Oxford, he considers such displays of wealth inappropriate, and prides himself on living 'the ordinary life of an undergraduate', and having his food cooked 'by the heavy and unaided hand of Mrs Batch, my landlady' (63). The Duke's slumming is only another facet of his sophistication: he sets himself off through the contrast with his humdrum context. More importantly, the 'simple way of life' – without servants or luxury – which he adopts at Oxford is part of the dandy's parodic imitation of

25 At least, it does in the Edwardian period. Previously, it meant particular or scrupulous, but it also had a range of other, remarkably diverse, meanings in different periods. Compare Henry Tilney's comment in Austen's *Northanger Abbey* about the debased meaning of the term: 'Oh! It is a very nice word indeed! It does for every thing' (95).
26 Michael Murphy remarks: 'An uneasy feeling exists among critics that *Zuleika Dobson* is not really a novel', and proposes that it would be better read 'in terms of another genre of fiction – the medieval Romance' ('Medieval' 303, 304).

the monk: 'The dandy must be celibate, cloistral; [...] an anchorite, mortifying his soul that his body may be perfect' (33).

The dandy is the ultimate figure of sophistication, and before he meets Zuleika, the Duke of Dorset performs this role flawlessly:

In him the dandiacal temper had been absolute hitherto, quite untainted and unruffled. He was too much concerned with his own perfection ever to think of admiring any one else. Different from Zuleika, he cared for his wardrobe and his toilet-table not as a means to making others admire him the more, but merely as a means through which he could intensify, a ritual in which to express and realise, his own idolatry. (29)

The Duke thinks he has finally met his match in Zuleika, but in fact her temperament is the opposite of his: 'Her love for her own image was not cold aestheticism. She valued that image not for its own sake, but for the sake of the glory it always won for her' (15). In contrast to the Duke's complex blending of the ascetic with the gourmet, Zuleika's lifestyle is straightforwardly self-indulgent: she lives at 'the most exorbitant hotel in all Mayfair' (16), and travels with trunks full of costly finery and jewels. She aspires to distinction, but has no taste: 'She was one of the people who say "I don't know anything about music really, but I know what I like"'. Wishing to show her gratitude to all the young men who intend to die for her, she can think of nothing but 'to do my tricks' (157) – that is, to perform her inept conjuring on a platform. The Duke is tortured by Zuleika's worse than mediocre performance: 'her constantly reiterated catch-phrase – "Well, this is rather queer!" – was the most distressing thing of all' (163). Embarrassed by his own desire for such an unworthy object, he comments: 'You make me feel slightly unwell' (157).

Zuleika is an ineffective imitation of the goddess Aphrodite (or Venus) on whom she is ostensibly modelled,[27] and the admiration she inspires only indicates the degeneracy of modern taste:

Her features were not at all original. They seemed to have been derived rather from a gallimaufry of familiar models. From Madame la Marquise de Saint-Ouen came the shapely tilt of the nose. The mouth was a mere replica of Cupid's bow, lacquered scarlet and strung with the littlest pearls. No apple-tree, no wall of peaches, had not been robbed, nor any Tyrian rose-garden, for the glory of Miss Dobson's cheeks. Her neck was imitation-marble. Her hands and feet were of very mean proportions. She had no waist to speak of.

Yet, though a Greek would have railed at her symmetry, and an Elizabethan have called her 'gipsy', Miss Dobson now, in the midst of the Edvardian Era [sic], was the toast of two hemispheres. (9–10)

27 As Bonaparte points out, allusions to Venus or Aphrodite are frequent in the text; for instance, Zuleika's magical earrings, which change colour in response to her feelings, refer to Rubens' *The Toilet of Venus* (1612–15).

This mockery of the clichéd vocabulary of love poetry suggests that Zuleika herself is a cliché: merely a caricature of the femme fatale. This is reinforced by her incongruous name, in which the mythical, exotic allure of 'Zuleika' is contradicted by the plebeian tones of 'Dobson'.[28] Her imitative quality, and the fact that her actual worth is far less than her reputation suggests, connects her to the discourse of advertising which, as Bowlby suggests, is intimately linked to aestheticism, since the preoccupation of both was 'with making the object appear beautiful' (5). Beerbohm makes use of the advertiser's strategies of exaggeration; at the same time, he mocks those who are susceptible to such ruses. Zuleika, remarks Lawrence Danson, 'disappears in the language that describes her' (127).

Beerbohm's Zuleika has no sophistication, in the modern sense; instead, she is defined by sophistry. The Duke accuses her of this when she tries to persuade him to introduce some more of the undergraduates:

> 'Suppose unrequited love *is* anguish: isn't the discipline wholesome? Suppose I *am* a sort of furnace: shan't I purge, refine, temper? Those two boys are but scorched from here. [...] Cast them into the furnace for their own sake, dear Duke! Or cast [...] any one of these others!'
>
> 'For their own sake?' he echoed, withdrawing his arm. 'If you were not, as the whole world knows you to be, perfectly respectable, there might be something in what you say. But as it is, you can but be an engine for mischief; and your sophistries leave me unmoved. I shall certainly keep you to myself.' (101–102)

Zuleika's respectability (that is, her sexual inaccessibility) means that her erotic promise is illusory; similarly, her profession as a conjuror aligns her with the elaborate deception which underpins the Greek conception of sophistry. Through his susceptibility to Zuleika's illusion, his undiscriminating love for this undistinguished girl, and his melodramatic vow to die, the Duke temporarily sacrifices his chaste, single-minded dandyism and thus his sophistication, becoming an object of the narrator's pity. The Duke is 'furiously mortified' (29) by his sudden passion; the word 'mortified' contains,

---

28 The name 'Zuleika' occurs in several earlier texts. In Byron's poem 'The Bride of Abydos' (1813), Zuleika is a graceful Turkish virgin, beloved by a man she thinks is her brother, though he is actually her cousin. He saves her from a forced marriage, but both are later captured and killed. More relevant to Beerbohm's text is 'Yussuf and Zuleika' by the fifteenth-century Persian poet Jami. This Zuleika, a woman of outstanding beauty, falls in love with a man seen in a dream vision. She agrees to a marriage proposal sent by the Asis Potiphar, whom she expects to be the man she dreamed of, but it turns out she was dreaming of Yussuf, who is sold to her as a slave, and whose supernatural beauty makes all women in love with him. When she reveals her love, Yussuf flees (see Horne 381–401). This, of course, is a version of the story of Potiphar's wife, which occurs in both the Old Testament and the Koran (in the Koran, the wife is named Zuleika). Beerbohm repeats elements of this narrative, though the male and female roles are to some extent reversed, in that it is Zuleika who rejects the Duke once he confesses his love.

etymologically, the concept of mortality, and thus the Duke has relinquished his heroic stature and become mortal (see Bonaparte 6). He even briefly seeks a conventional form of happiness by his proposal of marriage to Zuleika. Following her rejection of him and his vow to drown himself, one of his fellow students, also bent on suicide, cries 'Happiness be hanged!', and the narrator observes: 'To the Duke this seemed a profoundly sane remark – an epitome of his own sentiments. But what was right for himself was not right for all. He believed in convention as the best way for average mankind' (131). The novel ironically repeats the conflation of love and death which defines the femme fatale, and the Duke, contemplating marriage one moment and death the next, will become conventional either way. Since his vow to die for Miss Dobson is also taken by all his fellow students, in his death he does not demonstrate his superiority, but rather becomes one of a crowd.

The Duke, however, finally distinguishes himself by dying not for Miss Dobson, whom he has by this point ceased to love, but for the sake of consistency. Bound by his vow, and by the decision of the gods who play a large part in the narrative and are responsible for sending the black owls, the Duke presents himself as fated to die young. He is fully aware of the picturesqueness of this scenario: 'The Duke, so soon as Zuleika's spell was broken, had become himself again – a highly self-conscious artist in life' (220). Reflecting that an early death often ensures a glorious posthumous reputation, he compares himself to Byron:

> Perhaps, had Byron not been a dandy – but ah, had he not been in his soul a dandy there would have been no Byron worth mentioning. And it was because he guarded not his dandyism against this and that irrelevant passion, sexual or political, that he cut so annoyingly incomplete a figure. He was absurd in his politics, vulgar in his loves. Only in himself, at the times when he stood haughtily aloof, was he impressive. (269)

The Duke similarly fails to guard his dandyism against an irrelevant passion: Zuleika is not, in reality, at all distinguished, and the Duke does not even succeed in enjoying her:

> For him, master-dandy, the common arena was no place. What had he to do with love? He was an utter fool at it. Byron had at least had some fun out of it. What fun had *he* had? Last night, he had forgotten to kiss Zuleika when he held her by the wrists. To-day it had been as much as he could do to let poor little Katie kiss his hand. Better be vulgar with Byron than a noodle with Dorset! he bitterly reflected… Still, noodledom was nearer than vulgarity to dandyism. It was a less flagrant lapse. And he had over Byron this further advantage: his noodledom was not a matter of common knowledge; whereas Byron's vulgarity had ever needed to be in the glare of the footlights of Europe. (269–70)

The Duke tries to regain his sophisticated position by emphasising that, while intensely preoccupied with his own image, he does not invite popular judgement on it: 'Never had he given ear to that cackle which is called Public Opinion. The judgement of his peers – this, he had often told himself, was the sole arbitrage he could submit to; but then, who was to be on the bench?' (86). Similarly, the cartoon persona of Beerbohm denies the validity of popular opinion through his gesture of ridiculing readers who would choose one of Heinemann's rather lowbrow novels instead of his own book. This exclusionary move (self-consciously and perhaps parodically aligned with the strategies of modernists) defines Beerbohm's audience as select.

Since the Duke temporarily lapses, the only character to retain the status of sophisticate throughout is the narrator. Indeed, the novel's real central character is not Zuleika nor the Duke, but the authorial persona. This persona is imaged, of course, in the drawings: while these pictures remained unpublished during Beerbohm's life, they complement the narrative so beautifully that it is difficult not to see them as integral to the book. But the narrator is also created as a personality in the text itself. This is achieved through self-reference and conversations with the reader ('Please don't interrupt me again. Am *I* writing this history, or are you?' [219]); through reflections on his own identity ('Ever since I can remember, I have been beset by a recurring doubt as to whether I be or be not quite a gentleman' [185]); and, more subtly, through a distinctive style, marked by uncommon and antiquated vocabulary, ornate and fanciful constructions. When the Duke has been humiliated by Zuleika throwing a jug of water over him, the narrator observes:

> He stood quite still, a figure orgulous and splendent. And it seemed to him as though the hot night, too, stood still, to watch him, in awe, through the open lattices of his window, breathlessly. But to me, equipped to see beneath the surface, he was piteous, piteous in ratio to the pretension of his aspect. Had he crouched down and sobbed, I should have been as much relieved as he. But he stood seignorial and aquiline. (196)

This style gains added effect through contrast. The sudden switches into a colloquial, comic tone are both self-conscious and self-mocking:

> Brief was the freshness of the dawn. From all points of the compass, dark grey clouds mounted into the sky. [...] Somewhere under cover of them the sun went his way, transmitting a sulphurous heat. The very birds in the trees of Trinity were oppressed and did not twitter. The very leaves did not whisper.
>
> Out through the railings, and across the road, prowled a skimpy and dingy cat, trying to look like a tiger.
>
> It was all very sinister and dismal. (206–207)

In his introduction to the 2002 facsimile edition of Beerbohm's illustrated copy of *Zuleika Dobson*, N. John Hall notes: 'Max is present in the "aesthetic" prose of every sentence, and, even more important, as the first-person narrator who manages – as in all his fiction – to be centre stage while telling the stories of fantastical people' (n.p.).

Beerbohm negotiates with his own celebrity image through his cartoons of himself, but also through the text of the novel.[29] When the Duke remarks on the 'literary flavour' of Zuleika's conversation, Zuleika replies that she has not in fact read much, and that her style is purely imitative: 'an unfortunate trick which I caught from a writer, a Mr Beerbohm, who once sat next to me at dinner' (100). Jonathan Goldman comments: 'Usual associations are made, justifiably, between Beerbohm and the duke. It is Zuleika, the omnisubjugator, however, whose effect on Oxford reflects that of Beerbohm's parrotry on notions of individuation' (303). The novel, indeed, is intensely preoccupied with celebrity, imitation, reputation, and distinction from the mass. In contrast to the Duke and the narrator, Zuleika is openly concerned with public opinion: 'it was only the crowd she cared for' (164). When she visits New York, she reads

> every line that was printed about her, tasting her triumph as she had never tasted it before. And how she revelled in the Brobdingnagian drawings of her, which, printed in nineteen colours, towered between the columns or sprawled across them! [...] Zuleika was the smiling target of all the snap-shooters, and all the snap-shots were snapped up by the press and reproduced with annotations: Zuleika Dobson walking on Broadway in the sables gifted her by Grand Duke Salamander [...]; chatting at the telephone to Miss Camille Van Spook, the best-born girl in New York; laughing over the recollection of a compliment made her by George Abimelech Post, the best-groomed man in New York [...]. Thus was Zuleika enabled daily to be, as one might say, a spectator of her own wonderful life. (18–20)

The newspapers construct Zuleika as exceptional, sophisticated and distinguished because she associates only with 'the best' people and has the best of everything. But the novel's narrator reveals her as ordinary in all respects apart from her remarkable sexual allure, describing her as middle-class (72), mediocre, banal and piteous (163). The unsophistication of the mass audience – that is, their inability to distinguish – is revealed through their adulation of Zuleika. Thus Beerbohm presents an apparently hostile account of the operations of celebrity culture. It seems to accord with the thinking of other early twentieth-century intellectuals, who were alarmed by their perception that

29 An account of Beerbohm's celebrity is beyond the scope of this discussion, but a quotation from A. G. Macdonell's *England, their England* (1933) concisely demonstrates the fascination he held for the public. The narrator mockingly lists the top attractions which draw American tourists as 'the Colosseum, the Venus de Milo, the outside of Mr Beerbohm's villa at Rapallo, or the fields at St Mihiel' (107).

the advent of mass media had transformed 'genuine' artistic fame based on achievement into a culture of high profile yet disposable celebrities, whose renown derived from cults of personality. But given Beerbohm's cultivation of his own public image, and his complex, intelligent negotiation with the celebrity processes which sought to define him, it could be unwise to read these passages as a straightforward denunciation of celebrity culture. They may also be mocking the exaggeratedly hostile responses to celebrity which were circulating among intellectuals at the time.

The dismayed reaction to the growing public obsession with the famous was directly related to anxieties about overpopulation and crowd behaviour, and about the sociological effects of the mass media, political democracy, and mass education. Among the fears expressed by writers such as D. H. Lawrence and T. S. Eliot (both influenced by Nietzschean thinking) were that universal literacy would result in a lowering of standards and a diminution of intellectual authority, and that the media would become a dominant influence, able to sway the easily-influenced crowd, and to govern them by emotional rather than rational appeal. Lawrence even entertained fantasies of mass extermination (Carey 11–12). Beerbohm addresses these issues very directly:

> If man were not a gregarious animal, the world might have achieved, by this time, some real progress towards civilisation. Segregate him, and he is no fool. But let him loose among his fellows, and he is lost – he becomes just a unit in unreason. If any one of the undergraduates had met Miss Dobson in the desert of Sahara, he would have fallen in love with her; but not one in a thousand would have wished to die because she did not love him. The Duke's was a peculiar case. For him to fall in love was itself a violent peripety, bound to produce a violent upheaval; and such was his pride that for his love to be unrequited would naturally enamour him of death. These other, these quite ordinary young men were the victims less of Zuleika than of the Duke's example, and of one another. A crowd, proportionately to its size, magnifies all that in its units pertains to the emotions, and diminishes all that in them pertains to thought. [...] To die for Miss Dobson was 'the thing to do'. The Duke was going to do it. The Junta was going to do it. It is a hateful fact, but we must face the fact, that snobbishness was one of the springs to the tragedy here chronicled. (151)

This apparently earnest analysis is undone by the excessiveness and idiocy of the event which follows. The suicides are too literal an image of sheep rushing off a cliff to be considered at all seriously. The fact that the 'mob' (154) here is the undergraduate population of Oxford might also warn us against taking Beerbohm's denunciation of crowd behaviour at face value, since this group is hardly representative of unintelligent, lower-class, feminised, mass humanity.

Beerbohm's invention of the Junta is also revealing: it is so very exclusive a social club that at one point, the Duke is its only member. Alone on each election night, he proposes and seconds various potential members, but they are all rejected, seemingly by a higher power: 'in every case, when he drew out the drawer of the ballot-box, [he] found it was a black-ball that he had dropped into the urn' (117). The Junta's dress code demands 'a mulberry-coloured coat with brass buttons', and the narrator notes: 'It is awful to think that a casual stranger might have mistaken [the Duke] for a footman' (116). Only the true sophisticate can read the sign of the mulberry coat, and understand that it is a mark of very high class which – like the Duke's insistence on the cuisine of an ordinary undergraduate – functions by eschewing obvious class markers. Though the Duke eventually manages to elect two additional members, the Junta remains a symbol of elitism taken to its logical (and absurd) extreme. Therefore, while Beerbohm may appear to be participating in the broader intellectual denunciation of crowd behaviour, it is equally possible to read these passages of *Zuleika Dobson* as parodies of the panicky, anti-democratic statements made by his modernist contemporaries.

As Felicia Bonaparte observes in her essay 'Reading the Deadly Text of Modernism', the unconvincing nature of Zuleika's tricks 'highlights the fictiveness of her art precisely as Beerbohm himself is highlighting, through his literary paradigms and his dialogues with the reader, the fictiveness of his own narration' (4). Beerbohm deliberately undermines the realistic illusion which other authors seek to foster; in this respect, his text makes sense in the context of modernism. Bonaparte suggests that *Zuleika Dobson* is in fact 'an inquiry into the nature of modernism' (2). To take this argument further, it might be suggested that the novel parallels modernist strategies in its (mis) matching of a grand mythic design with commonplace characters, and in its repeated implication that the modern is detached from the past yet can only be understood in the context of history. Rather than wholly embracing modernist forms, though, *Zuleika Dobson* reflects on techniques such as this, sometimes very explicitly (in the narrator's disquisitions on fiction and history), and also mocks them as he 'parrots his contemporaries and appropriates literary flavor' (Goldman 303). Beerbohm's performance of sophistication, then, is largely achieved through his self-conscious narration and its play with different literary modes and genres. The mass suicides are not really framed as tragic, since the excessive damage wrought by the decadent femme fatale, who literally causes hundreds of fatalities merely by arriving on the scene, moves the plot towards farce. The astonishment and reluctance of the figure of Melpomene (the tragic muse) in Beerbohm's accompanying cartoons empha-sise that this 'tragedy' is an improper one. Neither is the novel a genuine epic, in spite of its many allusions to the epic form.[30] It seems more accurate to class

30 Bonaparte notes that the text makes repeated reference to the gods and their wills, and contains

it as satire. Yet, like many books about the varieties of sophistication, it is such a slippery text that it is impossible to decide precisely what it is satirising. N. John Hall comments:

> *Zuleika Dobson* is fanciful though hard-edged satire, but of what? Of the new woman? Or the literary *femme fatale*? Of Oxford, university life, athleticism? Of rank, snobbery, the herd instinct? Of dandyism, or novels of dandyism (such as those of Bulwer Lytton and Disraeli)? Of aestheticism?

Similarly, Felicia Bonaparte argues that it is Beerbohm's instinct 'not so much to assert positions as to question them, to dislodge them, to entertain their antitheses, and to see what can survive the assault of his caprice' (1). In this, the text may be compared with many of the others discussed in this book: the sophisticated narrative, it seems, is one in which few fixed positions are taken, and which addresses a reader capable of accepting paradox. The sophisticated narrative is also one which aims to give pleasure, and pleasure of a very particular sort. E. M. Forster captured this aspect of *Zuleika Dobson*, writing that it possesses 'a beauty unattainable by serious literature' because '[it] is so funny and charming, so iridescent and yet so profound' (*Aspects* 173). Robert Scholes in *Paradoxy of Modernism* points out that Forster did not suggest that Beerbohm's kind of writing was in some sense lower than serious literature: 'For him it was higher in certain respects, reaching iridescence because it is light enough to get there, but also establishing its own connection with the beautiful and profound' (191). All the books considered in this chapter, it seems to me, reach iridescence because they are light enough to get there. Late Victorian and Edwardian literary visions of sophistication seem to have an especial lightness of tone, even though they often represent sophistication itself as potentially fatal.

---

numerous epic similes and epical sentence structures (Bonaparte 9).

3

Melancholy, modernity and the middlebrow: the twenties and thirties

I suffered a good deal, and had my heart broken. But it wasn't an innocent girlish heart. It was jagged with sophistication. I've always been sophisticated, far too knowing. That caused many of my rows with Elyot. I irritated him because he knew I could see through him.

– Amanda in Noël Coward's *Private Lives* (477)

If there has ever been an Age of Sophistication, it was surely the 1920s and 1930s. I begin with a defining image from that era: Coward and Gertrude Lawrence in *Private Lives* (1930) (Figure 2). For audiences in 1930, this image – or this play as a whole – would have suggested sophistication because of its modernity. Amanda's extreme modernness consists in her smoking (still a rebellious act for a woman),[1] her bobbed hair, and her peculiar situation in relation to her two husbands. The scene also suggests luxury (the silk jacket, the expensive items for consumption) and has a very poised, even posed quality. In the twenty-first century, the image suggests sophistication for an additional – perhaps contrary – reason: its black-and-white stylishness evokes the glamour of an earlier era. We feel nostalgic for the age of leisure, evening clothes and elaborately curled hair, when smokers sat at elegant dinner tables with long cigarette holders rather than huddling in rainy doorways. This picture, then, encapsulates the balancing between nostalgia and modernness which is typical of twentieth-century sophistication. Yet it also invokes the

---

1 The association of smoking with deviant sexuality had only just begun to diminish in the 1920s, partly as a result of cigarette advertisers' new focus on the female market and efforts to make smoking acceptable, partly because of a broader trend towards increasing social freedoms for women. In succeeding decades, partly due to the influence of Hollywood, smoking became extremely widespread. But it still clearly signals sophistication, distinction and modernness in Coward. On the cultural history of smoking, and its (gendered) connections with leisure and consumption, glamour and modernity, see Hilton; Tinkler.

113

Figure 2: Noël Coward and Gertrude Lawrence in *Private Lives*, 1930. Getty Images.

codes of romance (the intimate setting, the characters' complete absorption in one another, the sexual tension). The dynamic opposition between romantic sentiment and worldly disillusionment in Coward's play is typical of the early twentieth-century sophisticated text.

In his introduction to the first volume of *Play Parade: The Collected Plays of Noël Coward* (1934), Coward said of the critics who had begun to analyse his plays: 'They search busily behind the simplest of my phrases, like old ladies peering under the bed for burglars, and are not content until they have unearthed some definite, and usually quite inaccurate, reason for my saying this or that' (vii). Many of his phrases and dramatic lines are, indeed, quite simple, and do not seem to invite analysis or interpretation. And yet, while heeding this warning, I still feel curious about exactly how he turned his plays – and himself – into the epitome of sophistication. In what, precisely, does this sophistication consist? Can it be located in the texts of his plays, or is it the product of a complex inter-action between the performances we see on stage and the performed character of 'Noël Coward' as celebrity?

The paradoxical association, in Coward's public persona as well as in his work, of apparently opposite qualities emerges strikingly in a letter he received in March 1954 from the composer Hugh Martin, who had just visited the Gertrude Lawrence memorial exhibition at the Museum of the City of New York:

But it was the photographs of you that fascinated me. Watching you evolve from the ravishing young juvenile of 'Rain Before Seven' [...] through the matinée idol of *Private Lives* [...] – into something more beautiful than either: the sardonic, sentimental, sophisticated gentleman in the photograph Miss Lawrence kept so close to her pretty head when she was making up for *The King and I*. (Coward, *Letters* 710)

Although sophistication is often understood in terms of a rejection of the sentimental, in Coward, and in several of the texts I discuss later in this chapter, sophistication proves unexpectedly compatible with sentiment and romance. It is, perhaps, the self-consciousness about the conventions of romance which means that a play such as *Private Lives* can retain a witty, even 'jagged' element without destroying the intensely romantic mood or the belief in the permanence of a great love:

ELYOT: I went round the world you know after –
AMANDA: (*hurriedly*): Yes, yes, I know. How was it?
ELYOT: The world?
AMANDA: Yes.
ELYOT: Oh, highly enjoyable. [...]
AMANDA: How was the Taj Mahal?
ELYOT (*looking at her*): Unbelievable, a sort of dream.
AMANDA: That was the moonlight I expect, you must have seen it in the moonlight.
ELYOT (*never taking his eyes off her face*): Yes, moonlight is cruelly deceptive.
AMANDA: And it didn't look like a biscuit box did it? I've always felt that it might.
ELYOT (*quietly*): Darling, darling, I love you so. [...] You love me, too, don't you? There's no doubt about it anywhere, is there?
AMANDA: No, no doubt anywhere.
ELYOT: You're looking very lovely you know, in this damned moonlight. Your skin is clear and cool, and your eyes are shining, and you're growing lovelier and lovelier every second as I look at you. (498–99)

'Damned moonlight' seems the ideal form of illumination for a scene of romantic sophistication. Yet Amanda's loveliness is not simply an effect of the moonlight, though it may be enhanced by it. Likewise, the repartee does not conceal the feeling between Amanda and Elyot, but rather reveals the bond of their shared sophistication. Highly aware of the improbability of the romance plot into which they have suddenly been drawn, they succumb with a self-consciousness which actually makes their love seem *more* unusual, *more* fated and inevitable, than it would have done if they were younger and more subject to illusion.[2] During the hotel balcony scenes, the orchestra's insistence

2   This separates Coward from other writers associated with sophistication. Dorothy Parker, for instance, also combines sophistication with sentiment in unexpected ways, but she emphasises the repetitiveness and generic quality of love affairs (see Burstein), rather than focusing on the

on playing the 'sentimental, romantic little tune' which they both remember from the earlier phase of their relationship makes them aware of each other's presence, and brings them together. Amanda observes: 'Extraordinary how potent cheap music is' (496). The play, in the midst of its sophistication, acknowledges the power of the sentimental.

Coward, of course, defined the role of Elyot Chase himself when *Private Lives* premiered, and this merging of character, actor and author reveals the way he enlisted his own fictional creations in order to dramatise himself as sophisticated. His performance as singer was also crucial. Video footage of his cabaret acts reveals that his gestures and expressions were particularly camp in the later stages of his performance career;[3] written reviews suggest that his earlier style was likewise mannered and rather epicene, bringing out the artificial style and the transgression of gender boundaries which is often associated with sophistication.[4] The lyrics, too, reveal a range of different 'takes' on sophistication, combining and recombining it with romantic, comic and satirical elements in different proportions.[5] Songs such as 'I'll See You Again', 'Dearest Love', or 'Lover of My Dreams', for instance, create an entirely romantic mood, whereas 'Mad Dogs and Englishmen', 'Could You Please Oblige Us With A Bren Gun' and 'The Stately Homes of England' are miniature comedies of manners, caricaturing the English upper class. The pseudo-pastoral fantasy in 'World Weary' from the revue *This Year of Grace* (1928) is of particular interest:

> I'm world-weary, world-weary,
> Living in a great big town,
> I find it so dreary, so dreary,
> Everything looks grey or brown.
> I want an ocean blue, great big trees
> A bird's eye view of the Pyrenees
> I want to watch the moon rise up
> And see the great red sun go down

singularity of one relationship as *Private Lives* does.

3   I saw this footage in a montage at the 'Star Quality: Aspects of Noël Coward' exhibition, National Theatre, London (21 January–29 March 2008). (None of it is reproduced on the accompanying DVD set *The Coward Collection*.) For comments on Coward's earlier performance style, see Morley, 120, 168, 356 *et passim*; Tynan.

4   Amanda's and Elyot's sophistication divides them from their very ordinary new partners, Victor and Sibyl, both of whom attempt to set up conventionally gendered relationships. Elyot observes to Sibyl: 'You're a completely feminine little creature aren't you?' and she replies 'I like a man to be a man' (471), while Victor aspires to look after Amanda, and later, insists on fighting Elyot. In one telling contrast, Victor and Sibyl both hate sunburned women but think it suitable for a man, whereas Amanda and Elyot think a tan looks good on everyone.

5   Cole Porter's songs provide an interesting comparison to Coward in this respect: indeed, a recent dual biography by Stephen Citron was titled *Noël and Cole: The Sophisticates*.

Watching clouds go by through a wintry sky
Fascinates me,
But if I'm standing in the street
Ev'ry one I meet simply hates me. (Coward, *Essential* 51–53)

This seems perfectly to exemplify Georg Simmel's account of the blasé in his essay 'The Metropolis and Mental Life' (1903): 'There is perhaps no psychic phenomenon which is so unconditionally reserved to the city as the blasé outlook' (14). According to Simmel, this attitude is produced by overstimulation of the nerves in the city, resulting in an incapacity to react to new stimuli with much energy: 'The essence of the blasé attitude is an indifference towards the distinctions between things. [...] They appear to the blasé person in a homogeneous, flat and gray color with no one of them worthy of being preferred to another' (14). The blasé, world-weary outlook, then, is as fundamentally urban as sophistication itself. Coward connected all these terms when he wrote in 1957 to Beverly Nichols, who was preparing a book on the twenties: 'Were we happy in the Twenties? On the whole I think most of us were but we tried to hide it by being as *blasé*, world-weary and "jagged with sophistication" as we possibly could' (Coward, *Letters* 165).

The imagination of the blasé character in Coward's song is not bounded by the urban. He wishes for open spaces, sea, sky, and even a farm: 'I want a horse and plough, chickens too / Just one cow with a wistful moo' (52). This is of course deliberately silly; nevertheless, it connects with Simmel's comment about the way urban life is understood in terms of its contrast with an imagined rural sphere:

> To the extent that the metropolis creates these psychological conditions – with every crossing of the street, with the tempo and multiplicity of economic, occupational and social life – it creates in the sensory foundations of mental life, and in the degree of awareness necessitated by our organization as creatures dependent on differences, a deep contrast with the slower, more habitual, more smoothly flowing rhythm of the sensory mental phase of small town and rural existence. Thereby the essentially intellectualistic character of the mental life of the metropolis becomes intelligible as over against that of the small town which rests more on feelings and emotional relationships. (12)

But Simmel's city is not defined purely through its opposition to the rural, since it also connects with, and impacts on, the regions beyond its borders: 'The most significant aspect of the metropolis lies in this functional magnitude beyond its actual physical boundaries', and 'its inner life is extended in a wave-like motion over a broader national or international area' (17).

In her discussion of 'The Metropolis and Mental Life' in relation to the work of Dorothy Parker and Mina Loy, Jessica Burstein argues: 'Simmel's reading of the metropolitan imagination, with its networks that at once exceed and connect, maps the means by which sentimentalism traffics with modernity'. Moving on to consider the specific artistic and literary practices of modernism, she suggests: 'If we understand modernism as fundamentally linked to the urban experience, we can understand sentimentalism in the same way: imagined as the provinces of modernity, but in fact so closely linked as to be at its heart' (243). Burstein engages with the complex relationship between modernism and the sentimental, inserting 'sophistication' as an additional term in the debate. While Suzanne Clark, in *Sentimental Modernism* (1991), urges 'that we should restore the sentimental *within* modernism' (4), Burstein argues a different position: 'It's less useful to think of modernism as refusing sentimentalism, or, in a revisionist account, embracing it, than to understand modernism as privileging urbanity, with its concurrent aggrandizement of sophistication, pleasure, and boredom' (228).[6] The logic which sets up straightforward oppositions between sentimentality and modernism or else between sentimentality and sophistication is false, as the examples of Coward, Parker and Loy all demonstrate.

Burstein also writes that 'sophistication works by relentlessly defining itself against its immediate past, or immediate context' (234); she might have added that this could also serve as a preliminary definition of modernism. Modernism often operates through the mechanisms of sophistication, and the two words are often associated (usually in passing) by critics. To cite a few of the many available examples: Randall Stevenson refers to 'modernism's technical sophistication' (196), while Malcolm Bradbury and James McFarlane define modernism as '[the] movement towards sophistication and mannerism, towards introversion, technical display, internal self-scepticism' (26). According to Michael Tratner, '[the] very use of "primitive" images in modernist works becomes a marker of the sophistication and technical complexity of the artists and writers' (60). Daniel Albright points out that '[some] composers heard in jazz a music that had already attained Modernist goals (sophistication, sinuosity, planar textures)' (376), whereas George Hutchison notes that the work of Harlem Renaissance artists has sometimes been dismissed as 'an inferior attempt at white modernist sophistication' (443). All these critics, and numerous others, see modernism as sophisticated because of its formal complexity.

Sean Latham is one of the few to consider other dimensions of modernist sophistication, which he analyses in terms of taste and cultural capital. He argues that modernists 'struggled to deflect attention away from their elitism, typically seeking some sort of solace in an idealized aesthetic realm

6   See also Sedgwick's discussion of sentimentality (150–56).

in which the signifiers of taste and sophistication might reach their referents in a genuine work of art' (3). This, of course, was impossible, and they were forced into negotiations not only with the marketplace but also with the operations of a snobbery which they at once denied and participated in. Woolf, for instance, 'presents snobbery as a persistent problem plaguing the act of aesthetic creation within an increasingly segmented and commodified cultural market place', but at the same time, she 'reconstructs the snob as a typically ironic intellectual performer capable of self-consciously exploiting the complicated flows of social and cultural capital'. Eventually, 'she founders on the disorienting effects of her own suddenly acquired fame' (63). At the same time, modernist formal practices began to be imitated and appropriated as signs of sophistication by middlebrow artists and audiences. This process was already being satirised by the mid-twenties – on 13 April 1924, the *Oakland Tribune* printed the following paragraph:

How to Appear Sophisticated

1. Express yourself in free verse, the crazier and the more meaningless the better.
2. Refer familiarly to H. L. Mencken, Theodore Dreiser, D. H. Lawrence, the intelligentsia, and your bootlegger.
3. Interlard your stuff with French phrases, such as may be found in any First French book.
4. Allude often to Freud and play up his jargon.
5. Emit an occasional cynicism about books, jakes, yokels, morons, etc. (qtd in Nardini 8)

A decade later, the modernist aesthetic had been more thoroughly appropriated by middlebrow authors. Latham comments that Stevie Smith's *Novel on Yellow Paper* (1936), a book written at the request of her publisher, clearly evokes the stream-of consciousness style of Woolf and Stein, and 'became a best-seller precisely because it drew so successfully upon a modernist literary practice that had, by the late thirties, become a commodified object of taste and sophistication' (6).[7]

The commodification of taste and sophistication is an important aspect of middlebrow culture, and indeed, it is in the realm of the middlebrow that sophistication is most insistently invoked and explored in early twentieth-century culture. Nina Miller, in her chapter on the Algonquin Round Table in *Making Love Modern*, writes:

The periodical forms of popular modernism – cartoons, newspaper columns, farcical sketches, short fiction, and the glossy magazines of urban life – comprised the most prominent area in the 1920s for the negotiation of modern selfhood, a

---

7 Latham perhaps underestimates Smith; for a reassessment of her as an intermodernist (rather than a wannabe modernist) see Bluemel 27–66.

selfhood that came to be (and in many ways, still is) defined by irony, urbanity, and humor. More than any other discursive project of the time, middle-brow culture made modern selfhood its explicit and relentless business. Meeting modernity head-on, it answered the crisis of value and dislocation with the heartbreakingly (and deceptively) simple panacea of style. (88)

Miller's account of New York middlebrow sophistication is, however, only partially compatible with the interwar English version which I have outlined using Coward as an example. She interprets sophistication in the framework of 'Modern Love', a set of media and literary discourses 'concerned with negotiating the new social terrain defined by the modern woman and the focus on heterosexual couples, as opposed to the actively reproductive family' (109). The cultural meaning of the liberated New Woman of the 1920s, Miller writes, derived principally from 'her forthright sexuality and sophistication', which 'lent her an aura of modernness highly desirable to an era significantly self-identified with the modern world of technological innovation, personal style, and fast-paced living' (8). Here there are certainly connections with the more attractive young female characters of Coward or Evelyn Waugh, Winifred Watson or, a little later, Nancy Mitford. But Modern Love, according to Miller, 'took its driving force from the assumption that gender relations were permanently and intrinsically flawed', and 'rendered a heterosexual world whose chief appeal was perhaps the opportunity it offered for cynical detachment from a common obsession; in the process, it flatteringly inscribed its readers as sophisticates' (109). Therefore, 'sophistication meant cynicism and a barbed wit' (109). Though certainly accurate in the context of the Algonquin Round Table, this would be insufficient or misleading as a general definition of early twentieth-century sophistication. It is certainly at odds with the version legible in Coward, or in British middlebrow fiction, in which detachment does not necessarily imply cynicism, and wit is by no means always bitchy. Indeed, Coward once wrote in a letter to Arnold Wesker: 'Once and for all you really must stop calling me "cynical"', citing a dictionary definition – 'A captious, sneering, fault-finding person, especially one who attributes human conduct to low motives of self-interest' – to prove that the label is incorrect (*Letters* 240). Cynicism, I would suggest, is not a necessary component of sophistication, just as sentimentalism is not necessarily excluded by sophistication. Indeed, middlebrow literature, music, art and cinema often achieve a delicate blending of such apparently incompatible ingredients as sentiment and sophistication, optimism and disillusionment, frivolity and engagement, conservatism and subversion.

The blending of styles is also an important middlebrow strategy, and is exemplified with particular clarity in American music. In his book on the birth of concert jazz, John Howland writes:

> In the 1920s and 1930s, the foremost exponents of symphonic jazz in the form of dance band arranging and popular concert works were Paul Whiteman and his chief arranger, Ferde Grofé. Whitemanesque symphonic jazz was a stylistically heteroge-neous idiom that referenced jazz, syncopated popular music from Tin Pan Alley to Broadway, African American music, and the 'light' classics. The *jazz* component of symphonic jazz paralleled 1920s journalistic uses of the term [...] to imply a mildly irreverent interbreeding of white and black and high and low music. The *symphonic* characterization references the music's heightened theatricality, its comparatively complex multithematic formal structures, and especially its 'sophisticated' intro-ductions, interludes, and codas, its unexpected modulations and dramatic cadenzas, and its emphasis on orchestrational and stylistic variety. The hybrid symphonic jazz sound developed an unusual cultural breadth that spanned the concert hall, jazz and dance bands, radio orchestras, Tin Pan Alley, Broadway musical theater, the variety prologue shows of the deluxe movie palaces, and certain genres of film music [...]. In each of these contexts, the proponents of symphonic jazz sought to endow contemporary popular music with an aura of glamour and cultural refine-ment. (2)

It was precisely this cultural breadth, however, which evoked hostility from 'highbrow' music circles: 'During the 1930s and 1940s, most contemporary critics damned this miscegenation of concert hall culture, entertainment intent, jazz, dance band arranging, Tin Pan Alley tunes, and quasi-symphonic instru-mentation as mongrel, middlebrow culture' (Howland 3). This is connected to a broader concern, which intensified during this period, with keeping art 'pure' and separate from entertainment. Indeed, the rise of specifically middlebrow forms of sophistication is directly linked to the fragmentation of the cultural field and the stratification of audiences in the early twentieth century. Constant Lambert wrote in *Music Ho!* (1934):

> Elgar was the last serious composer to be in touch with the great public. Sophisti-cated composers are either becoming more sophisticated, like Alban Berg, or they are deliberately turning their sophistication to popular account, like Kurt Weill. In the early nineteenth century one could be a great poet and yet a popular figure. [...] But now [...] while the highbrow poet, through his no doubt sincere complexity, has lost all save a small section of the old middlebrow public, the lowbrow poet – the type of writer who in the nineteenth century produced *Champagne Charlie* and now produces revue lyrics – has, through his social and technical sophistication, gained the greater part of it. (198)

Although this comment, like many other accounts of the development of 'brow' hierarchies, presents a narrative of decline, it is interesting in that it points to different varieties of sophistication – one roughly corresponding to 'difficulty'

(Berg) and the other to something smoother, more broadly appealing, and yet skilful and distinctive (the revue writer).

In both British and American contexts, however, the complexity and impact of middlebrow culture is still seriously underestimated and under-analysed by critics. I have argued elsewhere that the middlebrow is characterised by an intense interest in style, taste, imitation and social performance;[8] all these preoccupations are related to sophistication – indeed, they are primary themes of my present study. Nicola Humble in her groundbreaking book *The Feminine Middlebrow Novel, 1920s to 1950s* (2004) also points to the connection between middlebrow and sophistication:

> [W]hat I call the 'feminine middlebrow' in this period was a powerful force in estab-
> lishing and consolidating, but also in resisting, new class and gender identities [...]
> it is its paradoxical allegiance to both domesticity and a radical sophistication that
> makes this literary form so ideologically flexible. (2–3)

Humble's book, which considers about sixty novels by authors such as Rosamund Lehmann, Rose Macaulay, Elizabeth Bowen, Elizabeth Taylor, Dodie Smith, and Nancy Mitford, is part of a recent revival of interest in British and American middlebrow culture. This area of cultural production is now receiving new attention from critics and historians aiming to reconstruct the tastes and ideologies of the 1920s and 1930s, to explore novelists' interventions in discourses of class, gender and domesticity, or to challenge 'modernism's self-serving narratives of cultural centrality', as Ann Ardis puts it (9).[9] Many of these critics explore middlebrow writers' engagement with modernity, and especially with changing class structures and gender economies. Politically, this body of literature is complex: while its authors and readers mostly belonged to the middle classes, the actual novels are as likely to subvert as to reinforce values which are taken to be constitutive of interwar middle-class ideology. They complicate accepted ideas about the home and family, women and work, sexual behaviour, taste and propriety. Something similar happened in cinema, as avant-garde film separated itself as far as possible from commercial Hollywood models, and middlebrow cinematic forms evolved in the space between. As Lawrence Napper argues throughout his book *British Cinema and Middlebrow Culture in the Interwar Years* (2009), middlebrow film was by no means necessarily uniformly conservative; indeed, it negotiated with ease between modernity and tradition, and often posed substantial challenges

---

8   *Women, Celebrity* 5; see also the rest of the introduction.
9   For recent work on middlebrow culture, see Ardis; Botshon and Goldsmith; Erica Brown; Deen; Earnshaw; Grover; Light; Radway; Rubin; Scholes. For a much fuller list of references, see the annotated bibliography on the Middlebrow Network website: < www.middlebrow-network.com>.

to established social and cultural orders.[10]

The middlebrow engagement with modernity brings with it a sustained focus on moments of change, especially in relation to adolescence and developing sexuality, and it also produces retrospection and, sometimes, nostalgia. These two impulses are closely related. The 'younger generation', 'flaming youth', 'Bright Young Things' and so on were buzzwords of the interwar years, and the sense of a gulf between the generations was much exacerbated by the break in cultural continuity caused by the First World War. Young people evoked reactions ranging from fascination to fear, and were the subject of intense attention and debate in the media and in literature. In the US especially, as Paula Fass writes in *The Damned and the Beautiful: American Youth in the 1920s*,

> [the] young had come to represent the unhinging of the social order, and the journals of the twenties were filled with an image of youth out of control, of energy released from social restraints, and of raw forces unleashed. [...] Those energies, which had once been drawn into socially necessary channels through work and child-rearing, appeared now to threaten social order as adult enterprises were delayed and leisure time expanded. [...] Not surprisingly, traditionalists equated the unharnessed energies of youth with license, and sexual license above all. (20–21)

In the British and American literature of the period, the forms of licence which young people seized, not only in terms of sex but also in terms of drinking, smoking and unchaperoned socialising, were often associated with sophistication. Evelyn Waugh makes this association rather sardonically: his Bright Young Things consider themselves sophisticated, but many of them appear merely ridiculous.[11] Scott Fitzgerald's twenty-somethings have much more pathos, but their sophistication is equally imaginary. Other texts direct their mockery at the older generation's intolerant cant about 'the younger generation'. This is dramatised, for instance, in T. S. Eliot's *The Family Reunion* (1939), during a conversation among several ageing aristocrats:

VIOLET: They bathe all day and they dance all night.
    In the absolute *minimum* of clothes.
CHARLES: It's the cocktail drinking that does the harm:
    There's nothing on earth so bad for the young.
    All that a civilised person needs
    Is a glass of dry sherry or two before dinner.

10 The introduction to Napper's book makes this argument in detail; the discussion is specifically tailored to the subsidised British cinema industry, though some of the points would also apply to certain groups of American films.
11 Angela Lyne in *Put Out More Flags* (1942) is a rare exception: she manages to be perfectly sophisticated without trading on it, or inclining to excess, and her sophistication is never debunked by Waugh. Angela 'wore the livery of the highest fashion, but as one who dressed to inform rather than to attract [...]. Her smartness was individual' (25).

> The modern young people don't know what they're drinking,
> Modern young people don't care what they're eating;
> They've lost their sense of taste and smell
> Because of their cocktails and cigarettes.
> [*Enter* DENMAN *with sherry and whisky.* CHARLES *takes sherry and* GERALD *whisky.*]
> That's what it comes to.
>   [*Lights a cigarette.*]
> IVY: The younger generation
> Are undoubtedly decadent. (286)

Eliot invokes the clichés of Jazz Age sophistication (cocktails, cigarettes, decadence) in order to reveal the failure of the middle-aged to achieve wisdom, and to ridicule contemporary debates about taste, civilisation and cultural decline. By 1939, these debates no doubt seemed increasingly trivial in the context of political crises, but even as early as the twenties, Scott Fitzgerald could evoke youth culture in the context of decadence and impending doom.

Writers from the popular through to the high modernist explored these issues, and the tone of reflections on youth culture, generational divides and coming of age ranged from the scathingly satirical to the gently melancholic. At the melancholic end of the scale is a writer who, though twenty years older than Fitzgerald, came to prominence at the same time: Sherwood Anderson. His story 'Sophistication', from *Winesburg, Ohio* (1919), focuses on two eighteen-year-olds, George Willard and Helen White, living in a small town. The narrator generalises from George's experience of adolescence:

> There is a time in the life of every boy when he for the first time takes the backward view of life. Perhaps that is the moment when he crosses the line into manhood. The boy is walking through the street of his town. He is thinking of the future and of the figure he will cut in the world. Ambitions and regrets awake within him. Suddenly something happens; he stops under a tree and waits as for a voice calling his name. Ghosts of old things creep into his consciousness; the voices outside of himself whisper a message concerning the limitations of life. From being quite sure of himself and his future he becomes not at all sure. If he be an imaginative boy a door is torn open and for the first time he looks out upon the world, seeing, as though they marched in procession before him, the countless figures of men who before his time have come out of nothingness into the world, lived their lives and again disappeared into nothingness. The sadness of sophistication has come to the boy. (234)

Sophistication arises, in this story, from reflection and self-awareness: 'In youth there are always two forces fighting in people. The warm unthinking little animal struggles against the thing that reflects and remembers, and the older, the more sophisticated thing had possession of George Willard' (240).

But although this sentence seems to oppose mental life to sensuality, the story actually shows that the adolescent's sudden consciousness of mortality actually leads into the realm of the erotic. The awareness of death and time passing brings a desire for physical connection with another person: 'When the moment of sophistication came to George Willard his mind turned to Helen White' (235).[12]

Anderson juxtaposes this conception of sophistication (which the characters in the story are unable to articulate) with another view of it, which they do express directly. George, Helen and others speak of sophistication as a function of urban experience: George, for instance, 'was about to leave Winesburg to go away to some city where he hoped to get work on a city newspaper and he felt grown up' (234). But in fact, the growing up is taking place in Winesburg itself: George is simply 'walking through the street of his town' when sophistication comes to him. Helen has already been away to Cleveland to study: 'She thought that the months she had spent in the city, the going to theaters and the seeing of great crowds wandering in lighted thoroughfares, had changed her profoundly' (236). The narrator implies, though, that 'the change in her nature' (236) actually came not from the experience of the city but from her consciousness of her maturing body, which brings both heightened sexual desire and a frightening sense of mortality. A third character who associates sophistication with the urban is the college instructor who is a guest of Helen's mother: 'Although he had also been raised in an Ohio town, the instructor began to put on the airs of the city. He wanted to appear cosmopolitan' (238). But he fails to perceive that people live just as intensely in a small town as in the city, and obtusely asks Helen: 'Your life is still bound up with the life of this town? There are people here in whom you are interested?' (239). Anderson dismantles the conventional opposition between the sophisticated, liberating city and the regressive, repressive small town; like Georg Simmel, he emphasises the threads which bind the city to its provinces. In 'Departure', the last story of *Winesburg, Ohio*, George Willard leaves his home town for the city, but on the journey he does not think of his future. Rather, in a sort of mise-en-abyme of the book itself, a series of vivid images of Winesburg life pass through his mind:

He thought of little things – Turk Smollet wheeling boards through the main street of his town in the morning, a tall woman, beautifully gowned, who had once stayed overnight at his father's hotel, Butch Wheeler the lamp lighter of Wines-

12 Whalen notes the ambiguity of Anderson's account of what George and Helen experience together, and what 'sophistication' means to them, and surveys the views of several critics (57–58). Ciancio suggests that it is the reconciliation of 'the despair that comes from learning that man is a finite and grotesque creature' with 'knowledge of "the sweetness of the twisted apples", a more genuine and elevating kind of sophistication that both presupposes and negates the first' (1005).

burg hurrying through the streets on a summer evening and holding a torch in his hand, Helen White standing by a window in the Winesburg post office and putting a stamp on an envelope. (247)

The town appears idyllic in this passage, and the story is intensely nostalgic because it describes a way of life that the younger generation is anxious to leave behind. Even as he indulges in these retrospective musings, George is on a train speeding towards his new city life. The 'backward view of life' explored in *Winesburg, Ohio* connects it with many other texts from this period, because literature in the years following 1918 is often preoccupied with the lost stability, order and even innocence of the pre-war world.

The complexities of this looking backward are exemplified in Edith Wharton's *The Age of Innocence* (1920), which I discuss in the first section of this chapter, alongside F. Scott Fitzgerald's more clearly modernist novel, *The Beautiful and Damned* (1922). This section on American fiction of the twenties takes its impetus from Sherwood Anderson, exploring points of view on sophistication which are tinged with melancholy. In *The Age of Innocence*, which is set mainly in the 1870s but with a final chapter unfolding around the turn of the century, the performance of innocence actually requires an underlying sophistication. The narrative contrasts two kinds of sophistication: the concealed knowingness and worldliness of the New York leisure class and the overt style, cultural knowledge and cosmopolitanism of the European aristocracy. My discussion of this novel picks up on themes introduced earlier in the readings of Fanny Trollope and Henry James, particularly the notion of an American leisure class, which emerged towards the end of the nineteenth century as industrial fortunes multiplied, and leisure came to be seen as 'essential to the United States's view of itself as a civilized nation, that is to say, a society led by a group of cultivated people who were knowledgeable about manners and the finer things in life' (Montgomery 8). Wharton examines the American effort to acquire sophistication by appropriating European upper-class social practices. James and Trollope had also reflected on this, but Wharton's book is distinct from theirs because it is historical fiction, and therefore contains implicit reflections on post-First World War America. Wharton also shares with Trollope and James a preoccupation with the gendering of sophistication, and this theme, as well as that of the American leisure class, emerges once again in *The Beautiful and Damned*. Fitzgerald's Anthony Patch sees himself as a natural aristocrat and declines to work, relying on the prospect of inherited wealth and devoting himself to aesthetic and romantic pursuits. Like Coward's characters, he tries to combine sophistication and sentiment; unlike them he fails because he is not sufficiently self-conscious about his own romance.

Curious combinations of nostalgia and extreme modernness are exhibited in the remaining three texts discussed in this chapter: Stella Gibbons's *Cold Comfort Farm* (1932), Winifred Watson's *Miss Pettigrew Lives for a Day* (1938), and *Vanity Fair* magazine, which was edited by Frank Crowninshield from 1914 until 1936. As Nina Miller remarks: '*Vanity Fair*, the vanguard journal of the new sophistication, had begun its active promotion of wit and urbanity for New York and the nation as early as 1914' (91), yet the magazine often harked back to a lost (European) aristocratic era. *Cold Comfort Farm* is so very modern that it is set in the future, but its heroine, Flora Poste, refuses to earn her own living and prefers Victorian family structures to contemporary ones. Watson's novel is the most firmly contemporary of the texts discussed in this chapter, but even Miss Pettigrew insists on old-fashioned woollen underwear beneath her new evening gown. These are all texts which trade in humour, though in diverse styles. Miller's remark about the Algonquin Round Table would be extremely applicable to Gibbons's novel and to *Vanity Fair*:

> Highly marketable in a culture of self-conscious sophistication, humor also had distinct rhetorical advantages for the imperatives of this subculture. Principally, it afforded them licence for detachment: they could be clever without the implication of intellectualism, critical without affiliation with any positive ideological model, and ironic in relation to themselves, rendering their own social identifications indeterminate. (90–91)

Miss Pettigrew Lives for a Day, though also self-conscious about sophistication, is unusual in exploring it in the context of relationship and warmth, rather than detachment and self-absorption. Miss Pettigrew receives an education in sophistication from a new friend, just as Elfine Starkadder is educated by Flora in *Cold Comfort Farm*. These narratives of makeover explore whether sophistication can be learned, and whether it requires a change of values or only of surface style. Such questions also underlie *Vanity Fair*'s complex address to its supposedly elite, but actually aspirational, readership.

I would propose that the early twentieth century is the richest era of all in terms of the varied and complex elaboration of sophistication in different contexts. There is an enormous range of books, films, poems, songs, and periodicals which could potentially belong in this chapter. I could, for instance, have chosen an entirely different set of literary texts, say, Virginia Woolf's *Orlando* (1928), Evelyn Waugh's *Vile Bodies* (1930), Rose Macaulay's *Potterism* (1920), Ronald Firbank's *The Eccentricities of Cardinal Pirelli* (1926), and T. S. Eliot's *Sweeney Agonistes* (1926–27). Or I could have emphasised different themes – instead of focusing primarily on class and secondarily on gender, it would have been equally interesting to explore the impact of sophistication on constructions of homosexuality in early twentieth-century writing, or on constructions of race in the literature of the Harlem Renaissance. Visual sophistication also deserves further investigation: this could encompass art, photography, advertisements and especially film. Of particular interest are films from the silent era in which sophistication was defined visually by actresses such as Louise Brooks, Anna May Wong and Vilma Banky. With the advent of sound in the thirties, voice added a new dimension to Hollywood's definition of feminine sophistication; Greta Garbo, Bette Davis and Marlene Dietrich would be among the most obvious choices to discuss in this connection, but there are dozens of other actors, male and female, whose style was predicated on sophistication.

To make the most of the available space, then, I have attempted to establish an approach to the study of early twentieth-century literature in relation to sophistication which I hope might be applied in future to other authors and other kinds of texts. I have sought to give coherence to the chapter by concentrating primarily on the middlebrow literature of the period, while also pointing towards relationships among modernist, middlebrow and popular cultures. My choice of texts is also designed to illuminate the shifting meaning of the word 'sophistication' in the early twentieth century. Although it occurs quite frequently in the literature of this era, there are still many texts which address it only through indirection. I have chosen two texts in which the term itself is repeatedly used and reflected on: *The Beautiful and Damned* and *Miss Pettigrew Lives for a Day*. In the others, *The Age of Innocence*, *Cold Comfort Farm* and *Vanity Fair* magazine, the word itself occurs only occasionally, and the idea is diffused among other concepts such as civilisation and cosmopolitanism.

Sophistication was still very much a contested term in the interwar years, though the competing meanings were different from those which prevailed in earlier eras, and more clearly incompatible. Within a single text, it is often used as a term of both praise and criticism. For instance, Monica Dickens writes in her novel *Mariana* (1940) of her heroine Mary's ill-advised yearning for 'the shoddy sophistication of frocks in the small dress shops of Kensington High Street' (113) but also describes, much more admiringly, Mary's mother's appearance, 'like a sophisticated mermaid in a green crêpe dress that clung to her all the way down and then kicked out in a fishtail train' (335). The criticism here still depends, as it did in earlier periods, on the association of sophistication with fraudulence and inauthenticity; the praise invests sophistication with a new – and distinctly erotic – desirability. At the same time, the mermaid is a duplicitous figure, and this reveals the way that traces of the older meaning of sophistication persist in modern usages. In the texts discussed in this chapter, sophistication's affiliation with sex is more affirmative (at least potentially) than it was in earlier eras; on the other hand, the fear of tawdriness and lack of discernment – whether in the choice of a dress or of a lover – endures. In the eighteenth and nineteenth centuries, sophistication was a dangerous quality; at best a doubtful good. By the later twentieth century, the word had become, unambiguously, a term of approbation. It is in the earlier and middle parts of the twentieth century, and especially in the decades between the wars, that sophistication was most in flux, most debated, most fascinating.

'Playing a part before sophisticated witnesses': *The Age of Innocence* and *The Beautiful and Damned*

In her memoir *A Backward Glance* (1934), Edith Wharton writes:

> Not until the successive upheavals which culminated in the catastrophe of 1914 had 'cut all likeness from the name' of my old New York, did I begin to see its pathetic picturesqueness. [...] The small society into which I was born was 'good' in the most prosaic sense, and its only interest, for the generality of readers, lies in the fact of its sudden and total extinction, and for the imaginative few in the recollection of the moral treasures that went with it. Let me try to call it back ... (6–7)

Like *A Backward Glance*, Wharton's novel *The Age of Innocence* (1920) is an attempt to call back this lost social environment. It balances between nostalgic evocation of the 1870s and 1880s of Wharton's childhood and critique of the underlying cruelty and primitivism of this society. But the title *The Age of Innocence* has complex resonances, and may be read as at least partially ironic, since the old New York society which the novel examines is not really presented as innocent but as intensely sophisticated. Its rules and rituals are highly complicated, and it deploys subtle strategies of surveillance and coercion in order to preserve the power of a small elite of established families and to legitimise their dominance through reference to European social systems.

In *A Backward Glance*, Wharton points to what she sees as '[t]he really vital change' which divides the postwar era from late nineteenth-century America: 'in my youth, the Americans of the original States, who in moments of crisis still shaped the national point of view, were the heirs of an old tradition of European culture which the country has now totally rejected' (6). Before this eventual rejection, however, many aspects of European culture were enthusiastically embraced by America's elite. In the last decades of the nineteenth century and the early years of the twentieth, the haute bourgeoisie consolidated and extended their power by purchasing and displaying the trappings of European aesthetic and cultural sophistication, and by adopting social practices to match. As Maureen E. Montgomery explains in *Displaying Women: Spectacles of Leisure in Edith Wharton's New York* (1998):

> Architects and their patrons drew heavily upon a European aristocratic inherit-
> ance of French châteaux, Italian palazzi, and English country houses [...]. European
> art treasures, antiques, marbles and so on were purchased wholesale and shipped
> back to the United States [...]. European structures and aristocratic accoutrements
> harking back to courtly societies were thus imported and adapted to the needs of
> a powerful, wealthy business elite attempting to impose its leadership by *buying*
> history. (65)

This attempt by the newly rich families of north-eastern America to eschew the
vulgarity of the new exemplifies the dynamic between nostalgia and modernness in early twentieth-century constructions of sophistication. On the one
hand, the Parisian-style houses on Fifth Avenue, and the art treasures they
contained, conferred distinction; on the other hand, their owners were actually
participating in a fashionable practice, and in effect copying their neighbours
as well as imitating their transatlantic ancestors.

Wharton's old New Yorkers subscribe to aristocratic and racist notions
of inheritance, breeding and civilisation. Montgomery writes that etiquette
manuals around the turn of the century were concerned with how the
recently established American leisure class could counter European perceptions of Americans as 'savage' or uncivilised. The discourses of these manuals,
Montgomery notes, are underpinned by 'a formulation of national identity
[...] rooted in an Anglo-American and racist construction of "civilization"'.
Such texts contributed to 'the maintenance of a white Anglo-Saxon Protes-
tant elite confronted with the growing ethnic diversity of America's population and the challenge of wealthy Jewish families to the de facto segregation
practiced by high society' (8). Indeed, anxious references to foreignness rever-
berate throughout *The Age of Innocence*, and betray the preoccupation with
racial fitness which marked the late nineteenth-century society analysed by
Wharton. The figure of Julius Beaufort, who 'passed for an Englishman' (70)
but is probably Jewish, is the focus for many of these anxieties. His wealth has
gained him access to the best society: he is, in fact, far richer than the members
of the social elite whom he regularly entertains at his mansion. But they remain
suspicious of him, and at the time of his spectacular downfall, all those who
have associated with him feel implicated in, and contaminated by, his disgrace.

Beaufort inspires distrust not simply because of his possible racial origins
but also because he is a banker. The social elite in the novel shore up their
power by distancing themselves not only from the influence of the foreign but
likewise from the labour of wealth creation. Admittedly, many of the leading
members of New York society do have professions – including the novel's
protagonist, Newland Archer, who is a lawyer. He rarely does any actual work,
however, and conceives of himself as a gentleman of leisure:

He had dawdled over his cigar because he was at heart a dilettante, and thinking over a pleasure to come often gave him a subtler satisfaction than its realisation. This was especially the case when the pleasure was a delicate one, as his pleasures mostly were; and on this occasion the moment he looked forward to was so rare and exquisite in quality that – well, if he had timed his arrival in accord with the prima donna's stage-manager he could not have entered the Academy at a more significant moment than just as she was singing: 'He loves me – he loves me not – *he loves me!* – ' and sprinkling the falling daisy petals with notes as clear as dew. [...]

'*M'ama ... non m'ama ...*' the prima donna sang, and '*M'ama!*', with a final burst of love triumphant, as she pressed the dishevelled daisy to her lips and lifted her large eyes to the sophisticated countenance of the little brown Faust-Capoul, who was vainly trying, in a tight purple velvet doublet and plumed cap, to look as pure and true as his artless victim. (58–59)

Newland quite clearly presents himself as a sophisticate, and here he is gently mocked for his overstrained ideas and posturing. The cigar or cigarette is often used to signal sophistication in literary and visual texts from the later nineteenth century onwards, and in lingering over his, Newland emphasises his superiority to the tightly scheduled, hurrying lives of the middle and lower classes. He also displays his cultured familiarity with the opera by arriving in the middle, an act apparently nonchalant but in fact carefully calculated.

In the quoted passage, the word 'sophisticated' is displaced onto Faust; nevertheless, the quality unmistakably attaches to Newland, just as 'artless' attaches to his fiancée May, who is introduced in the following paragraph. Her artlessness, indeed, is just as much a self-conscious pose as Newland's sophistication:

Newland Archer, leaning against the wall at the back of the club box, turned his eyes from the stage and scanned the opposite side of the house. Directly facing him was the box of old Mrs Manson Mingott [...] filled by her daughter-in-law, Mrs Lovell Mingott, and her daughter, Mrs Welland; and slightly withdrawn behind these brocaded matrons sat a young girl in white with eyes ecstatically fixed on the stage-lovers. As Madame Nilsson's '*M'ama!*' thrilled out above the silent house [...] a warm pink mounted to the girl's cheek, mantled her brow to the roots of her fair braids, and suffused the young slope of her breast to the line where it met a modest tulle tucker fastened with a single gardenia. She dropped her eyes to the immense bouquet of lilies-of-the-valley on her knee, and Newland Archer saw her white-gloved finger-tips touch the flowers softly. He drew a breath of satisfied vanity and his eyes returned to the stage. (59–60)

May, clearly, is part of the performance which Newland has come to see; she dresses the part of the innocent maiden and blushes appropriately in response to the dual stimulation of the passionate song and her fiancé's gaze. She cannot, of course, return his bold stare, and instead lowers her eyes to the lilies-of-the valley, traditional symbols of purity and – since Newland has sent them – symbols also of his power to define her. (By contrast, he later sends the woman who almost becomes his mistress, Ellen Olenska, a box of yellow roses, which in the language of flowers signify infidelity.) May is later proved to possess considerably acuity, even cunning, yet always presents herself, as she is required to do, in terms of innocence and unsophistication. Though Newland feels it appropriate that his wife should possess these qualities, they also irritate him. During an archery competition in which May is victorious, he overhears a conversation between two of his acquaintances:

> 'Gad,' Archer heard Lawrence Lefferts say, 'not one of the lot holds the bow as she does;' and Beaufort retorted: 'Yes; but that's the only kind of target she'll ever hit.'
>
> Archer felt irrationally angry. His host's contemptuous tribute to May's 'niceness' was just what a husband should have wished to hear said of his wife. The fact that a coarse-minded man found her lacking in attraction was simply another proof of her quality; yet the words sent a faint shiver through his heart. What if 'niceness' carried to that supreme degree were only a negation, the curtain dropped before an emptiness? (224)

In this text, as in so many others from this period, the word 'nice' designates the opposite of sophistication, and in this passage, 'niceness', though respectable and necessary, nevertheless appears unalluring in contrast to sophistication. Newland certainly underestimates his wife's underlying sophistication, which is demonstrated in her ability to negotiate the complicated and dangerous system that is New York society, and to collude with her family in manipulating her husband.

May's superficial innocence successfully conceals a considerable degree of knowingness, while Ellen, on the other hand, appears cosmopolitan and even glamorous, yet eventually reveals herself as almost heroically pure and self-sacrificing. In two early scenes, Newland Archer visits Ellen in her rather shabby house which, by the skilful deployment of furnishings brought back with her from Europe, she has 'transformed into something intimate, "foreign", subtly suggestive of old romantic scenes and sentiments' (111). Although not literally foreign, Ellen, who married a Polish nobleman, has been away from New York for many years. Now separated from him, she returns to what she considers a place of safety, only to find her hometown an indecipherable and menacing place. Although she is actually too innocent to operate successfully in the upper echelons of New York society, she is considered to be quite the opposite. Newland is simultaneously dismayed and baffled by what he sees as her excess of sophistication. On his second visit to her house, he sees intrigue everywhere: even the maid seems to him to be 'smiling mysteriously' (138), while Ellen holds out her hand to him 'in a way mysteriously suggesting that she expected him to kiss it' (139). He finds her 'attired in a long robe of red velvet bordered about the chin and down the front with glossy black fur' (139). Reminded of the fashionable portraits he has recently seen in Paris, Newland reflects: 'There was something perverse and provocative in the notion of fur worn in the evening in a heated drawing-room, and in the combination of a muffled throat and bare arms; but the effect was undeniably pleasing' (139). Ellen is associated with Frenchness, and placed in an erotically charged atmosphere; these things, together with her familiarity with European art, literature and music, and her ability to converse in several languages, reinforce the impression of her sophistication. But in Wharton's fictional worlds, sophistication is a heavily gendered quality, desirable only in men. Newland Archer prides himself on his knowledge of French literature and Italian art, but is disconcerted to find that Ellen shares these tastes.

The narrative demonstrates, however, that there are two kinds of sophistication: the kind which Ellen embodies (that is, culture, style, cosmopolitanism, and perceptiveness) and the kind which New York society depends on and yet conceals (knowingness, worldliness, performative skill). In the later stages of the novel, Ellen's sincerity is explicitly contrasted with the dissembling sophistication of the fashionable set. Following a meeting with Ellen in which she acknowledges their mutual love, yet imposes severe constraints on their relationship, Newland reflects:

> It was the perfect balance she had held between their loyalty to others and their honesty to themselves that had so stirred and yet tranquillized him; a balance not artfully calculated, as her tears and her falterings showed, but resulting naturally from her unabashed sincerity. It filled him with a tender awe, now the danger was over, and made him thank the fates that no personal vanity, no sense of playing a part before sophisticated witnesses, had tempted him to tempt her. (251)

The 'sophisticated witnesses' are men such as Lawrence Lefferts, 'the foremost authority on "form" in New York' (62). The characterisation of Lefferts demonstrates once again the gendering of sophistication: Ellen's striking style of dress evokes suspicion, whereas Lefferts is admired because he 'knew how to wear such good clothes so carelessly and to carry such height with so much lounging grace' (62). Lefferts, the epitome of masculine sophistication, has a string of affairs and yet retains his position as a social leader, while Ellen, merely suspected of affairs which never actually take place, is eventually rejected by New York society. Even Newland Archer, who loves her, vacillates between desire and distrust.

Wharton's *The Age of Innocence* and *A Backward Glance*, along with Anderson's *Winesburg, Ohio* and Willa Cather's *O Pioneers!* (1918) and *A Lost Lady* (1923), are among the most significant fictions of nostalgia published in the twenties.

These texts contrast in many ways with the works which are usually considered more representative of the decade, such as the novels of F. Scott Fitzgerald. Works such as *The Great Gatsby* (1925), *The Beautiful and Damned* or 'The Diamond as Big as the Ritz' (1922) are often described as being very much of their time, intimately bound up with the particular cultural moment of America's postwar boom. But a closer reading uncovers that in Fitzgerald's work, too, the dynamic between modernity and nostalgia is continually evident. It is often forgotten that *The Beautiful and Damned* is set mainly in the 1910s, with the Armistice of 1918 occurring at a late stage in the story. Despite this, the novel does belong in many ways to the twenties: perhaps because its atmosphere combines the hedonism of the Jazz Age with the postwar longing for a lost era of stable values and meaningful endeavour. In Fitzgerald's fiction, the concept of sophistication is addressed more directly than it is in Cather or Wharton; indeed, in *The Beautiful and Damned*, the word occurs in the very first paragraph:

> In 1913, when Anthony Patch was twenty-five, two years were already gone since irony, the Holy Ghost of this later day, had, theoretically at least, descended upon him. Irony was the final polish of the shoe, the ultimate dab of the clothes-brush, a sort of intellectual 'There!' – yet at the brink of this story he has yet gone no further than the conscious stage. As you first see him he wonders frequently whether he is not without honour and slightly mad, a shameful and obscene thinness glistening on the surface of the world like oil on a clean pond, these occasions being varied, of course, with those in which he thinks himself rather an exceptional young man, thoroughly sophisticated, well adjusted to his environment, and somewhat more significant than anyone else he knows. (9)

As in most of the texts discussed in this book, sophistication consists partly in the ability to adjust to one's environment and function successfully in it. Anthony considers that he has this quality at the start of the narrative, when his environment is one of luxury and leisure, but later, when forced to work for a living, submit to the discipline of an army camp, and adopt a more economical lifestyle, he finds himself entirely unable to adapt. His sophistication, then, is not so 'thorough' as it initially appears, perhaps because his sense of irony is 'theoretical', merely part of the coolly disdainful attitude he cultivates. If he had had a proper sense of irony, he would have been able to apply it when contemplating his own life, and he would eventually have understood the ridiculous idealism and romanticism of his own hopes.

Yet the narrator does not seem entirely to lament Anthony's naivety: indeed, it is often presented as one of his more appealing qualities. The passage quoted above continues:

> This was his healthy state and it made him cheerful, pleasant, and very attractive to intelligent men and to all women. In this state he considered that he would one day

accomplish some quiet subtle thing that the elect would deem worthy [...]. Until the time came for this effort he would be Anthony Patch – not a portrait of a man but a distinct and dynamic personality, opinionated, contemptuous, functioning from within outward – a man who [...] knew the sophistry of courage and yet was brave. (9)

On this first page of the novel, then, both 'sophistication' and 'sophistry' occur: Anthony thinks he can tell the difference, but the kind of sophistication he embraces actually retains strong elements of disingenuousness and specious argument. He deceives himself with sophistry, and even begins to use it to deny the value – and even the possibility – of the very accomplishment which he initially aspired to. He tells Gloria, 'if I hadn't met you I *would* have done something. But you make leisure so subtly attractive' (175). Gloria laughs in response: 'she resented his sophistry as at the same time she admired his nonchalance', and she won't blame him for idling 'so long as he did it sincerely, from the attitude that nothing much was worth doing' (175).

Confident of inheriting his grandfather's fortune (which was made on Wall Street), Anthony sees no need to earn money and despises all effortfulness and profit-mindedness. This leads him to say to his friend Dick Caramel, an aspiring writer: 'I'd feel that it being a meaningless world, why write? The very attempt to give it purpose is purposeless'. Dick replies: 'Well, even admitting all that, be a decent pragmatist and grant a poor man the instinct to live. Would you want every one to accept that sophistic rot?' (25). The third man present during this conversation, Maury Noble, responds:

I believe that everyone in America but a selected thousand should be compelled to accept a very rigid system of morals – Roman Catholicism, for instance. I don't complain of conventional morality. I complain rather of the mediocre heretics who seize upon the findings of sophistication and adopt the pose of a moral freedom to which they are by no means entitled by their intelligences. (26)

It is unusual, even in this period of intense preoccupation with sophistication, to find fictional characters actually discussing it. The other texts considered or mentioned in this study very rarely allow characters to comment on the subject: Miss Pettigrew and Amanda in *Private Lives* are among the very few exceptions. Maury's view is not really upheld by the logic of the narrative; indeed, it is immediately deflated by a parenthetical aside in the form of a stage direction: '(*Here the soup arrives and what Maury might have gone on to say is lost for all time*)' (26). The arrogance of Maury and Anthony is certainly satirised in the novel, and yet in these early chapters at least, their rhetoric is often momentarily persuasive, and they occasionally approach heroism in their desire to transcend the banalities of mainstream American culture.

Particularly interesting in this context is the episode titled 'Admiration', in which Anthony and Gloria Gilbert, whom he is courting, tire of the familiar shows in the fashionable theatre district, and visit a cheap cabaret in a downmarket area. Anthony is both fascinated and repelled, and the narrator articulates and elaborates upon his point of view, saying of the patrons of this kind of nightclub:

> They have made sure that the place has three qualifications: it is cheap; it imitates with a sort of shoddy and mechanical wistfulness the glittering antics of the great cafés in the theatre district; and – this, above all, important – it is a place where they can 'take a nice girl', which means, of course, that every one has become equally harmless, timid, and uninteresting through lack of money and imagination.
>
> There on Sunday nights gather the credulous, sentimental, underpaid, over-worked people with hyphenated occupations; book-keepers, ticket-sellers, office-managers [...]. With them are their giggling, over-gestured, pathetically pretentious women [...] whose starved fancies are only too willing to believe that the scene is comparatively gay and joyous, and even faintly immoral. (61)

Again, 'niceness', in combination with sentimentality (used here in a very pejorative sense), designates a kind of unthinking, emotionally based respect-ability which is presented as the opposite of sophistication.[13] Though the narrator criticises the nightclub patrons harshly enough for their enjoyment of this imitation glamour, he is even more severe on them for attempting to disavow their own pleasure. Anthony and Gloria watch a girl come in to join a group:

> By gesture she was pretending [...] that she belonged to a class a little superior to the class with which she now had to do, that a while ago she had been, and presently would again be, in a higher, rarer air. She was almost painfully refined – she wore a last year's hat covered with violets no more yearningly pretentious and palpably artificial than herself.
>
> Fascinated, Anthony and Gloria watched the girl sit down and radiate the impres-sion that she was only condescendingly present. For *me*, her eyes said, this is practi-cally a slumming expedition [...]. – And the other women passionately poured out the impression that though they were in the crowd they were not of it. (62)

Anthony, with the self-assurance of his Harvard education and his anticipated wealth, conceives himself to be on a social plane far above these people, yet he too is 'slumming', and he too is no doubt projecting an appearance of conscious superiority. Gazing at Gloria, he dwells on their separateness from

13 Compare this sarcastic 1925 passage from *The New Yorker*: 'New York is a most sophisticated city. It is fastidious, aesthetic. It is open to criticism, perhaps, as to its morals and its business methods, but you've got to hand it to the metropolis for its insistence upon good taste. It elects and re-elects John F. Hylan for Mayor. Its choice in literature is the illustrated *News*. Its favorite play is "Abie's Irish Rose". The explanation of all this is found in every Fifth Avenue bus. It is because we love nice things' (Professor 19).

the crowd: 'they two, it seemed to him, were alone and infinitely remote, quiet. Surely the freshness of her cheeks was a gossamer projection from a land of delicate and undiscovered shades' (63). But to his horror, Gloria destroys the illusion by saying 'I belong here' and 'I'm like these people' (63). She explains with apparent pride that she has a streak of 'cheapness' and admires 'gaudy vulgarity' (64), but Anthony ignores these clues to her tastes because he is absorbed in aestheticising her: 'Anthony for the moment wanted fiercely to paint her, to set her down *now*, as she was, as with each relentless second she could never be again' (64). The impossibility of enjoying the moment, the 'now', while simultaneously seeking to preserve it constitutes the whole tragedy of *The Beautiful and Damned*. Anthony and Gloria, terrified of growing old, actually destroy their youth prematurely with cigarettes, alcohol and extravagant partying.

Like the girl with the violets on her hat, Anthony longs for sophistication and thinks he has achieved it, yet while he can unmask the girl as pretentious, only the narrator can reveal the extent of Anthony's self-deception. The section closes with this paragraph:

> Out of the deep sophistication of Anthony an understanding formed, nothing atavistic or obscure, indeed scarcely physical at all, an understanding remembered from the romancings of many generations of minds that as she talked and caught his eyes and turned her lovely head, she moved him as he had never been moved before. The sheath that held her soul had assumed significance – that was all. She was a sun, radiant, growing, gathering light and storing it – then after an eternity pouring it forth in a glance, the fragment of a sentence, to that part of him that cherished all beauty and all illusion. (64)

The reference to 'deep sophistication' is tinged with an irony which Anthony himself cannot understand. The meaning he projects onto Gloria's physical being derives entirely from his own imagination and not at all from her flimsy, rather inane and wholly selfish personality. Anthony achieves a veneer of sophistication, but beneath it he is – in spite of his intelligence – a romantic, sentimental fantasist. The spell of Gloria's beauty, the narrator remarks, 'coloured the banality of his words and made the mawkish seem sad and the posturing seem wise' (96). And yet the lyricism of Fitzgerald's prose makes Anthony's illusions almost irresistible, so that the reader, too, is temporarily allured by Gloria, or rather, by the visions of beauty which she inspires in her lover. Anthony's self-absorption, then, is intensified rather than reduced by his romance with Gloria. The blankness of her personality allows him to see in her the reflection of his own fantasies, while her beauty provides the confirmation of his own aesthetic discernment.

His self-admiring quality is an essential element of his dandiacal identity. Anthony's father is 'a dandy of the nineties' (11) and Anthony sees himself very much as a twentieth-century dandy. He amasses 'a rather pathetic collection of silk pyjamas, brocaded dressing-gowns, and neckties too flamboyant to wear; in this secret finery he would parade before a mirror in his room or lie stretched in satin along his window seat' (13). This is almost like a scene of furtive cross-dressing, and it reveals the discrepancy between the civilised, but fairly ordinary, figure that Anthony cuts in the world and his hidden self-image. In his imagination, Anthony is a figure of excessive, flamboyant, almost perverse sophistication. Having travelled quite extensively in Europe, he admires old world culture and considers himself 'thoroughly un-American' (12). Yet his desire for more clothes, larger rooms, and vaster wealth than his peers clearly identifies him with the national ideal of progress. In *Public Opinion* (1922), Walter Lippmann wrote that the American stereotype of progress demanded that 'what is small shall be big, what is slow shall be fast, what is poor shall be rich, what is few shall be many; whatever is shall be more so'. He added: 'The ideal confuses excellence with size, happiness with speed, and human nature with contraption' (71–72). Anthony and Gloria, too, live at high speed in terms of their social life, and do everything on a grand scale: Gloria 'goes, goes, goes' (Fitzgerald 37), while Anthony chooses an apartment with 'immense' rooms and fills his wardrobe with 'sufficient linen for three men' (15). In the first year of marriage, they 'danced and splashed through a lavish spring' (160). In these ways, they proclaim their careless superiority to the despised realm of commerce, prices and profits. Yet the descriptions of their excessive consumption are couched in the language of advertising. In Anthony's bathroom, there is 'a rich rug, [...] a miracle of softness, that seemed almost to massage the wet foot emerging from the tub' (16), and the bath-tub is 'equipped with an ingenious bookholder' (15). Before getting into the bath, he watches himself in the mirror as he adopts 'an athletic posture like the tiger-skin man in the advertisement' (20). These passages demonstrate Anthony's susceptibility to commercial rhetoric, and subtly remind the reader that, notwithstanding his scholarly and romantic poses, his class position is 'founded sheerly on money' (10). Thus, his social status is fragile and contingent, and when old Adam Patch cuts his grandson out of his will, Anthony begins a gradual descent from leisured man-about-town to alcoholic, penniless bum. By the time the will has been successfully contested, he has lost his wits.

'An artist in living flesh': *Cold Comfort Farm*

Stella Gibbons's immensely successful first novel is set, as the title page announces, 'in the near future'. Its heroine, Flora Poste, loses both her parents at nineteen and unexpectedly finds herself without any income to speak of. Following a short stay in London with her rich and fashionable friend Mrs Smiling, she goes to live on a decaying Sussex farm with her cousins, the Starkadders, who are parodic representations of characters from the regional novels which were in vogue in the years following the First World War.[14] Flora's character is defined by sophistication: this is so clearly evident that the cover blurb for the most recent Penguin edition begins by introducing 'sensible, sophisticated Flora Poste'. However, this description has been applied retrospectively to Flora; the word which resonates through the actual text of *Cold Comfort Farm* is not 'sophisticated' but 'civilised'. For Gibbons, these are not synonymous terms, yet with hindsight, her use of 'civilised' seems intimately connected with the discourses of sophistication which were unfolding in the early twentieth century.

'Sophisticated' only appears once in the narrative: when Flora is waiting on the street of the small Sussex town of Beershorn, she notes 'the spectacle of the Majestic Cinema immediately opposite. It was showing a stupendous drama of sophisticated passion called "Other Wives' Sins"' (95). This mocking remark questions the Hollywood publicists' use of 'sophisticated' as a positive term. They intend to suggest fascinating intrigue and irresistible sexual attractiveness, but Flora reads over-complication, showiness and posturing. These are all things which she vigorously resists in her own life. Flora's interpretation of 'sophisticated' was by no means outdated in 1932, because at this point the term was still very much contested and ambiguous. She does not, though, acknowledge its more attractive meanings; instead she substitutes her own term, 'civilised', which she uses to suggest worldliness, self-control, style and distinction.

Gibbons's narrator negotiates in rather perplexing ways among several key terms: alongside 'civilised', she interrogates and destabilises 'normal', 'natural', 'eccentric' and 'conventional'. Flora's own value system, while presented as simple and straightforward, is in fact extremely difficult to pin down, and her class position also appears unfixed. Flora's sophistication, indeed, inheres largely in her ability to elude classification, to operate across a series of incompatible social worlds, and to interpret a range of clashing discourses and sociolects. The basic theme of *Cold Comfort Farm*, as Gibbons herself expressed it in an article in *Punch* in 1966, was that of 'a sane person rearranging into peace and harmony the lives of some dismal and mistaken people' ('Genesis' 578). As Lynne Truss remarks in her introduction to the 2006 edition of the novel, 'Flora is like Lewis Carroll's Alice, unintimidated by

14 On Gibbons's response to regional fiction, see Hammill, '*Cold Comfort Farm*'; Horner and Zlosnik.

people who talk nonsense, refusing to be drawn into their mad world' (ix). But Flora goes beyond Alice in her ability to engage with the nonsense-talkers on their own terms in order to achieve her aims. For example, when she wants to get her religious maniac cousin Amos out of the way of her schemes at Cold Comfort, she suggests that he go on a preaching tour:

> 'I mun till the field nearest my hand before I go into the hedges and by-ways,' retorted Amos, austerely. 'Besides, 'twould be exaltin' meself and puffin' meself up if I was to go preaching all over the country in one o' they Ford vans. 'Twould be thinkin' o' my own glory instead o' the glory o' the Lord.' [...]
>
> 'But, Cousin Amos, isn't that rather putting your own miserable soul before the glory of the Lord? I mean, what does it matter if you *do* puff yourself up a bit and lose your holy humility if a lot of sinners are converted by your preaching? You must be *prepared*, I think, to sin in order to save others. [...] By *seeming* to be humble, and dismissing the idea of making this tour, you are *in reality* setting more value on your soul than on the spreading of the word of the Lord.'
>
> She was proud of herself at the conclusion of this speech. It had, she thought, the proper over-subtle flavour, that air of triumphantly pointing out an undetected and perfectly enormous sin lying slap under the sinner's nose which distinguishes all speeches intended to lay bare the workings of the religious mind. (Gibbons, *Cold* 90)

Flora deliberately employs sophistical arguments in order to counter the warped self-absorption of Amos's brand of religion; this is one of the strategic forms her sophistication takes.

From Amos's religious mania to his wife Judith's incestuous desire for their son Seth, from Aunt Ada's pretended madness to Reuben's lustful possessiveness towards the land, the Starkadders are all, in different ways, manipulative, unhinged and bizarre. This aspect of *Cold Comfort Farm* comes under the heading of mock-pastoral, since it debunks the idea that 'naturalness' is to be found among simple country folk. Nothing about the Starkadders can be understood as natural; they are all, in some sense, perverse. It is doubtful, however, whether 'naturalness' is itself presented as desirable – it is certainly not what Flora is in quest of. Though she repeatedly expresses approval of what is 'normal', she defines this in terms, not of naturalness, but of restraint and propriety. Mrs Smiling and Flora share a dislike of mess, posturing, emotionalism, 'wayward human nature' and 'grossness' (11), though their responses to the problem are dissimilar. Mrs Smiling, when confronted with the unpleasant aspects of human nature, 'pretended things were not so' (11), whereas Flora actively tries to counteract the grossness which she comes upon. This impulse is not, as she explains, an altruistic one: 'On the whole, I dislike my fellow-beings. I find them so difficult to understand. But I have a tidy mind, and untidy lives irritate me. Also, they are uncivilized' (20). In tidying up the lives of those around her, Flora achieves a degree of agency, self-determination and influence which would have been extremely unusual for a young woman in 1930s' Britain, and her ambiguous position in relation to class and family structures permits, rather than hampering, her independence.

Flora's identity is provisionally upper-middle-class, though she also identifies with aspects of upper-class culture. Her parents were people of leisure who travelled continuously, leaving their daughter to board in expensive private schools, but they left no money for her maintenance after their deaths. Mrs Smiling, by contrast, appears to come from an underprivileged background, though she is now – at only twenty-six – the widow of a racketeer. Mrs Smiling, 'like all people who have been disagreeably poor and have now become deliciously rich, had never grown used to her money and was always [...] positively revelling in the thought of what a lot of it she had' (17). Her moral outlook differs from her friend's. When Flora announces that she means to live off her relatives, 'Mrs Smiling gave her a shocked glance of enquiry, for, though civilized in her tastes, she was a strong-minded and moral woman' (13). The suggestion here is that civilisation (or sophistication) is difficult to reconcile with conventional morality; while Mrs Smiling attempts an uneasy compromise between the two, Flora herself is wholly committed to the 'civilised'.

Mrs Smiling is shocked, once more, when Flora explains that after an interval of independence, she will marry 'somebody whom I shall choose'. She continues:

> 'I have always liked the sound of the phrase "a marriage has been arranged". And so it should be arranged! Is it not the most important step a mortal creature can take? I prefer the idea of arrangement to that other statement, that marriages are made in Heaven. [...]'
> Mrs Smiling shuddered at the compelling, the almost Gallic, cynicism of Flora's speech. For Mrs Smiling believed that marriages should arise naturally from the union of two loving natures, and that they should take place in churches, with all the usual paraphernalia and hugaboo; and so had her own marriage arisen and been celebrated. (14–15)

Mrs Smiling, it is implied, retains the prudish yet sentimental outlook of her upbringing, while Flora's sophistication maps in interesting ways onto her curious class identity. Flora endorses many of the outward trappings of the upper class, such as arranged marriages, yet by proposing to arrange her own marriage herself, she claims far more autonomy than an upper-class girl of her era would be entitled to. Mrs Smiling sees this sophisticated position as perverse, and indeed, there is an important connection between sophistication and perversion, as Litvak points out:

> The class politics of sophistication are inseparable from its sexual politics. While

personal testimonies furnish ample proof that sophistication excites and frightens as much as, say, sexual perversion excites and frightens, a glance at the dictionary is all it takes to recall that *sophistication* in fact *means* 'perversion'. For though *sophistication* might nowadays be defined most readily as 'worldliness', as the opposite of 'naïveté', its older meaning, as well as its normative meaning, deriving from the rhetorical aberration known as sophistry, is 'corruption' or 'adulteration', and its opposite would be something like *naturalness*, which, if etymologically related to *naïveté*, enjoys a considerably better press. (4)

I have already suggested that the Starkadders are perverse. It seems strange that the same word may be applied to Flora, since her ordered, calm approach to life is continually contrasted with the Starkadders' disorderly, melodramatic emotionalism. Yet she is indeed perverse as they are perverse, because, like them, she resists assimilation into the normative structures of English middle-class life.

The social atomisation of early twentieth-century Britain was visible not only in the removal of nuclear families into individual suburban houses, but also in the proliferation of small flats for single women.[15] Mrs Smiling wants her friend to 'learn typing and shorthand, and then you can be somebody's secretary and have a nice little flat of your own' (Gibbons, *Cold* 14). Flora, however, is horrified by this vision of lower-middle-class clerkliness. She plans, instead, to retain her leisure by living with relations. Mrs Smiling, in her turn, considers this plan '*degrading*' (19), an opinion which suggests a distinctly middle-class ethos of self-reliance. Arriving at Cold Comfort Farm, Flora takes her place in a Victorian-style extended family structure, complete with servants. It fascinates her, and yet she works to dismantle it, because she cannot achieve power through this structure when she is not at its centre. The family revolves around Aunt Ada Doom, and Flora attacks Aunt Ada's consolidated power by picking off the individual family members who have previously been subservient to her. She sends Amos off on a preaching tour of America, Judith into therapy, and Seth to Hollywood, and marries off most of the remaining cousins. It only remains for Flora to transform Aunt Ada into an aviatrix dressed 'from head to foot in the smartest flying kit of black leather' (220) before she can leave the tidied-up farm herself. She then enters an apparently conventional marriage to Charles Fairford, yet there are peculiarities even here: Charles is her cousin, and this was a basis for marriage which the nineteenth century approved, as guaranteeing purity of blood, but which the twentieth century, with a better understanding of genetics, tended to reject. Also, in Gibbons's sequel, *Conference at Cold Comfort Farm* (1949), it is revealed that Flora has five children: again,

15 On the move to the suburbs, see Giles; Hapgood. On housing for single women, see Parsons 110–12; Vicinus 295.

the family structure she chooses has more in common with Victorian than 1930s' norms. She does not become a middle-class suburban wife, but more of a matriarch.

Despite all this, one important aspect of Flora's character does seem to align her with middle-class taste, and that is her preference for tidiness. In his *Theory of the Leisure Class*, Veblen explains that middle-class men who cannot afford to be gentlemen of leisure demonstrate their status by having their wives perform their leisure and consumption vicariously:

> The leisure rendered by the wife in such cases is, of course, not a simple manifestation of idleness or indolence. It almost invariably occurs disguised under some form of work or household duties or social amenities, which prove on analysis to serve little or no ulterior end beyond showing that she does not occupy herself with anything that is gainful or that is of substantial use. [...] Not that the results of her attention to household matters, of a decorative and mundificatory character, are not pleasing to the sense of men trained in middle-class proprieties; but the taste to which these effects of household adornment and tidiness appeal is a taste which has been formed under the selective guidance of a canon of propriety that demands just these evidences of wasted effort. The effects are pleasing to us chiefly because we have been taught to find them pleasing. (57–58)

As Veblen demonstrates, while the wife's performance of leisure indicated a clear nostalgia for a feudal social structure, it rapidly became a middle-class convention. On the surface, Flora conforms to this role: her desire for tidiness certainly determines the way she relates to her domestic environment. At one point, she spends a whole afternoon arranging her books, and at another, she insists on having her bedroom curtains washed, and feels an affinity with the visiting housekeeper, Mrs Beetle, because she 'seemed to perceive (however dimly) that curtains must be washed and life generally tidied up before anyone could begin to think of enjoying it' (Gibbons, *Cold* 71). Flora also engages in another staple activity of the socially aspirant housewife: pointless decorative needlework. On closer inspection, though, this practice appears to be a decoy. She does it while waiting for members of the Starkadder family to come into the kitchen, so that she can induce them to adopt the unfamiliar habit of taking afternoon tea. She is making a petticoat, but when Seth asks her what it is, she realises 'that he hoped it was a pair of knickers', and therefore replies 'that it was an afternoon tea-cloth' (82). The sewing is in fact part of the exaggerated performance of civilised domesticity which she puts on for the benefit of her uncouth cousins. It fits with the uncomprehending innocence she feigns when Seth talks to her about sex. In reality, she has heard his kind of conversation before 'at parties in Bloomsbury as well as in drawing-rooms in Cheltenham' and is 'merely a little bored by it all' (82). Flora, then, acts out the role of a nice middle-class girl in order to achieve her own ends, but her concealed knowingness marks her out as a sophisticate.

The underlying meaning of her preference for tidiness emerges in her remarks about Jane Austen: "'If you ask me,' continued Flora, "I think I have much in common with Miss Austen. She liked everything to be tidy and pleasant and comfortable about her, and so do I'" (19). As Avril Horner and Sue Zlosnik note, Flora is 'intent on resurrecting Austenian values in a world prey to the degeneracy of late Romanticism and clichéd Gothic' (168). This suggests that the kind of sophistication which Flora embraces is narrative sophistication, and not 'sophisticated passion' (Gibbons, Cold 95). As the author-within-the text, she is inspired by Austen when working out the 'plots' she will use to manipulate her characters (that is, her relatives). For example, one evening she is trying to work out a plan for luring Aunt Ada out from the room where she has spent many years pretending to be an invalid, and yet ruling the house. Flora 'opened Mansfield Park, at random, to refresh her spirits' and reads a line containing a reference to Fanny. Suddenly, a flash of inspiration comes to her, and immediately she has a clear plan in her head:

> Calmly, she detached a leaf from her pocketbook and wrote the following telegram:
> 'Hart Harris,
>   'Chauncey Grove,
>   Chiswick Mall.
> 'Please send at once latest number vogue also prospectus hotel miramar paris and very important photographs fanny ward love Flora.' (207)

Here, Austenian narrative sophistication suddenly gives way, through a connection which may be a little less 'random' than it seems,[16] to a much more flamboyant stylishness. Flora's telegram, its address demonstrating her intimacy with the English social elite (represented by the aristocratic Claud Hart Harris),[17] also points towards the contemporary, unashamedly commercial sophistication of high fashion, luxury, glamour and celebrity.

The novel repeatedly presents the hoarding of wealth as vulgar, while carefree expenditure on luxury can be sophisticated. Deliberately rejecting the

---

16 It is not simply that the name 'Fanny' reminds her of the actress Fanny Ward. In Mansfield Park, the maiden name of Fanny Price's mother is Fanny Ward. This may alert us to a deeper connection: Mansfield Park is the only one of Austen's novels to be explicitly concerned with the moral dimensions of luxury and expenditure, and it is arguably also (as I suggested in Chapter 1) intensely preoccupied with sophistication.

17 Chiswick Mall contained houses built by the earls (later dukes) of Bedford in the seventeenth century, and eighteenth-century Chiswick attracted numerous noble residents as well as artists and scholars. In the twentieth century, its working-class population expanded rapidly, but Gibbons refigures the geography of London in Cold Comfort Farm, reflecting imagined shifts in fashion which may have taken place by this point in the future: Lambeth is now stylish and Mayfair contains slums.

cautious economic practices of the working girl, Flora, after announcing her intention to live off her relatives, proposes to Mrs Smiling: 'I think we ought to dine out tonight – don't you? – to celebrate the inauguration of my career as a parasite. I have ten pounds and I will take you to the New River Club – angelic place!' (15). Later in the novel, Flora visits the New River Club again on a brief trip from Sussex up to London, and the narrator describes it further:

> It was the most haughty club in London. No one with an income of more than seven hundred and forty pounds a year might join. Its members were limited to a hundred and twenty. Each member must be nominated by a family with sixteen quarterings. No member might be divorced [...]. The Selection Committee was composed of seven of the wildest, proudest, most talented men and women in Europe. The club combined the austerities of a monastic order with the tender peace of the home. (145)

There is much of interest here. This club is ridiculously exclusive (as were the leading gentlemen's clubs of interwar London), but it is exclusive in a complicated way. The upper income limit would exclude *nouveau riche* capitalists and favour the English aristocrats who, by the 1930s, had generally fallen on hard times. This class bias is reinforced by the heraldic term 'quarterings': sixteen quarterings meant eight pairs of noble ancestors in the male and female lines. In gender terms, however, the club is improbably *in*clusive, and it also emphasises exceptional talent as much as impeccable pedigree (a rather subversive suggestion). In Gibbons's slightly futuristic London, the New River Club represents a form of sophistication which combines nostalgia for a disappearing social order with extreme modernity.

Flora's frequenting of the New River Club confirms her elite social status, and she 'designs' her cousin Elfine in order that she, too, may gain entry into this environment. In London, she takes her to a society hairdresser, Monsieur Viol, and a famous dressmaker, Monsieur Solide, who 'had dressed Flora for the last two years' (144). Frenchness is a repeated note in the definition of Flora's style and preferences, from her supposedly 'Gallic' cynicism to her favourite author (the fictional Abbé Faussemaigre) and artist (Marie Laurencin), and even her choice of the Hotel Miramar as Aunt Ada's destination. As in many other British texts from a whole range of periods, Frenchness becomes a code for sophistication. But rather than making Elfine over entirely in her own cosmopolitan, modern image, Flora chooses a 'look' for her cousin which combines a classical purity with a peculiarly English style of innocence: 'She must learn to be serious about horses. [...] She must learn to be long-limbed and clear-eyed and inhibited' (130). In London, Flora realises that she has succeeded:

> She had made Elfine look groomed and normal, yet had preserved in her personality a suggestion of cool, smoothly-blowing winds and of pine-trees and the smell

of wild flowers. She had conceived just such a change, and M. Viol and M. Solide, her instruments, had carried it out. An artist in living flesh could ask for no more. (146–47)

Since 'naturalness', as Litvak points out, is one of the possible opposite terms of sophistication, it is clear that Flora wants her reinvented Elfine to avoid excessive sophistication. After all, she is going to marry into the 'hunting gentry', who, as Flora notes, are 'slow on the uptake' (112, 128). Flora foresees that her protégée's life will be 'one of exquisite, sunny natural content. She would bear children and found a line of pleasant, ordinary English people who were blazing with poetry in their secret souls' (162). Though only two years older than her cousin, Flora acts as her guide and chaperone, and her attitude towards Elfine is, in the terms of pastoral, clearly that of the complex person towards the simple one. This is epitomised at the Hawk-Monitors' ball: 'Flora knew that she did not look so beautiful as Elfine, but, then, she did not want to. She knew that she looked distinguished, elegant and interesting. She asked for nothing more' (159). To refer back to Empson's account of pastoral, Flora recognises Elfine as in one way better than herself, and in another way, not so good.

Pastoral – and, more obviously, mock-pastoral – are crucial elements of *Cold Comfort Farm*, and are sometimes used in unexpected ways. The novel, of course, ridicules the clichés and untruths of literature about rural life – as Wendy Parkins argues, 'The force of the parody in *Cold Comfort Farm* lies in its awareness that representations of the "unspoiled" countryside found in regional novels were simply a deliberate exclusion of new social relations and practices that bound the country and the city' (87). The presence of the modern in supposedly backward rural Sussex is visible in Seth's addiction to the cinema, Amos's attraction to American styles of evangelism, and Mrs Beetle's plan to train up the four illegitimate children of her daughter Meriam into 'one of them jazz bands' which earn good money 'playin'' up West in night clubs' (Gibbons, *Cold* 72). But *Cold Comfort Farm* simultaneously evinces a serious appreciation of landscape and country pleasures, especially in the descriptions of Flora's solitary walks, and Gibbons exhibits real skill in landscape description. The novel's ambivalent attitude to the countryside is epitomised in the closing chapters describing Elfine's wedding, which present an idyllic pastoral vision, yet one which is counterpointed with comedy and invaded by urban modernity:

Midsummer Day dawned with a thick grey haze in the air and a heavy dew on the meadows and trees.

Down among the little gardens of the still-sleeping cottages of Howling an idyllic procession might have been observed making its way from flower-bed to flower-bed, like ravaging bees. It was none other than the three members of Mrs Beetle's embryo jazz-band, shepherded by the patriarchal form of Agony Beetle himself.

They had been commissioned to pick the bunches of flowers which were to decorate the church and the refreshment-tables up at the farm. A lorry load of pink and white rose-peonies, from Covent Garden, had already been discharged at the gates of the farm. (212)

The supplementation of home-grown flowers with London imports correlates with Howling's general openness to metropolitan culture, which arrives not only in the form of cinema and jazz, but also in the human shapes of Flora and Mr Mybug, a writer from Bloomsbury. Raymond Williams found in *Cold Comfort Farm* 'a suburban uneasiness, a tension of attraction and repulsion' towards the countryside, and concluded: 'what has to be said about that odd work is not easy' (*Country* 253). I have argued elsewhere that the novel is indeed suburban in terms of its point of view, its balancing between urban modernity and pastoral, between the conventional and the ex-centric (*Women, Celebrity* 167–78). But the text of the novel rigorously excludes suburban styles in order to enhance the stark opposition between the ultra-sophisticated central London milieu of the early chapters and the improbably primitive way of life at Cold Comfort.

The only characters who are dispatched to suburbia are the execrable Urk Starkadder and his new wife, a former servant. Urk and Meriam announce at the end of the novel that they 'would be honoured if Miss Poste would come to tea at "Bywaies", the villa which Urk had bought out of his savings from the water-vole trade' (Gibbons, *Cold* 227). This class-based hostility to the imitative gentility of the suburb belongs entirely to Flora, and does not coincide with Stella Gibbons's more complex, and largely sympathetic, view of the suburb. Unlike her heroine, Gibbons was firmly middle-class, and most of her later books are set in the North London suburbs, where she lived all her life. In novels such as *Miss Linsey and Pa* (1936), *My American* (1939), and *The Bachelor* (1944), Gibbons examines London and its environs, balancing an alternative or ex-centric perspective on interwar and wartime modernity with a continued investment in pastoral visions of England.[18] These fictions, like *Cold Comfort Farm*, upset hierarchies of class and disrupt dualities between intellectual and bourgeois; urban and rural; progressive and primitive; highbrow and lowbrow. In this sense, Gibbons reinvents the suburb as a crucial site for the development of a sophisticated middlebrow aesthetic, and *Cold Comfort Farm* anticipates these texts in its covert use of a suburban point of view.

---

18 See Hammill, 'Stella Gibbons'.

'A wicked feeling of sophistication': *Miss Pettigrew Lives for a Day*

Persephone Books, a London publishing company set up in 1999, 'revives books overlooked by the feminist publishing houses of the 1980s and 1990s because of their domestic slant' (Beauman 185) and each year republishes eight novels and non-fiction books from the early and middle twentieth century. Among their discoveries is Winifred Watson's *Miss Pettigrew Lives for a Day*, a comic yet subtle Cinderella story. Well received on first publication in 1938, *Miss Pettigrew* sold well in the UK and US and was also translated into French, but later fell into complete obscurity. In 2000, Persephone rescued it, and with such success that it not only became their top-selling title but was even made into a film in 2008, starring Frances McDormand.[19] The novel's plot concerns an impoverished, diffident forty-year-old governess, Guinevere Pettigrew, who – on applying for a new post – is sent to the wrong address and encounters a glamorous nightclub singer, Delysia LaFosse, with whom she spends an eventful day. Using common sense and quick thinking to rescue Miss LaFosse and her friend Edythe DuBarry from several fixes involving various young men, Miss Pettigrew earns their admiration and respect. Miss DuBarry, a beautician, gives her a makeover, and all three attend a party and later a night-club, where Miss Pettigrew intervenes to ensure that both her new friends become engaged to the right men. With her new clothes and hairstyle, and under the influence of the kindness and good humour she meets with, Miss Pettigrew acquires an increased confidence and social ease, even though she is continually surprised or confused by the modern ideas and forms of behaviour which she encounters.

Watson's first two novels were *Fell Top* (1935), which capitalised on the then-fashionable genre of the melodramatic rural novel, and *Odd Shoes* (1936), a historical story set in Victorian Newcastle. Henrietta Twycross-Martin, the only critic to have published anything on Watson to date, explains in her informative introduction to the Persephone edition of *Miss Pettigrew* that

> when presented with the draft version of *Miss Pettigrew Lives for a Day*, Methuen's readers were taken aback: what they wanted was more of the same, 'women's fiction' with passionate goings-on in rural settings of yore, not a West-End fantasy featuring a governess, a night-club singer, cocaine, cocktails and comedy. [...] Nothing in Winifred Watson's previous books could have prepared the Methuen readers for this change of direction, and what astonishes is the sheer fun, the light-heartedness

---

19 The novel was due to be filmed in 1939, when Watson sold the rights to Universal, but it was never produced. The 2008 film, by Focus Features and directed by Bharat Nalluri, starred Ciaran Hinds, Amy Adams and Lee Pace alongside McDormand. It follows the novel's plot reasonably closely, but is set a year later, as war was beginning. It turns Edythe into a villain and makes her Joe's lover, and has Miss Pettigrew abandoned at the end when Delysia and Nick board a ship to New York, though she is soon rescued by Joe.

and enchanting fantasy of an hour-by-hour plot that feels closer to a Fred Astaire film than anything else [...]. Sophisticated and naïve by turns, *Miss Pettigrew Lives for a Day* is also charmingly daring. (ix)

This last point must be disputed. It is not the *novel* which is naive and sophisticated by turns – it is the heroine. The novel is saturated with sophistication, and it is this, in fact, which constitutes its daring quality, and which shocked the Methuen readers.

'Sophistication' is a key word in *Miss Pettigrew Lives for a Day*, and occurs nine times over the course of a fairly short narrative. It encapsulates a range of qualities, particularly worldly wisdom, a refusal to be shocked, a stylish appearance, and easy, confident manners. Miss Pettigrew's outward transformation demonstrates, once again, that sophistication is not so much an innate quality as something which can be learned, practised and performed. Even before her initiation into the new world, she could already recognise and define sophistication, since she had spent so much time at the cinema. Repeatedly, she selects the word to name the manners, styles and images which she encounters in the company of Miss LaFosse. For instance, one of Delysia's lovers, Nick, resembles the seductive villain of innumerable Hollywood films and romance novels, and Miss Pettigrew observes his 'beautiful, cruel mouth, above which a small black moustache gave him a look of sophistication and a subtle air of degeneracy that had its own appeal' (27). Similarly, when she is talking with Delysia and Edythe, Miss Pettigrew thinks:

> And how they talked! She had never heard the like before. Their ridiculous inconsequence. Every sentence was like a heady cocktail. The whole flavour of the remarks gave her a wicked feeling of sophistication. And the way she kept her end up! No one would ever dream she was new to it. (70)

Talking with Delysia, Edythe and Nick, Miss Pettigrew feels as if she has been translated onto the set of a film. In the earlier scenes, she makes a faint effort to resist this: when another of Delysia's young men says to her, 'OK, sister. You win. I'll scram', she thinks 'severely' that this style of talking results from 'the contaminating effect [...] of too many cheap American films' (14). But a few minutes later, she herself remarks: 'You've said it, baby', adding that she has always longed 'to use slang. To let myself *go*' (24). This novel is, indeed, fantasy in that it suggests that the life represented by Hollywood can actually be lived out: watching Delysia with Nick, Miss Pettigrew reflects: 'And I *always* thought they exaggerated kisses on the films' (26). (The filmic quality of Winifred Watson's narrative, and its explicit preoccupation with cinema, meant that it translated well onto the screen, but the film is actually much less self-conscious about cinematic conventions than the novel is.)

Miss Pettigrew lets herself go to a considerable extent over the course of the day. First thing in the morning, on witnessing Delysia in the arms of Phil, who is just leaving after spending the night, 'Miss Pettigrew's virgin mind strove wildly for adjustment' (14). By the evening, she is herself being kissed in a taxi by a man named Joe, and responding with enthusiasm. Miss Pettigrew starts to acquire a degree of sexual sophistication by discarding her identity as a lady, that is, as someone who cannot accept gifts of jewellery or allow herself to be kissed. 'I find it much pleasanter not to be a lady,' she tells Joe. 'I have been one all my life. And what have I to show for it? Nothing. I have ceased to be one' (207). The tension between ladylike and sophisticated behaviour emerges repeatedly in the text. Miss Pettigrew observes at several points – though with decreasing levels of actual disapproval – that her new friend's rooms and habits are not those of a lady. On asking Miss LaFosse whether 'so much make-up is, well, lady-like' (163), she is told a story about the only time Miss LaFosse attempted ladylike behaviour, leaving off her lipstick and not showing her legs. The purpose was to try to ensnare a lord, but she had no success, and the lord in question married 'a bitch of a woman, all lipstick, legs and lust' (164). 'I learned my lesson', comments Miss LaFosse, and Miss Pettigrew does too: 'I see [...] there are many points to learn in collecting a husband. My ignorance is abysmal' (165).

Her attitude to marriage is radically altered as the narrative develops:

> 'A woman's got to look out for these men,' said Miss LaFosse darkly. 'If you don't you'll find yourself before the altar before you know where you are, and then where are you?'

Bang went all Miss Pettigrew's cherished beliefs: scattered her naïve imaginings that only the men dreaded the altar: gone forever her former unsophisticated outlook. 'I've lived too secluded a life,' thought Miss Pettigrew. 'I've not appreciated how my own sex has advanced. It's time I realized it.' (23–24)

Yet Miss Pettigrew actually proves to have a good deal of worldly wisdom, even though up until now it has been purely theoretical, derived largely from films and popular novels. She is able to advise Delysia intelligently about stratagems in relation to men, suggesting that of her three admirers, she select as a husband the one who is kind but also firm and courageous: Michael. By the close of the novel, although still committed to marriage as an ideal, Miss Pettigrew has entirely reconceptualised it. Seeing that neither Delysia nor Michael is meant for quiet domesticity, and that their marriage therefore won't entail settling down, she tells them: 'Once [...] I belonged to the settling-down brigade. It was my highest ideal of married bliss. But to-day I have learned a lot' (222). It is clear that Michael, though very manly, is not at all old-fashioned, and will be happy for his wife to continue with her singing career. As Twycross-Martin notes in an encyclopedia entry on Watson's novels: 'These optimistic books demonstrate a genial open-mindedness about sexual matters and a strong awareness that women may need careers as much as marriage' ('Watson' 268).

Miss Pettigrew and Miss LaFosse are constantly redefined against one another, with the balance of wisdom and sophistication shifting between them. Each, at times, takes on the childlike role. Miss Pettigrew realises that her new friend sometimes needs protecting: 'This lovely child looked to her to act' (Watson 11), and she rises to the occasion, preventing Delysia from allowing dangerous Nick the upper hand, and herself ejecting him from the flat by means of an effective imitation of the bombastic style of a former employer, Mrs Brummegan. At one point, Delysia says that if she could choose her own mother, she would choose someone like Miss Pettigrew. But in another episode, Miss Pettigrew, revealing her innocence in matters of relations between men and women, is indulged by the younger woman: 'There was the loveliest twinkle in Miss LaFosse's eyes, kindly, affectionate, but she veiled it discreetly. She wouldn't have hurt Miss Pettigrew for worlds' (35). Indeed, Miss Pettigrew repeatedly appears a child in an adult world, observing and trying to learn. When Miss DuBarry is mixing a cocktail, 'Miss Pettigrew watched her with veiled concentration' (70), and when Nick and Delysia are becoming amorous on the sofa, Miss Pettigrew 'sat up and began to take quite an interest in the technique' (33). As the day goes on, she adds considerably to the stock of knowledge she had already derived either from films or from her observation of the higher classes in the households of her employers.

Miss Pettigrew's secret familiarity with sophistication is at first concealed by her dowdy appearance and nervous manner, but in difficult situations, she can simulate it:

> 'I will take,' said Miss Pettigrew, with calmness, with ease, with assurance, 'a little dry sherry, if you please.'
> She considered the 'dry' the perfect touch. Not Sherry. Anyone could say that. 'Dry sherry.' That showed poise, sophistication, the experienced palate. It raised her prestige. She had no idea what the dry meant, but she remembered distinctly the husband of her last situation but one, who had always terrified her by his booming irritation, cursing this 'damned dry sherry' and she was quite sure that what he didn't like, she would. (34)

The counterpointing of internal discourse with outward behaviour is Winifred Watson's strategy for emphasising the performative nature of sophistication. Her heroine is often at a complete loss to understand what is happening around her, but retains her 'prestige' by boldly engaging in conversations 'without the faintest idea of what they were talking about' (69). She has entered a kind of wonderland, in which the ordinary rules of life seem to be suspended. It is apt, therefore, that Delysia, obliged to introduce her as-yet unknown visitor to Nick, chooses a name at random and says 'this is my friend Alice' (28). Carroll's Alice, too, uses words she does not understand, such as 'latitude' and 'longitude', in order to impress. And, like Alice, Miss Pettigrew finds herself physically transformed. Her new image succeeds because she does not try to remould herself in the image of Delysia LaFosse, who is at least fifteen years her junior. She borrows Delysia's clothes, but chooses carefully: in a move which demonstrates her latent sophistication, she selects elegant black velvet as opposed to the showy green and gold brocade which is initially offered. She also retains a commonsensical attitude even at romantic moments: during her episode with Joe in the taxi, they agree that woollen underwear is much better than silk for winter wear, and she concludes: 'They obviously had important tastes in common' (206). Her sensible bourgeois upbringing even gives her a touch of attractive eccentricity at times, such as when she and Edythe are clinking glasses: '"Mud in your eyes," said Miss DuBarry. Miss Pettigrew knew no happy rejoinders, so made one up. "Wash and brush up," said Miss Pettigrew' (71)

In acquiring an elegant, relatively restrained sophistication, Miss Pettigrew takes a different line from Delysia, who inclines to the kind of sophistication which is associated with excess. Not only does she have three lovers, but her personal style is also excessive. Edythe comments: 'If you weren't the kind of woman who can wear anything and look right, Delysia, you'd have no taste in clothes at all' (94), while Michael asks: 'My God, Delysia, who the devil furnished this room, it's like the seduction scene in *From Chorus Girl to Duchess*' (143). She retorts that she chose it herself, and he comments that her taste is deplorable. Yet since excess is, in some ways, very compatible with sophistication, I would argue that Miss LaFosse's apartment is an important dimension of her coding as sophisticated. In her living room,

> [b]rilliant cushions ornamented more brilliant chairs and chesterfield. A deep, velvety carpet of strange, futuristic design, decorated the floor. Gorgeous, breathtaking curtains draped the windows. On the walls hung pictures not ... not quite decent, decided Miss Pettigrew. Ornaments of every colour and shape adorned mantelpiece, table and stands. Nothing matched anything else. Everything was of an exotic brilliance that took away the breath. (4)

When Miss Pettigrew advances to the bedroom, she discovers that it is 'in great disorder. Cowebby stockings of various shades strewed the floor. Underwear, masses of silk and lace, hung out of drawers and draped chair-backs. Frocks were tossed on the bed' (59). The brilliance and disorder of the apartment directly contrasts with the respectable middle-class ideal of tidiness and conventional taste. In her untidiness, her movement among a variety of social circles (including those which would generally be deemed 'vulgar'), and her unashamed revelling in luxury, Miss LaFosse is distinguished in every possible way from the average middle-class woman. Her innate distinction and strong erotic appeal enable her to ignore the ordinary dictates of Good Taste.

Under the influence of Delysia and her circle, Miss Pettigrew, while preserving a rather more modest, orderly style of dress and behaviour, nevertheless rejects her repressively genteel upbringing and embraces the pleasurable possibilities which her parents always prohibited. Stealing a look at Joe in the taxi, she reflects:

> Big, bluff, hearty, a hint he could be a little brutal maybe, but also kind and considerate. He was not a gentleman. Her mother would have been shocked by him. [...] She was lowering her dignity as a well-bred gentlewoman in accepting his attentions, but she had sunk so low in one short day she simply didn't care whether he was vulgar or not. [...] She was quite shamelessly happy. (203–204)

The abandonment of shame takes place gradually over the course of the story. At the start, Miss Pettigrew is painfully conscious of her dowdy clothes and plain appearance, 'flushe[s] a painful red' (28) when the alluring Nick turns his gaze on her, and is 'petrified' when Edythe surveys her with her beautician's eye (72). She is also repeatedly shocked by Miss LaFosse's unrestrained behaviour with men. In the earlier part of the text, Miss Pettigrew imitates the sophisticated style she has witnessed without fully internalising the values which go with it. She continues to object to unladylike behaviour, and to suggest, though with rapidly decreasing conviction, that 'the path of virtue' (161) is the best one. But although the text does reveal that it is possible to perform sophistication without really embracing modern ideas about sexuality and pleasure, the situation has changed by the end of the story. Miss Pettigrew's approach to life has been fundamentally altered by her day with her new friends, and on the last page, she proclaims 'I have cast out fear. I am a new woman' (234). Her next question to Miss LaFosse is, 'Do you like me?' (234), and the positive response confirms that it is the way Miss Pettigrew has been treated throughout the day which has altered her. The friendliness, trust and admiration she has encountered have worked the transformation from a nervous, anxious, ineffectual woman to an increasingly confident and even charming one. This, then, complicates the earlier emphasis on the performativity of sophistication, so that the novel as a whole defines sophistication as a combination of innate and learned qualities, and as something which is forged through relationships and interaction.

'Frankly, we shall not try to interest everybody': *Vanity Fair* 1913–36

Early twentieth-century magazines are often categorised as either 'little' (avant-garde and modernist periodicals) or mass-market (large-circulation magazines publishing fiction, entertainment news, gossip, fashion features and so forth). But in between there was another group for which it is harder to find a label. In America, such magazines included *The Smart Set*, *Vanity Fair*, *The New Yorker*, *The American Mercury* and *Esquire*. Described collectively by Sharon Hamilton as 'American humor magazines with serious literary pretensions' (101), by George H. Douglas as 'smart' (1), and in other contexts as 'quality' or 'slick', these periodicals were influential taste-makers, and crucial to the circulation of discourses of sophistication in the period from the 1910s to the 1930s. Among the various editors of these periodicals, those most consistently associated with sophistication were Frank Crowninshield, editor of *Vanity Fair*, and H. L. Mencken and George Jean Nathan, co-editors of *The Smart Set* and subsequently of *The American Mercury*. While these magazines all eventually died, leaving the field to *The New Yorker*, edited by Harold Ross, their cultural influence in the early decades of the century was considerable. An analysis of the careers and reputations of editors such as Mencken and Crowninshield clearly reveals one of the paradoxes of modern sophistication: they were viewed as taste-makers for the nation, yet their preferences were defined in opposition to those of Americans in the mass. Critics who have written about Mencken and his contemporaries have tended to get tangled up in this apparent contradiction. Douglas, for instance, argues:

> As the decade of the 1920s dawned, the influence of the *Smart Set* and its two editors was stronger than ever. [...] America was ready, it seemed, for the very sorts of things Mencken and Nathan had been dishing out for years [... and] their charming and ever-amusing magazine seemed so perfectly suited to this confident and uproarious decade. [...] Circulation still lagged and income continued to be disappointing, but the two editors were relishing the rewards [...] of their literary power and celebrity. (86)

This passage inadvertently reveals that America was *not* ready for *The Smart Set*. The magazine may 'seem' to us to have been 'perfectly suited' to 1920s' America, but as the limited circulation and unprofitability prove, it appealed to an audience which was by definition a minority one. *The Smart Set* coincides, not with some mythical spirit which united American society in the 1920s, but with the version of the twenties which we like to remember. Indeed, Mencken and Nathan's power came much more from their celebrity status, from their visibility in the mainstream media (as opposed to in the smart magazines themselves) than from their actual writing. People read about them much more than they read them.[20]

The sophisticated New York magazines explicitly addressed a minority readership. An early advert for Condé Nast's *Vanity Fair*, which for its first four issues (September to December 1913) was titled *Dress & Vanity Fair*,[21] read:

> Our ambition is not towards a popular magazine with a big subscription list. We don't expect everybody to be interested in 'Dress & Vanity Fair', and, frankly, we shall not try to interest everybody. On the other hand, there are, we believe, a great number of people, who will thoroughly enjoy the cleverness, the variety, the dash and appreciate the fastidiousness and luxuriousness that shall in time make 'Dress & Vanity Fair' the most distinctive among all American magazines.[22]

There is a clear echo here of *The Smart Set*'s slogan, 'a magazine of cleverness' (although this word, as David Earle notes, was already becoming 'derogatory in the mouths of modernists' [23]). But *Vanity Fair* was more successful than *The Smart Set* in capitalising on its supposed selectness, and negotiating the tension (visible in the advertisement just quoted) between a rhetorical appeal to a discerning minority and the practical imperative to make a profit by selling copies to 'a great number of people'. Although *Vanity Fair* pretends to be exclusively addressing an already sophisticated metropolitan elite, it actually offers an education in sophistication designed for those who aspired towards membership of that elite. A 1918 advert promised that

> *Vanity Fair* binds between the covers of a single magazine, the table-talk of a dinner party – at which cosmopolitan, well-bred, cultivated people discuss the news of their varied world – its arts, sports, letters, operas, theatres, dances, music, fashions, humor and gaieties. [...] If you are a forward-minded American – and want to keep up with all the new movements of our day – and enjoy the work of our younger and more amusing writers and artists, you should read *Vanity Fair*.[23]

Thus, despite the magazine's reiterated suggestion that qualities of style and distinction are natural and inherent, its cross-class appeal actually depends on the assumption that such sophistication can be *learned*.

Nast was not entirely satisfied with his new magazine, and sought advice from the man of letters and champion of modernism Frank Crowninshield. In January 1914, Crowninshield took over as editor, and he continued until the magazine folded in 1936. Dropping 'Dress' from the title, he made *Vanity Fair* a far more culturally rich magazine than had been originally intended, while

---

20 See Earle, chapter 1, on *The Smart Set*'s relation to the contemporary magazine scene; see Leick on the reporting of the contents of 'smart' and 'little' magazines in the daily press.
21 Nast had recently purchased two New York magazines: *Dress*, a potential rival for his *Vogue*, and a gossipy, commercialised theatre weekly, *Vanity Fair*, because he wanted the rights to the title.
22 *Vogue* 42.7 (1 October 1913): 16.
23 *Vanity Fair* 10.7 (September 1918): 9.

retaining Nast's emphasis on high-quality photography. Seeking to consolidate its authority in the sphere of taste, *Vanity Fair* policed the boundaries of its supposedly select readership, occasionally publishing articles in foreign languages (usually French) or difficult modernist poems, and engaging frequently with experimental art. Thus the magazine invited serious attention to modernism and simultaneously flattered readers by implying that they were intelligent enough not to be intimidated by such material.

Vanity Fair was a very significant outlet for avant-garde art and literature, and introduced the American public to dozens of the writers and artists whose work now forms the modernist canon. Crowninshield and his various managing and literary editors – among the most influential of whom were Edmund Wilson and Robert Benchley – accepted contributions by authors including Jean Cocteau, Djuna Barnes, Gertrude Stein and D. H. Lawrence, and reproduced or photographed artwork by Pablo Picasso, Constantin Brancusi, Jacob Epstein, Frida Kahlo, Tamara de Lempicka and Georgia O'Keeffe. Images were commissioned from experimental photographers such as Man Ray and the Photo-Secessionists Baron de Meyer and Arnold Genthe, and from artists such as Fortunato Depero and Marie Laurencin. The design of the magazine drew on Surrealism, Vorticism, Futurism and Dada, and subsequently on Art Deco (see Murphy, 'One Hundred'). At the same time, the magazine was an important conduit of the expanding culture of celebrity in interwar America, and it printed many portraits and star profiles, together with a regular 'Hall of Fame' gallery celebrating achievement in the arts, entertainment and public life. There is a fascinating dynamic between the magazine's sustained attention to the stars of popular culture and its apparently contrary commitment to disseminating experimental art. I would suggest that the interactions between modernist and celebrity systems of value in the pages of *Vanity Fair* can be made intelligible through analysis of its organising framework of sophistication. The sophisticated reading position which the magazine constructs for its audience disrupts conventional cultural hierarchies because it is defined, on the one hand, by knowledge about modernists and confidence in speaking of them, and on the other, by a refusal to set modernists apart from other kinds of celebrities or to separate their work from other forms of cultural production.[24]

Lawrence Rainey suggests that *Vanity Fair*'s publication of modernist texts represented a commodification of 'the works of a literature whose ideological premises were bitterly inimical towards its ethos and cultural operations' (91), while Michael Murphy describes the magazine as 'a piece of market-driven mass culture' ('One Hundred' 68) and Mark Morrisson classes it with the *Ladies' Home Journal* and *Cosmopolitan* as a 'mass market magazine' (176).

24 For more on *Vanity Fair*'s relation to modernism, see Hammill, 'Sophistication'.

These critics maintain a fairly rigid division between 'little' and 'mass market', allowing no category to intervene between them. Therefore, they can only characterise *Vanity Fair* as an oddity; Morrisson, for instance, writes: 'one mass market magazine that made an exceptional effort to support modernist art and literature [was] Frank Crowninshield's *Vanity Fair*' (205). But all these judgements are based on a dualistic model of high and low culture which fails to acknowledge the middle ground: that is, the range of cultural production which lay between the experimental and the popular, and engaged with both. The books and periodicals falling into this range relate to the literary market-place in particularly complex ways, and indeed, *Vanity Fair* was never straight-forwardly a product of the market economy, even though it was launched as a sister magazine to Nast's profitable *Vogue*. Crowninshield's showcasing of modernism put off conservative readers, raised production costs, and entailed distinct commercial risks. For instance, several regular advertisers protested when he reproduced paintings by Van Gogh, Matisse and Picasso, which they termed 'decadent and distorted' (Bradlee 11). Despite advertising revenues of around $500,000 a year, very few issues of *Vanity Fair* (which was priced at 35 cents) actually made a profit. Circulation was always somewhat restricted, varying between about 86,000 and 99,000, and the magazine was expensive to produce.[25] But, as Terence Pepper notes, 'Nast's attachment to the title placed editorial excellence above all else and he was able to subsidize its high produc-tion values due to the financial success of his other periodicals' (19).

Vanity Fair, then, provided a middle space, located between the author-centred production model of the avant-garde magazines and the market-driven arena of the daily papers and mass-circulation weeklies. It addresses a reader who is literate in both high and popular culture, and who possesses or aspires to possess wit, discriminating tastes, style, and current knowl-edge. In the early twentieth century, the term 'sophistication' functioned as a shorthand for these qualities. But the more complex resonances revealed by the etymology of 'sophistication' are also relevant here. Litvak proposes that 'the distinction between snobbery and distinction [... is] precarious: natural-ized or not, *sophistication* – which means adulteration or denaturing before it means refinement – is by definition pseudo' (62). Anxieties about this 'pseudo' quality surface in *Vanity Fair* in various forms, and are particularly visible in its satiric features and cartoons, which often mocked intellectual posturing or fashionable bohemian slumming.[26] The ambivalence of the term 'sophistica-

25 On circulation, see Hamilton 26; Peterson 271. Leick says of *Vanity Fair* 'the many discussions and reprints of its (uncopyrighted) articles in the daily press accounted for many more readers' (Leick 129).

26 There are many examples of these. See for instance the witty cartoons by 'Fish' (Anne Harriet Fish), often captioned by Dorothy Parker or by Crowninshield, which epitomise *Vanity Fair*'s occasional

tion' also corresponds to the magazine's ambivalent positioning in relation to the marketplace, and the idea of fraudulent mixing of commodities may seem to be (implicitly) invoked by those critics who object to the proximity of film stars and experimental poets in *Vanity Fair*'s pages.[27]

This proximity is particularly visible in the 'Hall of Fame' features, which juxtaposed modernist artists, writers and musicians with popular culture celebrities. Among the experimental artists who appeared were Rachmaninov and Yeats (1920), Proust (1923), Picasso, Mann, Diaghilev and Hemingway (1928), Woolf and Strachey (1929), Klee and Hindemith (1930), Joyce (1931), Stravinsky and Shostakovich (1935). The pictures in these features were accompanied by captions indicating the subjects' newsworthiness and describing their careers over the longer term. Reasons for nominations to the Hall of Fame ranged from commercial, artistic or political success through aristocratic descent to wit, charm and glamour. Murphy remarks on *Vanity Fair*'s 'especially skillful appraisal of and traffic in the celebrity values of the most important "bohemian" figures, photographed stylishly by serious "art" photographers' ('One Hundred' 62). The magazine laid claim to highbrow culture by assuming its readers' familiarity with the key figures of modernism and bohemia. At the same time, the Halls of Fame make meaning through diversity; Jaffe remarks that the similar spreads in British *Vogue* represent a 'gallery of mixed worthies knowingly juxtaposing the elite and the popular', and point to 'the kind of qualified re-integration of high and low forms first undertaken by Gilbert Seldes' (237 n. 2). This sort of celebrity-watching was deliberately eclectic, advocating a generous understanding of culture and beauty which could at once value the elegance of Greta Garbo, the popular appeal of Pearl Buck, and the stylistic innovation of James Joyce.

Vanity Fair's eclecticism was, however, combined with an emphasis on discrimination. While stars from Gertrude Lawrence to Gertrude Stein earn inclusion in the Hall of Fame because they are widely discussed and admired, nevertheless the detailed captions suggest that their true value will only be understood by sophisticated elites. For example, Clara Bow, star of the 1927 film *It*, is permanently associated with an elusive quality, 'it', which is usually identified with sex appeal. Some might mistake 'it' for 'sophistication', but not *Vanity Fair*. Far from seeing Bow's appeal as inimitable, they described her, in the caption to a 1928 photograph, as representative of 'the *genus* American

---

scepticism about the modernist celebrity. Fish reduces the stars of bohemia to a series of 'types'. For more detail on Fish, Parker and their satire of pseudo-sophistication, see Hammill, *Women, Celebrity* 37–39.

27 Bishop, for instance, noting that Eliot considered three possible venues for the American publication of *The Waste Land*, remarks: 'in *Vanity Fair*, *The Waste Land* would have been next to pictures of movie stars; in *The Little Review*, in good company but isolated from the mainstream' (311).

girl, refined, washed, manicured, pedicured, permanent-waved and exalted herewith'. She is also referred to as 'the little lady prancing and dancing', and the clichéd style of her autobiography is ridiculed. In contrast to Clara Bow's rather infantile charms, *Vanity Fair* presents the nightclub hostess Texas Guinan (also featured in 1928) as a true original, with a 'genius' for words: 'She sits atop the piano in a kind of savage Parcae glory, maintaining an unceasing and genuinely funny running comment, keeping everything going'.[28] According to *Vanity Fair*, Guinan's unpretentious brand of sophistication attracts 'those who know they're wise and those who are willing to get wise', while Bow's appeal is far more general:

> Ladies, and gentlemen (not to mention children): regard, observe and otherwise behold [...] the vivacious, the audacious, the orchidaceous Clara Bow! Feast your weary optics upon this super-flapper of them all – the hyper-reality and extra-ideality of a million or more film goers.[29]

The inclusion of the Bow portrait brings *Vanity Fair* into momentary alignment with movie fan magazines, even as the sarcastic caption, with its parodic citation of Hollywood promotional discourses, seeks to distance the magazine from mass-market celebrity.

While pandering to public interest in the famous, *Vanity Fair* nevertheless maintained a certain scepticism towards the modern celebrity system. The 'Hall of Fame' was occasionally replaced by a 'Hall of Oblivion', nominating people who should be quickly forgotten, and many features and stories lampooned would-be stars or analysed cultures of publicity.[30] Crownin-shield also encouraged satire of the excesses of modernists and their imitators, and this scepticism is crucial to the pose of sophistication which *Vanity Fair* constructed for itself and its readers. Many modernists were named in its high-profile 1923 symposium on 'The Ten Dullest Authors', in which widely read journalists and authors such as H. L. Mencken, Edna Ferber and George Jean Nathan challenge the dominance of modernist aesthetics by repeatedly selecting Lawrence, Stein, Whitman and Proust among their nominations for 'the Most Unreadable of the World's Great Writers'. In addition, *Vanity Fair* printed numerous parodies of the very modernist writers whose work it had previously published (see Leick). The parodies compromise modernist cultural authority, but simultaneously contribute to the fame of elite artists by citing the recognisable conventions of their work. They interpellate an audience already familiar with avant-garde texts, flattering readers by implying that they are too sophisticated to be intimidated by experimental writing, but that

28 Parcae: Roman goddesses of fate.
29 Portraits reprinted in Amory and Bradlee 153 (Bow) and 142 (Guinan).
30 For two among many examples, see Ross; Wells.

they can also recognize the *over*-sophistication (speciousness, obscurity) of certain highbrow postures.

Vanity Fair – like modernism itself – continually marketed itself in terms of novelty and making new: one advert characterised it as a 'forward-marching magazine', while another ran: 'We promise you, solemnly, that *Vanity Fair* is not just one more magazine; or even a new magazine of an old kind – but an ALTOGETHER NEW KIND OF MAGAZINE. It is an entertaining magazine for Moderns'.[31] The rhetorical modernness of *Vanity Fair*, *The Smart Set* and others is, though, interestingly balanced against their endemic nostalgia. *Vanity Fair*, of course, shares its name with a novel set in the eighteenth century, and was openly modelled on the British *Sketch* and *Tatler*, sharing their visual appeal and elite atmosphere.[32] The *Tatler* took its name from Richard Steele's paper, set up in 1709 to report on gossip heard in the London coffeehouses, and both papers were fascinated by the British aristocracy, and by the disappearing world of entitlement, leisure and ritual which they embodied. Crowninshield was fond of evoking the atmosphere of Georgian and Regency London: for instance, he ran features on characters such as Beau Brummell and David Garrick, and referred often to characters, styles and etiquette from this era. His conception of sophistication was a very well-mannered one, as Anita Loos noted in the first volume of her autobiography:

> Crownie's magazine, together with *Smart Set*, had an enormously civilizing effect on the United States; but while Mencken's policy was to boot our native land into an awareness of culture, Crownie's was to lead us there with a gentle, properly gloved hand. (145)

Crowninshield's repeated evocation of a lost age appears to contradict *Vanity Fair*'s claim to be a harbinger of the new, yet I would suggest that the logic of sophistication actually depends on a continual negotiation between an impulse towards novelty and a contrary longing for a past era of elegance and intellectual polish. This approach is epitomised by contributors such as Noël Coward, who combined the ultra-modern, brittle style of the twenties with a nostalgic vision of aristocratic English life. P. G. Wodehouse, a regular contributor, similarly offers access to a rose-tinted country-house world, complete with witty butlers and dotty or dastardly lords.

Of course, the aristocratic way of life retained a precarious existence in England itself during the interwar years, but for American readers of *Vanity*

31 *Vanity Fair* 10.7 (September 1918): 9; and 5.5 (January 1916): 11.
32 'In London alone there are seventeen papers like the "Sketch" and the "Tatler". In America there is not one. [...] It is along the lines of these English publications that we have planned "Dress & Vanity Fair".' Advert in *Vogue* 42.7 (1 Oct. 1913): 16. The London illustrated weekly *Vanity Fair*, which folded in February 1914, was also an influence.

Fair (and, indeed, for middle-class readers everywhere) it was pure fantasy. Its appeal derives partly from the fact that its elite is small and membership cannot usually be achieved through the mechanisms of the marketplace. Frank Crowninshield repeatedly published texts which celebrated upper-class manners, houses and lifestyles, and with these gestures of his 'properly gloved hand', he partially concealed the economic basis of his operation and disguised the primarily middle-class identity of his readership. This was essential because, as Litvak explains in his discussion of Thackeray's *Vanity Fair*,

> [it] is customary to see Thackeray as an emblematic figure in the process whereby the Victorian gentleman displaces the Regency dandy as an arbiter of taste. But, once the ambitious, endemically imitative middle class buys into sophistication as a cultural value, as both a means and an index of social success, the arbiter of taste risks becoming [...] redundant. Or, as *Time* magazine lamented in the title of the 8 August 1994 cover story, 'Everybody's Hip (and That's Not Cool)'. (62)

Similarly, generalised, or mass, sophistication would put the smart magazines out of business, and thus editors such as Crowninshield often retreat defensively into an imagined feudal England where sophistication was only available to a tiny elite.

Balanced against *Vanity Fair*'s fascination with Englishness is its growing emphasis on New York as a centre of urbanity and style. Reviews and features began to focus increasingly on the New York cultural and social scene. A promotional text written by Dorothy Parker describes the magazine as a 'whole course of study in the art of being a New Yorker' and 'a Who's Who in New York'. The advertisement is in the form of a story about a soldier who has returned from the war to find that 'change was all about him'. He can no longer find his way about or recognise the current celebrities: 'It seems as if wisps of hay were sticking out of my hair. If I could just get a good working knowledge of the places to go and the people who go there!' he exclaims (D. P.). Parker's copy promises that *Vanity Fair* will teach similarly bewildered readers to navigate the public and social spaces of New York successfully.

Harold Ross's *The New Yorker*, founded in 1925, also made a major contribution to the development of a distinctively urbane Manhattan sensibility during the interwar years, even though many of the staff were actually provincials and did not have access to the more privileged clubs and social sets of New York. In his book on the history of the magazine, Ben Yagoda observes: '*The New Yorker* was sophistication in the form of a weekly magazine,' explaining: 'It was knowing, a trifle world-weary, prone to self-consciousness and irony, scornful of conventional wisdom or morality, resistant to enthusiasm or wholehearted commitment of any kind, and incapable of being shocked' (57). The word 'sophistication' resonates throughout Yagoda's book, and in fact, through the whole history of the magazine itself, which was launched with a prospectus in which Ross wrote:

> It will not be what is commonly called radical or highbrow. It will be what is commonly called sophisticated, in that it will assume a reasonable degree of enlightenment on the part of its readers. [...] The *New Yorker* will be the magazine which is not edited for the old lady in Dubuque. [...] the *New Yorker* is a magazine avowedly published for a metropolitan audience and thereby will escape an influence which hampers most national publications. It expects a considerable national circulation, but this will come from persons who have a metropolitan interest.[33]

'Sophisticated' here is equated, first, with a rejection of everything provincial (that is, everything represented by the old lady from Dubuque, who would be frequently referred to in the text of *New Yorker* articles)[34] and second with 'enlightenment'. 'Note the wearied distaste behind "what is commonly called sophisticated"', observes Jessica Burstein, adding: 'Not far behind is the cloaked presumption that *The New Yorker*'s audience won't be entirely ready for it; only a "reasonable degree of enlightenment" will be expected' (238). In order to clarify what 'enlightenment' meant to city intellectuals around this time, it is useful to turn to H. L. Mencken. One of his regular features in *The American Mercury*, 'Americana', consisted of unintentionally funny extracts from regional newspapers, each headed with a sardonic introduction. For example:

> ALABAMA
> Final triumph of Calvinism in Alabama, October 6, 1923
> Birmingham's exclusive clubs – and all other kinds – will be as blue hereafter as city and State laws can make them. Commissioner of Safety W. C. Bloe issued an order today that Sunday golf, billiards and *dominoes* be stopped, beginning tomorrow. ('Americana' 48)

When the 'Americana' features from 1925 were reprinted in book form, Mencken's introduction explained that their purpose was 'to make the enlightened minority of Americans familiar, by documentary evidence, with what is going on in the minds of the masses – the great herd of undifferentiated good-humored, goose-stepping, superstitious, sentimental, credulous, striving, romantic American people' (Mencken v–vi). Mencken's series of opposite terms for enlightenment might also serve as a definition of unsophistication.

Both *The New Yorker* and *The American Mercury* are important to the development of the sophisticated aesthetic in magazine publishing, yet it is *Vanity*

---

33 Harold Ross, Prospectus for *The New Yorker*. *The New Yorker* Records, 1924, Box 1, Manuscripts and Archives Division, The New York Public Library. Typescript pages 1, 3. Quoted in Burstein 238.
34 On the significance of the old lady from Dubuque, see Burstein. She suggests that 'the relation of Dubuque to the city is analogous to the relationship of sentimentalism to modernity' (243).

Fair which is most perfectly representative of early twentieth-century sophistication. *The American Mercury* was unillustrated, politically oriented and very American-centred, explicitly rejecting the European emphases of its competitors.[35] Mencken's concern with sophistication extended only to its intellectual aspects. *The New Yorker*, though rather more cosmopolitan than the *Mercury*, remained anchored in the New York context. It combined current affairs coverage with arts reviews, and was illustrated only with cartoons and drawings. But *Vanity Fair* strongly emphasised transatlantic cultural exchange and also visual style and self-fashioning, and was sumptuously illustrated with photographs, sketches and even paintings. As Pepper writes, *Vanity Fair*'s 'informative, sophisticated and sometimes irreverent pages [...] set the standard for the "smart" magazines of the era' (18–19). In its middlebrow cultural eclecticism, its combination of nostalgia and modernity, and its preoccupation with urbanity, *Vanity Fair* played a defining role in the elaboration and mediation of early twentieth-century sophistication.

35 The first editorial explains the editors' intention to stress 'American ideas, American problems and American personalities' (Mencken and Nathan).

4

Nostalgia, glamour and excess: the postwar decades

In 1950, T. H. White wrote at the beginning of *The Age of Scandal*: 'Well, we have lived to see the end of civilization in England. I was once a gentleman myself' (9). He goes on, with a mixture of archness and conviction, to measure the modern age against an idealised past:

> I believe that the peak of British culture was reached in the latter years of George II: that the rot began to set in with the 'Romantics': that the apparent prosperity of Victoria's reign was autumnal, not vernal: and that now we are done for. [...] I have written this book in the effort to give one last, loving, and living picture of an aristocratic civilization which we shall never see again. (11)

White suggests that the glory of the British Age of Scandal (the 1770s and 1780s) might elude the representational conventions of modern popular culture. 'As for their women,' he writes, 'in contrast to the dowdy blue-stockings who consorted with the poets of the nineteenth century, the beauties who were the contemporaries of Walpole lived through romances of such intricacy and splendour that Hollywood in delirium would scarcely do them justice' (139). Indeed, the late eighteenth century represents, for White, an escape from the popular:

> It was inevitably an age of intimacy and of nicknames. [...] It was because the people were aristocrats. The gossips lived in a small society which scarcely touched the middle classes of Wesley, nor the peasantry, nor the Mob. Literature had for the first time since Elizabeth become the medium instead of the plaything of the gentry. They moved in the tight world of the Drawing-rooms and of the Birthdays, knew each other as well as the boys at a public school in England might know each other today, chatted about the latest scandal, and, because they had learned to be literate, they wrote it down. (18)

In this representation, the social elite of England coincides with its intellectual elite, and this doubly privileged set of people live in an atmosphere of luxury. It is hardly surprising that, in the context of austerity Britain, this vision was suggestive of Hollywood fantasy. In 1950, 'intellectuals' had long since become identified with university academics rather than social elites, and many British aristocrats had been discredited by their involvement (or rumoured involvement) with appeasement and Nazi collaboration. Political power was no longer connected with inherited wealth, and global capitalism was already the dominant force.

White's mythologisation of the Age of Scandal exemplifies a broader postwar lament for the loss of aristocratic sensibilities, manners, entitlement and distinction. This is the nostalgia of a democratic age. Books and films which adopt or explore this attitude evoke periods ranging from the Renaissance to the 1930s, though the eighteenth century seems to have an especial appeal as it escapes the earnestness of the Victorian age but is modern enough to be reasonably accessible to late twentieth-century minds. This chapter focuses on the 1950s and 1960s in order to form a complement to Chapter Three. Comparisons have always been drawn between the post-First World War and post-Second World War periods, in terms of politics, economics and consumerism, and culture.[1] The important point for the purposes of my discussion, though, is that both periods exhibited nostalgia for the lost social structures of aristocracy and leisure. The early twentieth century was nostalgic for the eighteenth century;[2] the 1950s and 1960s were nostalgic for both the 'peak' of aristocratic culture in the eighteenth and nineteenth centuries and for its last days in the interwar years.[3]

1   Discussion of such similarities is beyond the scope of this study, but obvious examples in the American context, for instance, include the economic growth and consumerism that marked both the twenties and the fifties; the two Red Scares; and parallels between the Lost Generation and the Beat Generation.

2   As Chapter Three suggested, this nostalgia was legible in *Vanity Fair* magazine; it is further evident in such varied contexts as Coward's comedy *The Marquise* (1927), set in 1730s' France; Cleone Knox's *The Diary of a Young Lady of Fashion in the Year 1764–1765* (1925), which was believed on first publication to be a real diary; the dress designs of Jeanne Lanvin (sometimes including imitation panniers); the drawing style of fashion illustrators such as Robert Bonfils (see Blackman 46, 47, 55); the 1920s' revival of Chinoiserie, which had been popular in eighteenth-century France and England; or the earlier phases of Art Deco, described by Bevis Hillier as '[the] feminine, somewhat conservative style of 1925, chic, elegant, depending on exquisite craftsmanship and harking back to the eighteenth century' (9).

3   Following the Second World War, the 1920s and 1930s were reconstructed by Hollywood for international audiences as an era of glamour, hedonism and jollity – *Singin' in the Rain* (1952), *Auntie Mame* (1958), *Some Like It Hot* (1959), *A House is Not a Home* (1964), *Thoroughly Modern Millie* (1967) and so on. European films sometimes represented the interwar years in images of decay: *Indifferenti* (*Time of Indifference*, 1964) dramatises the disintegration of a rich Italian family in the twenties. In literary texts, and especially autobiographies, though, the era was presented as one of high sophistication. The Left Bank society of the twenties was extensively memorialised: Morley Callaghan's

In this chapter, then, the theme of nostalgia culminates. I suggested in Chapter Three that the interwar years might be seen as the Age of Sophistication: this would imply that by the fifties and sixties, sophistication was already beginning to be associated as much with history as with modernity. Indeed, many postwar representations of sophistication are melancholic in tone and pervaded with images of degeneration, and this is certainly true of the three novels I discuss below. I begin with Françoise Sagan's *Bonjour Tristesse* (1954), which centres on an amoral teenager, Cécile, and her world-weary, hedonistic father Raymond. Reprising elements of earlier novels by Laclos and Colette, *Bonjour Tristesse* created something of a scandal because both the eighteen-year-old author and the seventeen-year-old heroine seemed too sophisticated for their years. The slightly precocious sexuality of Sagan's heroine is, though, hardly shocking in comparison to the extremely premature sexual experience of Dolores Haze in Vladimir Nabokov's *Lolita* (1955), my second text. The child, 'Lolita', is appropriated into – and literally sophisticated by – the parodic thriller scripts of Clare Quilty's plays and plots, the highly literary, intensely self-conscious written confession of her adoptive father, Humbert Humbert, and the consumerist fantasies of American popular culture. In my third section, I consider Giuseppe di Lampedusa's *Il Gattopardo* (*The Leopard*, 1958), which is set mainly in 1860s' Sicily. Lampedusa's hero, the Prince of Salina, a figure of high breeding, cultivation and wisdom, represents the last of his kind; his nephew Tancredi is a transitional figure; while his young grandson has replaced aristocratic sophistication with mere middle-class worldliness. The fourth book included in this chapter, Genevieve Antoine Dariaux's handbook of chic, *A Guide to Elegance* (1964), while not so explicitly preoccupied with cultural decline, is an intensely nostalgic text, and encodes into its recommendations on dress a whole conservative ideology of class, sexuality and gender. Yet while Dariaux insistently evokes a disappearing world of feminine leisure, her vision of elegance as simultaneously modern and timeless closely matches the notion of sophistication current in later twentieth-century culture.

Although only *Lolita*, among my four chosen books, could be considered for Susan Sontag's canon of camp, her comments are nevertheless relevant here: 'Aristocracy is a position vis-à-vis culture (as well as vis-à-vis power) [...]. For the aristocratic posture with relation to culture cannot die, though it may persist only in increasingly arbitrary and ingenious ways' (290–91). All four

---

That Summer in Paris was published in 1963; Ernest Hemingway's A Moveable Feast appeared posthumously the following year; and John Glassco eventually found a publisher for his Memoirs of Montparnasse in 1970. Hollywood memoirs proliferated also; they included Anita Loos's A Girl Like I (1966), Colleen Moore's Silent Star (1968) and Lillian Gish's Lillian Gish: The Movies, Mr Griffith and Me in 1969. One of the outstanding English memoirs of the era is Jessica Mitford's Hons and Rebels (1960).

of the texts discussed in this chapter are deliberately anachronistic in their privileging of a leisured lifestyle, and their rejection of the modern emphasis on effort and endeavour, profit and progress. In addition, aristocratic cultural values are embraced directly in Lampedusa's lament for the disappearing way of life of the Sicilian nobility, and rather mockingly in Humbert Humbert's fantasy of himself as a degenerate aristocrat – 'youngish but sickly, [...] maybe a viscount' (273).[4] Sophistication, in these texts, is cultivated through a concentration on the aesthetic and the erotic, on style and sensuality, to the exclusion of more practical or materialistic preoccupations.

None of the three novels offers unmediated access to a perspective outside the sophisticated. There are no innocent, naive or childlike narrators or protagonists in these books, and any critiques of the sophisticated worldview (such as that offered by Father Pirrone in *The Leopard* or Cyril in *Bonjour Tristesse*) are contained within, and subordinated to, the sophisticated narrative. At the same time, all three exhibit nostalgia for the lost innocence of a past which is located before the start of the story. Sagan's Cécile sadly remembers the time before sadness, when she emerged carefree from her convent school and knew nothing of the coming complications of sex, jealousy and death. Humbert Humbert continually remembers his lost childhood sweetheart, Annabel, comparing his pure and equal erotic relation to her with his corrupt, coercive, relation to her substitute, Lolita. The Prince of Salina, compelled to engage with the forces of modernity which are invading Sicily, is nostalgic for a pre-modern era of true nobility and political stability, an 'old world' (Lampedusa, *Leopard* 124) which disappeared during his youth. In all these texts, the value of what has been lost is increased by the contrast with the violence of the present: the wars in *The Leopard*, the death of Raymond's fiancée in *Bonjour Tristesse* and the violation of Lolita as well as the melodramatic death of her lover Quilty. Violence, in the three novels, brings out the persistent theme of cultural degeneration, and intensifies nostalgia for a purer past.

Scholarship on nostalgia from a range of disciplines has consistently linked it to social transformation. George Steiner has suggested that the decline in religious faith generates 'nostalgia for the absolute', a phrase he used as the title of his 1974 Massey Lectures, later published as a book. From a sociological point of view, Fred Davis understands nostalgia as a 'restitutive link' (36) by which groups and individuals can preserve their identities in the face of displacement, urbanisation or demographic change. Susan Stewart in *On Longing* (1984) refers to 'the social disease of nostalgia' (23), and her study is especially relevant because she focuses on narrative:

4 Even *A Guide to Elegance* closes with a rather ostentatious list of acknowledgements, including names such as 'Comtesse de Gramont', 'Vicomtesse de Ribes' and so on (223).

> By the narrative process of nostalgic reconstruction the present is denied and the past takes on an authenticity of being, an authenticity which, ironically, it can only achieve through narrative.
>
> Nostalgia is a sadness without an object, a sadness which creates a longing that of necessity is inauthentic because it does not take part in lived experience. Rather, it remains behind and before that experience. Nostalgia, like any form of narrative, is always ideological: the past it seeks has never existed except as narrative, and hence, always absent, the past continually threatens to reproduce itself as a felt lack. (23)

Irony, a rhetorical trope which often structures narratives of sophistication, is frequently found in conjunction with nostalgia in a contemporary context. Linda Hutcheon writes:

> Our contemporary culture is indeed nostalgic; some parts of it – postmodern parts – are aware of the risks and lures of nostalgia, and seek to expose those through irony. Given irony's conjunction of the said and the unsaid – in other words, its inability to free itself from the discourse it contests – there is no way for these cultural modes to escape a certain complicity, to separate themselves artificially from the culture of which they are a part. (206)

She suggests that irony is particularly compatible with nostalgia because just as nostalgia consists of a 'structural doubling-up of two different times, an inadequate present and an idealized past', so 'irony too is doubled: two meanings, the "said" and the "unsaid" rub together to create irony' (198).[5]

As Hutcheon's comments imply, the politics of nostalgia are not necessarily straightforwardly conservative. Numerous critics have developed typologies of nostalgia which differentiate between, for instance, 'restorative nostalgia' which aims to reconstruct and preserve, and 'reflective nostalgia', a more playful version which evolves new patterns from 'shattered fragments of memory' (Boym 41, 49). In an alternative model, 'simple nostalgia', the belief that things were better in the past, may be distinguished from 'second-order or reflexive nostalgia', which involves the critical analysis of versions of history, while 'third-order or interpreted nostalgia' leads to a questioning of the meaning of nostalgic emotion (Davis 27, 21, 24). Certainly, the encounter between nostalgia and sophistication in the books discussed in this chapter leads to an intense self-consciousness about the origins and effects of longing for the past.

It is also possible to separate directly experienced nostalgia for a personal past from shared longing for a cultural past, such as an era of perceived greatness or the lost homeland of displaced generations of ancestors. Forms of nostalgia based on nationalism, the pride of an embattled class, or an

---

5   On irony and postmodernism, see also David Kolb's *Postmodern Sophistications: Philosophy, Architecture, and Tradition*, 36–50. This book, in addition, relates postmodern theory and design to the traditions of Sophist thought (see especially 130–45).

immigrant consciousness are legible in *The Leopard* and *Lolita*. Indeed, the international focus of the selection of texts in this chapter is intended to counterbalance the Anglo-Saxon emphasis elsewhere in the book. In previous chapters, I discussed Anglo-American perceptions of the French as arbiters of style, and noted the way in which cosmopolitanism may operate as a marker of sophistication. Here, I take a different approach, exploring a range of inter-national perspectives on sophistication by comparing two French authors with an Italian and a Russian-American. The bilingual Dariaux writes in English in order to purvey French chic to British and American readers; Sagan, by contrast, wrote in French, but since her novels were almost immediately translated into English, she rapidly became an icon of French sophistication for Anglophone audiences. Lampedusa's novel is, in many ways, specific to the context of 1860s' Sicily, yet it also resonates more broadly with historical narratives of the decline of aristocratic power and the rise of the middle classes across Europe. In *Lolita*, as Thomas Frosch notes, the 'central structural figure is displacement, or incongruity'. He continues:

> Often cultural or geographical incongruity appears in such local details as Charlotte's calling her patio a 'piazza' and speaking French with an American accent; but more generally it appears in Humbert's Old World, European manner – aristocratic, starchy, and genteel – set in a brassy America of motels and movie magazines and in his formal, elegant style of speaking posed against Lolita's slang. But Humbert is not only out of place, he is also out of time, since he is still pursuing the ghost of that long-lost summer with Annabel. (45–46)

Frosch nicely captures the connections between nostalgia and displacement, as well the link between cosmopolitanism and alienation.

This chapter, like the preceding ones, explores the different words used to name sophistication and related concepts. However, my focus on the evolution of the English word 'sophistication' is necessarily reduced here because I am working with one novel in French and one Italian novel in translation.[6] There is an Italian word 'sofisticatezza', roughly equivalent to 'sophistication' in the sense of 'elegance', but it is not widely used and does not appear in the original text of *Il Gattopardo*. The untranslatability of the word into a French context is explained by Litvak in his discussion of Proust:

> Yet, for all that Proust represents 'sophistication', the closest thing to an equivalent term in his text, *la mondanité*, or worldliness (in French, unlike English, *sophistication* retains the negative meaning of 'adulteration'), acquires an almost equally negative charge. [...] (Why is it, by the way, that, if you can't really say *sophistication* in French, you can't really say *naïveté* in English? *Problème à resoudre*.) (78)

---

6 *The Leopard* has been very widely read in its English version, so that the translation may be consid-ered an influential text in its own right.

Sagan, therefore, does not use 'sophistication' either. Dariaux, writing in English, does use it occasionally, but she prefers the French term 'chic'. My discussion of *A Guide To Elegance* considers the relationship between these two concepts, while the section on Lampedusa picks up on Litvak's distinction between worldliness and sophistication, and the reading of *Bonjour Tristesse* begins by considering the French word 'ennui'.

'A charming little monster': *Bonjour Tristesse*

'Sur ce sentiment inconnu dont l'ennui, la douceur m'obsèdent, j'hésite à apposer le nom, le beau nom grave de tristesse' (Sagan 9).[7] This is the opening of Françoise Sagan's *Bonjour Tristesse*, and it has been described as 'a vintage Sagan sentence' (Pace). In the English translation by Irene Ash, it is rendered as: 'A strange melancholy pervades me, to which I hesitate to give the grave and beautiful name of sorrow' (9). This creates rather a different effect. First, 'tristesse' is more usually translated as 'sadness', whereas 'sorrow' would be 'chagrin'. It is sadness which is the defining note of Sagan's narrative; the weightiness of sorrow is far beyond the experience of her irresponsible characters, and the mood of the story is not one of grief. Rather, it intersperses melancholy with joyousness, and dwells as much upon beauty and desire as upon loss. The French sentence also includes three ideas which are missing from the English version: obsession, sweetness and boredom. All these are much more compatible with sadness than with sorrow. 'L'ennui', indeed, is a little more subtle than 'boredom': it includes a suggestion of world-weariness, and is therefore often associated with sophistication. Its rather untranslatable quality accounts for its occasional usage in English texts or discourses.

The narrator of *Bonjour Tristesse*, Cécile, is seventeen, just a year younger than Sagan was when the novel was published, and she recounts the events of the past summer, which permanently changed her. The French version of Sagan's opening sentence evokes the mysterious, indefinable quality of the new feeling which the narrator experiences ('ce sentiment inconnu'); even 'tristesse', she says, does not quite capture her rather shameful combination of 'l'ennui, le regret, plus rarement le remords' (9). Actually, the change in Cécile might be best described using Sherwood Anderson's phrase 'the sadness of sophistication'. For the preceding two years, Cécile has shared a carefree, unregulated and amoral lifestyle with her father, Raymond, a widower with a string of mistresses. She discovers that this way of living is under threat, because

7 For quotations in French, the equivalent passage from the English translation is given in a footnote. Therefore, my bracketed page references refer to the French edition of *Bonjour Tristesse* for quotations in the main text and to the English edition for quotations in the footnotes.

her father has abandoned his latest, youthful mistress, Elsa, in favour of the mature, intelligent and poised Anne, whom he decides to marry. During the fateful summer, spent at a seaside villa, Cécile takes her first lover, Cyril, and subsequently manipulates him, as well as her father, Elsa, and Anne, in order to prevent the projected marriage. She succeeds, but the unintended result is that Anne, distraught at having witnessed her fiancé kissing Elsa in the woods, instantly leaves the villa to return to Paris. On the way she drives off the road and is killed.

Before they learn of her death, Cécile and her father, full of remorse, have begun composing a letter begging her to return and telling her that they love and need her. But afterwards, they return to their former hedonistic ways and both take new lovers: 'La vie recommença comme avant, comme il était prévu qu'elle recommencerait' (126).[8] The only difference is that sometimes Cécile wakes in the night and remembers Anne. The novel concludes by describing these solitary retrospections:

> ma mémoire parfois me trahit: l'été revient et tous ses souvenirs. Anne, Anne! Je répète ce nom très bas et très longtemps dans le noir. Quelque chose monte alors en moi que j'accueille par son nom, les yeux fermés: Bonjour Tristesse. (127)[9]

Cécile may acquire the sadness of sophistication (or perhaps the sophistication of sadness) during the summer when she is seventeen, but it almost seems as though she was never innocent. She recounts that two years earlier, on leaving the convent where she was educated, she had discovered the nature of her father's lifestyle, but was undismayed, since she found his ways entirely congenial: 'Mais bientôt sa séduction, cette vie nouvelle et facile, mes dispositions m'y amenèrent' (9–10).[10] Her father is sophisticated in the sense of ignoring bourgeois morality – 'Il refusait systématiquement les notions de fidélité, de gravité, d'engagement' (15) – and also in that he is frivolous, lively and yet easily bored: 'C'était un homme léger, habile en affaires, toujours curieux et vite lassé [...] généreux, gai' (10). Although lazy and somewhat passive, Cécile and her father are by no means unintelligent, and while they are both content to associate with the attractive but rather dim Elsa, they are more strongly attracted by the intellectual Anne.

Anne, possessed of 'l'ironie, l'aisance, l'autorité' (19), embodies a cultured, orderly sophistication, quite different from the frivolous, sensual kind which belongs to Cécile and her father. In the juxtaposition of these two versions, the

---

8   'Life began to take its old course, as it was bound to' (108).
9   'my memory betrays me: that summer returns to me with all its memories. Anne, Anne, I repeat over and over again softly in the darkness. Then something rises in me that I welcome by its name, with closed eyes: Bonjour tristesse!' (108)
10 'his charm, my new easy life, and my own disposition led me to accept it [his lifestyle]' (9).

scope and complexity of the idea of sophistication can be seen. Cécile admires Anne's taste and poise, and remembers that while paying her a visit two years previously, she had rapidly learned to dress tastefully and live elegantly:

> En une semaine, elle m'avait habillée avec goût et appris à vivre. J'en avais conçu pour elle une admiration passionnée qu'elle avait habilement détournée sur un jeune homme de son entourage. Je lui devais donc mes premières élégances et mes premières amours et lui en avais beaucoup de reconnaissance. A quarante-deux ans, c'était une femme très séduisante, très recherchée, avec un beau visage orgueilleux et las, indifférent. (13)[11]

At times, Anne seems so opposite to Cécile and her father that it is difficult to see how all three might be described using the same term, sophistication. Yet the fact that they are all, though in different ways, sophisticates explains the attraction which they have for one another. They each resist the sentimentality and moral platitudes of an unreflective mainstream culture, and they each appreciate fine food, wine, clothes and other luxuries. Their mutual attraction is, however, mingled with distrust:

> elle fréquentait des gens fins, intelligents, discrets, et nous des gens bruyants, assoiffés, auxquels mon père demandait simplement d'être beaux ou drôles. Je crois qu'elle nous méprisait un peu, mon père et moi, pour notre parti pris d'amusements, de futilités, comme elle méprisait tout excès. (13)[12]

The question of whether sophistication is compatible with excess has been raised in earlier chapters. Here, it is clear that Anne's cultured elegance depends on restraint, whereas Cécile's hedonism and knowingness lead her inevitably towards excessive, self-indulgent behaviour.

She is anxious about Anne's plan to marry Raymond because she fears that the older woman will place limits on their pleasures. During the summer spent at the villa, Cécile is supposed to be preparing to retake a school examination, but rarely does any work. Anne says it is essential that she gain the diploma in October, but Raymond disagrees:

> – Pourquoi? intervint mon père. Je n'ai jamis eu de diplôme, moi. Et je mène une vie fastueuse.
> – Vous aviez une certaine fortune au départ, rappela Anne.

11 'Within a week she had dressed me in the right clothes and taught me something of life. I remember thinking her the most wonderful person and being quite embarrassingly fond of her, but she soon found me a young man to whom I could transfer my affections. To her I owed my first glimpse of elegance and my first flirtation, and I was very grateful. At forty-two she was a most attractive woman, much sought after, with a beautiful face, proud, tired, and indifferent' (12).

12 'Her friends were clever, intelligent, and discreet; ours, from whom my father demanded only good looks or amusement, were noisy and insatiable. I think she rather despised us for our love of diversion and frivolity, as she despised all extremes' (12).

– Ma fille trouvera toujours des hommes pour la faire vivre, dit mon père noble-
ment.

Elsa se mit à rire et s'arrêta devant nos trois regards.

– Il faut qu'elle travaille, ces vacances, dit Anne en refermant les yeux pour clore
l'entretien.

J'envoyai un regard désespéré à mon père. Il me repondit par un petit sourire
gêné. (29)[13]

Raymond and his daughter strongly resist the middle-class ethic of work
and self-improvement which Anne embraces. But Cécile's alternatives are
restricted: she does not have the independent income which would permit
a leisured lifestyle, and though she sees her father's proposition as 'noble',
he is in fact assigning her to a permanently dependent role.[14] Elsa's presence
during this exchange is important, since she and Anne represent Cécile's
possible futures: as either a kept mistress with a succession of lovers or a self-
supporting professional woman.

In a review of the English translation of Sagan's third novel, *Dans Un Mois,
Dans Un An* (1957),[15] Whitney Balliett wrote that Sagan proposes 'that all
endeavor, no matter how furious, is futile' and described the novel as 'another
minor variation on degeneration among the *demi-haut monde* of Paris' (100). In
Bonjour Tristesse, too, the futility of endeavour is starkly demonstrated in Anne's
sudden death (which ends her successful career) and Cécile and Raymond's
return to their usual mode of sensual sloth. And yet, though Anne apparently
has so little permanent effect on the other two, Cécile does admit the logic and
attraction of the older woman's thoughtful, refined way of life. Anticipating
Anne's arrival at the villa, she muses:

je savais que dès l'arrivée d'Anne la détente complète ne seriat plus possible. Anne
donnait aux choses un contour, aux mots un sens que mon père et moi laissions
volontiers échapper. Elle posait des normes du bon goût, de la délicatesse et l'on ne
pouvait s'empêcher de les percevoir dans ses retraits soudains, ses silences blessés,
ses expressions. C'était à la fois excitant et fatigant, humiliant en fin de compte car
je sentais qu'elle avait raison. (16)[16]

---

13 'Why should she?' my father interrupted. 'I never got any diplomas and I live a life of luxury.'
   'You had quite a fortune to start with,' Anne reminded him.
   'My daughter will always find men to look after her,' said my father grandiloquently.
   Elsa began to laugh, but stopped when she saw our three faces.
   'She will have to work during the holidays,' said Anne, shutting her eyes to —put an end to the
      conversation.
   I gave my father a despairing look, but he merely smiled sheepishly. (25)
14 'Noble' is given as 'grandiloquent' in the English translation, which – though not a dictionary translation – may be more in accord with the way a modern reader might interpret the scene.
15 The translation, by Frances Frenaye, was titled *Those Without Shadows* and appeared in 1958.
16 'I knew that once she had come it would be impossible for any of us to relax completely. Anne gave
   a shape to things and a meaning to words which my father and I prefer to ignore. She set a standard

Anne's sophistication is an evolved, mature, worldliness; Raymond's is a form of degeneracy. Cécile is caught between the two, but Anne's influence comes too late to reform her. She can perceive that her way of life is superior ('je sentais qu'elle avait raison'), but she finds living up to Anne's standards of taste and manners not only exciting but also exhausting. Despite her youth and health, Cécile is frequently exhausted and she also eats little and is too thin. She often quotes to herself a line from Oscar Wilde's *The Picture of Dorian Gray*: 'Sin is the only real colour-element left in modern life',[17] and this suggests that she not only recognises but also welcomes her degeneracy.

Cécile is not especially well read; Wilde and Henri Bergson (whom she has to study for her examination) are the only authors she quotes in her narrative. Nevertheless, the influence of numerous others can be discerned in the larger structure of the novel. Reviewers and critics have compared Sagan to a range of writers, including Choderlos de Laclos, Benjamin Constant, Raymond Radiguet, Jean Cocteau, Colette, Nancy Mitford, Evelyn Waugh and Willa Cather. Some of these comparisons are rather more convincing than others; I would choose Laclos and Colette as Sagan's most obvious literary ancestors. Laclos's *Les Liaisons Dangereuses* (1782), like *Bonjour Tristesse*, centres on amorous intrigues and concerns a young, convent-educated girl named Cécile who is gradually debauched over the course of the story. In Laclos's novel, too, the adolescent girl comes under the sway of a mature, worldly woman, the Marquise de Merteuil. But while in *Bonjour Tristesse*, Anne tries to improve Cécile's chances of thriving in the world by encouraging her to work for her examinations, avoid sexual relationships and look after her health, the situation is the opposite in *Les Liaisons Dangereuses*. Cécile Volanges is literally ruined by the complicated machinations of the older woman, who arranges for her to be seduced by the Vicomte de Valmont. The Marquise's purpose is revenge on her former lover, the Comte de Gercourt, who intends to marry Cécile because he wants a virginal wife fresh from the convent. But following Valmont's ministrations, Cécile Volanges provides without embarrassment, as Valmont puts it, services which one would hesitate to demand from a professional ('ce qu'on n'ose pas même exiger de toutes les filles dont c'est le métier' [311]).[18] Valmont also tells his 'pupil' scandalous stories about her mother, an approach which he considers essential if one wishes to deprave a young girl, since 'celle qui ne respecte pas sa mère ne se respectera pas elle-même'

---

of good taste and fastidiousness which one could not help noticing in her sudden withdrawals, her expressions, and her pained silences. It was both stimulating and exhausting, but in the long run humiliating, because I could not help feeling that she was right' (15).

17 Wilde, *Dorian Gray* (29); quoted in the English edition of *Bonjour Tristesse* on p. 21.

18 My English phrase is that used in the 1988 film version directed by Christopher Hampton.

(298). Mlle de Volanges does indeed become depraved, but she never attains the knowing, world-weary sophistication of Sagan's Cécile. She remains a child in many ways, and she is always very easily influenced. Madame de Merteuil has no difficulty in persuading her that she should not feel guilty over her affair with Valmont, that she should take sensual pleasure whenever possible, and even that she could use the liaison as an opportunity to manipulate her mother into breaking off the engagement with Gercourt.

Sagan's Cécile resembles her eighteenth-century namesake in that contact with the world of sophisticated adult sexuality causes her to embrace sensuality and abandon integrity; at the same time, she is a little like Madame de Merteuil in her plotting and cynicism. The Marquise is a pre-eminent strategist, playing off her lovers, friends and protégées against one another. Sagan's Cécile similarly succeeds in manipulating everyone around her, but she is much clumsier than Madame de Merteuil in her intriguing, and not at all vengeful. She does feel, though, that her father has inspired her with 'un cynisme désabusé sur les choses de l'amour' (23).[19] This attitude is often associated with sophistication, but it is actually only compatible with one of the more unusual forms of sophistication: the amoral, self-obsessed form which belongs to characters such as the Marquise de Merteuil, or Lord Illingworth in Wilde's *A Woman of No Importance*. Virtually all the sophisticated characters in the texts discussed in this book are, at some point, susceptible to romance and (at least temporarily) serious about it: even Henry Crawford and Elyot Chase fall in love. But Françoise Sagan's teenage heroine remarks, during her final encounter with her first lover: 'Je le regardai: je ne l'avais jamais aimé. Je l'avais trouvé bon et attirant; j'avais aimé le plaisir qu'il me donnait; mais je n'avais pas besoin de lui' (124).[20]

Bonjour Tristesse certainly draws on the cynicism of the libertine tradition, and also on earlier French accounts of adolescent desire. Brendan Gill wrote in 1955 that Sagan might be compared to Colette 'in her combination of candour and cunning' (114), and, indeed, one novel which must surely have influenced *Bonjour Tristesse* is Colette's *Le Blé en Herbe* (1923). Both books are set in the liminal space of the seaside, and in both, the long summer holiday is the occasion for the adolescent's entry into sexuality. The experiments in love are partly a response to the environment: Cécile remarks on the way she is influenced by 'la présence de la mer, son rythme incessant, le soleil' (22).[21] Colette's protagonists, Vinca and Phil, are sixteen and fifteen, and they are enclosed in

---

19 'a cynical attitude towards love' (21).
20 'I looked at him: I had never loved him. I had found him gentle and attractive. I had loved the pleasure he gave me, but I did not need him' (106).
21 'the presence of the sea with its incessant rhythm' (20).

an entirely innocent, even though intensely sensual, world of adolescence, a space apart, in which they can embark on a shared journey of erotic discovery:

> Il y eut ainsi une série de jours immobiles, sans vent, sans nuages, [...] des jours si divinement pareils l'un à l'autre que Vinca et Philippe, apaisés, pouvaient croire l'année arrêtée à son plus doux moment, mollement entravée par un mois d'août qui ne finirait pas.
>
> Vaincus par la félicité physique, ils pensèrent moins à la séparation de septembre. (32)[22]

Cécile too, has a young lover, Cyril, but she does not seek to escape with him; rather, she draws him into the adult intrigues in which she is herself so deeply involved. While Colette explores the sense of loss associated with the end of childhood, the melancholy of *Bonjour Tristesse* is of a different kind. There is little idealising of youth in Sagan's novel; indeed, the precocious Cécile appears to be that dismaying creature, a sophisticated child.

It is revealing that she rarely associates with people of her own age, because she prefers her father's friends:

> je fuyais ces étudiants de l'Université, brutaux, préoccupés d'eux-mêmes, de leur jeunesse surtout, y trouvant le sujet d'un drame ou un prétexte à leur ennui. Je n'aimais pas la jeunesse. Je leur préférais de beaucoup les amis de mon père, des hommes de quarante ans qui me parlaient avec courtoisie et attendrissement, me témoignaient une douceur de père et d'amant. (11)[23]

Since the author was barely older than her protagonist, the judgement of Cécile as unpleasantly precocious was extended to Sagan herself, and explains the hostile elements in the book's somewhat mixed reception. It was awarded the prestigious Prix des Critiques in May 1954, but François Mauriac, in an editorial in *Le Figaro*, questioned this award on the basis of the book's amorality and shamelessness. Like many other critics, he fully acknowledged Sagan's artistic achievement, writing of 'this cruel book, whose literary merit shines out from the first page and is indisputable'. But the ambiguity of the response to Sagan's success is epitomised in Mauriac's description of her as 'a charming little monster'.[24] The novel was a *succès de scandale* and, as Janet Flanner noted in one of her 'Letter from Paris' columns for *The New Yorker* in July 1954, it was

22 'There was a series of still days, without wind, without clouds [...], days so divinely identical that Vinca and Philippe, at peace, almost believed the year to be ending at its sweetest moment, softly held in check by an August that would last forever. Overcome by physical contentment, they thought less of the separation of September.' (My translation.)

23 'Usually I avoided university students, whom I considered rough, and only interested in themselves and their own problems, which they dramatized, or used as an excuse for their boredom. I did not care for young people, I much preferred my father's friends, men of forty, who spoke to me with courtesy and tenderness, and treated me with the gentleness of a father or a lover' (10–11).

24 These extracts are quoted, in English, in Flanner 48.

'required vacation reading' in France (47). The English translation, published the following year, reached the first place on the *New York Times* bestseller list, and this made Sagan the youngest author ever to achieve that feat. By 1958, 810,000 copies had been sold in France and more than a million in the US, and the novel had been translated into twenty languages (Pace).

Sagan's star appeal has, to a significant extent, determined the reception of her works. As is usual with a writer whose first novel makes a sensation, critics were reluctant to admit her later work to be of a comparable quality. Her second novel, *Un Certain Sourire*, published in 1956, was widely admired, but her subsequent books were often thought to represent a decline. However, as Maeve Brennan noted in a review of *La Chamade* (1965):

> A new novel by Françoise Sagan is an event because of the excitement that is gener-
> ated when talent and good fortune work together in one person towards success.
> Miss Sagan is a natural writer who has grown content to chatter, but she remains
> significant because she made her first appearance marked as an Original who is also
> a Star, and because among her many imitators there has not been one who has come
> anywhere near echoing the seductive individuality of 'Bonjour Tristesse'. (66–67)[25]

Sebastian Faulks, in a long profile published in *The New Yorker* in 1998, remarks that Sagan presents an idealised France in which 'personal responsibilities count for nothing against the joy of intrigue and stylish living' (148), 'a ficti-tious world of sex, sophistication and the tinkle of champagne glasses' (150). This fictional world, in combination with her personal style and celebrity, have turned Sagan into an embodiment of French sophistication or, as Faulks puts it, 'a representative of the spirit of Frenchness to the rest of the world' (146).

'An artist and a madman': *Lolita*

It is above all in its style that *Lolita* is sophisticated. And seductive. But it is also about sophistication, and about seduction, and the narrative enacts both. Humbert Humbert is among the most sophisticated characters in modern literature; at the same time, he is Lolita's fool.

The distinctive qualities of Nabokov's narrator, in comparison to other sophisticated males, are his self-mockery and self-revelation. The urbane figures in, for instance, Wilde's or Coward's plays maintain a flawless poise and detachment, but Humbert Humbert achieves a much more astonishing feat. He reveals – even emphasises – his own ineptness, clumsiness, cowardice,

---

25 One imitator of interest was Michèle Bernstein, a founding member of the Situationist International with her first husband, Guy Debord. Her roman à clef, *All the King's Horses* (1960), was inspired
   by the recent scandalous successes of *Bonjour Tristesse* and of Roger Vadim's film version of *Les
   Liaisons Dangereuses*. The book rewrites and parodies Laclos and Sagan.

sordid manoeuvrings and utter subjection to his own physical desires, and yet manages to remain distinctive, even fascinating. The elements of his sophistication are wit (his narrative is extremely funny), distinction (his taste and intelligence are continually set off by the banality of everyone around him), knowingness *and* knowledge, cosmopolitanism, a commitment to aesthetic rather than moral values, and most importantly a prose style which, in its teasing circumlocutions and astonishing inventiveness, both allures and in some way dominates the reader. The narrative certainly addresses a sophisticated reader: that is, one who is not prevented from reading the book by moral recoil, and who is not dismayed by grammatical convolutions, untranslated conversations in French, dense literary allusiveness or unfamiliar vocabulary.

Favonian, phocine, remindful, incurvation, nympholept, girleen: Humbert Humbert continually uses recondite and archaic words in his narrative, as if the resources of ordinary modern English were not enough to express the excesses, the singularity of his desires and sensations.[26] He even invents words, notably 'pederosis' (55), which refers to the solitary pleasure he experiences when looking at the young girls he calls nymphets.[27] The unusual vocabulary produces an effect at once intellectual and playful, and evokes the highly specialised nature of the narrator's tastes and mental universe. (Specialisation can be a form of sophistication, since it suggests a superiority to, or distinction from, mainstream preferences.) Humbert records his long confession while confined in a mental institution, and writing becomes for him both an evocation of, and ultimately a substitute for, sexual pleasure: 'Oh, my Lolita,' he laments, 'I have only words to play with!' (32). His imagery is remarkably vivid, sometimes even surreal: 'Out of the lawn, bland Mrs Haze, complete with camera, grew up like a fakir's fake tree' (41). In phrases such as this, the ordinary becomes monstrous, and Humbert constructs a barrier of words around his own fastidiousness: viewing Mrs Haze's bathroom, he notes 'limp wet things overhanging the dubious tub (the question mark of a hair inside); and there were the expected coils of the rubber snake, and its complement – a pinkish cozy, coyly covering the toilet lid' (38). The vulgar and the banal become, in Humbert's vision, obscene and revolting, and thus he reverses the conventional perception which would classify Mrs Haze as respectable, and himself as vile.

In the sophisticated aesthetic, certain things are designated obscene which would not ordinarily be; conversely, there is an acceptance of some images, ideas and behaviours which would conventionally be considered taboo.

26 These words appear on pages 16, 17, 18, 19, 42.
27 The words 'nymphet' and 'nympholept' were not invented by Nabokov, though they were very obscure before his book appeared, and 'nymphet' had a rather more innocent meaning.

During a scene in which Humbert is plotting to achieve orgasm in his nymph-et's presence without her noticing, Dolores – or Lo – shows him a picture in a magazine: 'a surrealist painter relaxing, supine, on a beach, and near him, likewise supine, a plaster replica of the Venus di Milo, half buried in sand. Picture of the Week, said the legend. I whisked the whole obscene thing away' (58). A few moments later he is massaging her upper thigh and realising 'there seemed to be nothing to prevent my muscular thumb from reaching the hot hollow of her groin – just as you might tickle and caress a giggling child – just that' (61). He manages to present the tasteless drawing as more obscene than his sexual desire for children. Nabokov remarks in his 1956 reflection piece 'On a Book Entitled *Lolita*' that 'in modern times the term "pornography" connotes mediocrity', adding: 'Obscenity must be mated with banality because every kind of aesthetic enjoyment has to be entirely replaced by simple sexual stimulation' (311). On the other hand, in more conventionally acceptable liter-ature, aesthetic enjoyment has often been subordinated to moral considera-tions. But in *Lolita*, the aesthetic almost entirely displaces both the moral and the sexually stimulating. Humbert's mental world is constructed according to the inverted norms of Oscar Wilde, in which beauty substitutes for goodness. In *Shopping with Freud*, Rachel Bowlby says of *Lolita*: 'As with *Dorian Gray*, this is the story of a connection between eroticism, youthful aesthetic perfection and the pleasures of limitless consuming' (4). But while Wilde's plays and fictions remain committed to surfaces and appearances, Nabokov plumbs the depths of a madman's psychology. On careful consideration, Humbert Humbert might appear at once heroically sophisticated and quite unhinged, but it is often difficult to consider him carefully at all, because of the almost blinding effects of his style.

Writing itself is, indeed, the basis of his defence. Describing the first night he spent sharing a bed with his nymphet, during which he had planned to achieve his own satisfaction merely by touching her during her drugged sleep, he insists: 'The gentle and dreamy regions through which I crept were the patrimonies of poets – *not* crime's prowling ground' (*Lolita* 131). And when he arrives at the point (six a.m.) when she unexpectedly seduces him, he suddenly terminates his narrative, giving no details and simply saying: 'But really these are irrelevant matters; I am not concerned with so-called "sex" at all'. He explains this with reference to the distinction of the true artist: 'Anybody can imagine those elements of animality. A greater endeavor lures me on: to fix once for all the perilous magic of nymphets' (134). He mocks the vigilantes who insist on the potential of sexually explicit art to deprave readers, and conversely on the uplifting quality of morally improving litera-ture, remarking to some imagined middle-aged, male readers: 'It would never do, would it, to have you fellows fall madly in love with my Lolita!' (134). This is, of course, a very disingenuous comment, since the immensely lyrical passages evoking Lolita's charms seem expressly designed to make readers fall in love with her, so that they will find themselves aligned with Humbert's point of view.

Humbert Humbert is the most relentlessly self-conscious of narrators. His sophistication is intensely performative: on the first page, he addresses his readers, who will pass judgement on him: 'Ladies and gentlemen of the jury, exhibit number one is what the seraphs, the misinformed, simple, noble-winged seraphs, envied. Look at this tangle of thorns' (9). The envious seraphs are taken from Edgar Allan Poe's poem 'Annabel Lee', the most important among the many intertexts for Humbert's narrative. All the allusions display his specialised knowledge, but he also mocks his own excessive literariness, exclaiming after a particularly apt quotation: 'Well-read Humbert!' (70). Emphasising his own good looks in order to account for the amorous behaviour of Charlotte, Lo and other women, he comments: 'Of course, such announcements made in the first person may sound ridiculous' (104). He adds that he is nevertheless obliged to include such reminders about his appearance, 'much as a professional novelist, who has given a character of his some mannerism, [...] has to go on producing that mannerism every time the character crops up' (104). In this rather dizzying form of narrative sophistication, the distinctions between author, narrator and character become very blurred, and the role of the audience is augmented: 'Imagine me,' he pleads to his reader, 'I shall not exist if you do not imagine me' (129).[28]

Autoeroticism is Humbert's natural mode. His passion for Dolores Haze does not, at least in the earlier phases of the story, affect his complete self-absorption:

> I knew I had fallen in love with Lolita forever; but I also knew she would not be forever Lolita. She would be thirteen on January 1. In two years or so she would cease being a nymphet [...]. The word 'forever' referred only to my own passion, to the eternal Lolita as reflected in my blood. (65)

His unusual, carefully nurtured and beautifully expressed passion is what, in Humbert's view, lends him distinction. His possession of Lolita, he suggests, places him '*beyond happiness*. For there is no other bliss on earth comparable to that of fondling a nymphet. It [...] belongs to another class, another plane of sensitivity' (166). He positions himself in a realm apart from the coarse, unsophisticated pleasures of other men, and likewise represents his later

---

28 He also revels in the coincidences which make the story of his life sound like a novel, and the way that the lies he invents later turn out to be truths, in the manner of Wilde's *The Importance of Being Earnest*.

experience of trauma as exceptional: 'the atrocious, unbelievable, unbearable, and, I suspect, eternal horror that I know' (169). Humbert also considers his own mind to be uniquely interesting. He suggests that '[the] able psychiatrist who studies my case – and whom by now Dr. Humbert has plunged, I trust, into a state of leporine fascination' (166) will be anxious for him to make love to Lolita on a beach, and thus achieve 'release from the "subconscious" obsession of an incomplete childhood romance with the initial little Miss Lee' (167). The inverted commas are telling: Humbert presents himself as the most supremely conscious of men, aware of the tiniest sensation, appreciative of the most elusive delicacies of scenery, of expressions, of little girls' bodies. Nothing which he narrates can be read as revealing something which he did not intend: of betraying anything of his subconscious. The sophisticate has no subconscious, or if he does, it is not accessible to the prying of psychologists, or indeed, of readers. Every possible 'Freudian' interpretation of his experiences is commented on by Humbert himself; indeed, he revels in pointing out the coarse obviousness of such generalised models, and revealing their inapplicability to individual cases: 'We must remember that a pistol is the Freudian symbol of the Ur-father's central forelimb' (216); 'no yearnings of the accepted kind could I ever graft upon any moment of my youth, no matter how savagely psychotherapists heckled me' (287).

And how are we to read Lolita's own personal style? At a late stage in the narrative, Humbert is tortured by 'the nightmare of unknown betrayals within the innocence of her style, of her soul, of her essential grace' (233). Indeed, her attraction for him seems to derive from her combination of sensuality and the remaining traces of childishness which he construes as innocence, and this results in such paradoxical phrases as 'her shameless innocent shanks' (60). In comparison to the Victorian child-heroines and child-authors discussed in Chapter 2, Dolores Haze is both more and less sophisticated. She is not precociously clever like Daisy Ashford, or wise and socially adept like Alice, but she is far more sexually knowing, deliberately provocative and unsentimental than any fictional child before her. Humbert is persuaded that all nymphets have a 'demoniac' or 'delinquent' quality (16, 23), and emphasises Lo's flirtatiousness and cynicism as well as describing her as 'dimly depraved' (92). Yet he also recognises the innocence which she has not fully relinquished: 'my innocent little visitor soon sank to a half-sitting position upon my knee' (48). Her combination of childish ignorance and adult knowingness is exemplified in the scene at the Enchanted Hunters motel: though she initiates her sexual relations with her stepfather and even confesses that he is not her first lover, she also believes Humbert when he claims that adults don't have sex.

In an important passage, inserted just before the description of how he and Lo first became lovers, Humbert reflects on her difference from his dead childhood sweetheart Annabel:

> in my old-fashioned, old-world way, I, Jean-Jacques Humbert, had taken for granted, when I first met her, that she was as unravished as the stereotypical notion of 'normal child' had been since the lamented end of the Ancient World [...]. The whole point is that the old link between the adult world and the child world has been completely severed nowadays by new customs and new laws. [...] I really knew very little about children. After all, Lolita was only twelve, and no matter what concessions I made to time and place – even bearing in mind the crude behaviour of American schoolchildren – I was still under the impression that whatever went on among those brash brats, went on at a later age. [...] I should have understood that Lolita had *already* proved to be something quite different from innocent Annabel. (124–25)

The familiar contrast between American crudeness and old-world delicacy is mockingly invoked, and then complicated by a second contrast, between the unexpected sexual sophistication of the child and the naivety of the middle-aged man. In the larger patterns of the narrative, Lo's amorous precocity is constructed as an effect of American consumerism and the sexualised imagery of advertising: 'She it was to whom ads were dedicated: the ideal consumer, the subject and object of every foul poster' (148). During her extended travels across the States with Humbert, she is 'automatically stirred' by the injunctions of adverts and the promise of gift shops, ice-cold drinks and so forth, and 'entranced' simply by the words 'novelties and souvenirs' (148). Rachel Bowlby comments: 'It is Lolita who is the poetic reader, indifferent to things in themselves and entranced by the words that shape them into the image of a desire that consumption then perfectly satisfies' (49). She is not, on the other hand, in any way satisfied by her sexual relations with Humbert; he is offended by her preference for other pleasures, which he considers deeply unsophisticated: 'Mentally, I found her to be a disgustingly conventional little girl. Sweet hot jazz, square dancing, gooey fudge sundaes, musicals, movie magazines and so forth – these were the obvious items in her list of beloved things' (148). Her affection can, to some extent, be purchased: it is only after Humbert displays the suitcase full of new clothes which he has got for her that 'she crept into my waiting arms, radiant, relaxed, caressing me with her tender, mysterious, impure, indifferent, twilight eyes – for all the world, like the cheapest of cheap cuties. For that is what nymphets imitate – while we moan and die' (120).

Of course, we never have access to Lo's point of view, so it is impossible to be quite certain how much of her supposed depravity is projected onto her by Humbert, in order to excuse or mitigate his own vice. He is not, though, an unreliable narrator, and in any case, we do hear Lo's spoken voice quite often in his narrative. Her incipient sophistication, it seems, does indeed derive from her ability to imitate, to play, by turns, the roles of sweet little girl, petulant adolescent, and lascivious mistress. She can imitate different voices and styles too, and is quite capable of engaging in cynical banter with her stepfather. Telling him about her experiences at the summer camp, she parodies its publicity material:

'The Girl Scout's motto,' said Lo rhapsodically, 'is also mine. [...] My duty is – to be useful. I am a friend to male animals. I obey orders. I am cheerful. [...] I am thrifty and I am absolutely filthy in thought, word and deed.' (114)

At the same time, and perhaps unsurprisingly, given her age, she can't appreciate Humbert's extreme amorous and linguistic sophistication, refusing all unusual erotic manoeuvres and asking him to speak English whenever he uses long words:

She had entered my world, black and umber Humberland, with rash curiosity; she surveyed it with a shrug of amused distaste [...]. Never did she vibrate under my touch [...]. To the wonderland I had to offer, my fool preferred the corniest movies, the most cloying fudge. To think that between a Hamburger and a Humberger she would – invariably, with icy precision – plump for the former. (166)

Although he calls her his fool, it is in fact he who is abject, enslaved, reduced to planning every day solely with a view to keeping her in a good temper, bribing her with endless presents, and forced to go with her to the fast food restaurants and trashy movies which she loves. Eventually, she begins to charge him several dollars for sexual favours. It is at this point that he first refers to her as 'my sophisticated young mistress' (187). Her strategies have become more sophisticated; so also have her tastes. Though by this point she no longer cares for Humbert, her initial crush on him, and the time spent in his company, have clearly moulded her. She is in some ways older than her years, and boys her age invariably bore her.

Lo even picks up some of Humbert's language: her headmistress observes that her vocabulary comprises 'a two-hundred-forty-two word area of the commonest pubescent slang fenced in by a number of obviously European polysyllabics' (194). She also learns from other sources: she swears at her stepfather 'in language that I never dreamed little girls could know, let alone use' (170), and at this moment, he appears more naive and innocent than she does. Finally, she is allowed to take part in a play: 'By permitting Lolita to study acting I had, fond fool, suffered her to cultivate deceit' (229). Lo outsophisticates her fool, tricking him into taking her on a trip which will deliver her into the arms of her lover, Clare Quilty, the author of the play she has been rehearsing. But Lo achieves no real freedom through this move: she is simply transferred to the control of a different author. Humbert has determined her roles over the past two years; now, she speaks from the script of another highly literate child-molester who, in many respects, is Humbert's double, the pervert within, whom he kills at the end.[29] Under Quilty's tuition, Lolita 'like a hypnotic subject or a performer in a mystic rite, produced sophisticated versions of infantile make-believe' (230). Her new sophistication, then, is a continuation of her child's play, which returns us to Mark Backman's point that '[p]retending and imitating are the most essential kinds of child's play', while adults 'employ these skills with greater subtlety and precision' because they have conscious objects in view when acting (9). Humbert's own sophistication is intensely performative as well as manipulative, but his nymphet eventually outdoes him in performance.

The Lolita who is invented and cherished by Humbert is an exotic creature who does not belong in the ordinary realms of suburban America. After their joyride, when they settle in the small town of Beardsley and Lo starts school, her stepfather observes with disappointment: 'she seemed to me better adapted to her surroundings than I had hoped she would be when considering my spoiled slave-child and the bangles of demeanour she naively affected the winter before in California' (188). This brings us to a paradox: adaptability is one facet of sophistication, but a sophisticate must always remain distinct from her or his background. Lo is apparently starting to fit in a little too well in Beardsley. Humbert, though, manages to keep up his performance as a sedate widower while retaining a touch of eccentricity – at one point a small boy remarks to him: 'First time I've seen a man wearing a smoking jacket, sir – except in movies, of course' (189). Humbert is proud of his improbably elegant clothes, but also of his unfamiliarity with the rituals of bourgeois life:

> My west-door neighbor, who might have been a businessman or a college teacher, or both, would speak to me once in a while as he barbered some late garden blooms or watered his car, or, at a later date, defrosted his driveway (I don't mind if these verbs are all wrong). (179)

As well as taking pains to display his arcane knowledge, then, Humbert also exults in his areas of ignorance – and this, too, is a facet of sophistication, and an element of his identity as a European gentleman of leisure, disdainful of convention, sentiment and effort.

29 Numerous critics have discussed Quilty's status as Humbert's double: see for instance Frosch. There is even, as Raine remarks, 'the further innuendo that Humbert is being written by Quilty': the highly literary clues left in a series of hotel registers lead Humbert to suspect that he is 'the subservient pawn of Quilty's narrative ebullience' (328, 329).

In most of the novel, Humbert is evidently persuaded that ordinary, consensual morality can provide no guidance and no protection to someone like himself. But at the end, there is a change. Humbert begins to acknowledge his guilt more fully, and he also ceases to view his former mistress simply as the embodiment of an ideal (the perfect nymphet). She takes on a more human, and more suffering form. After a gap of several years, he rediscovers Dolores, now seventeen and married, and realises that he loves not simply the nymphet enshrined in his memory, but the young woman she is now: 'I insist the world know how much I loved my Lolita, *this* Lolita, pale and polluted, and big with another's child, but still gray-eyed, still sooty-lashed, still auburn and almond' (278). The sudden sincerity and grief in this chapter contrasts markedly with the earlier phases of the narrative (though it has been antici-pated by many forward-references throughout). There is even a touch of sentimentality in the last pages of the book, and it is significant that at this stage, Humbert begins to ridicule his own image as a sophisticate much more harshly, and less playfully, than he did before, seeing himself through the eyes of Dolores's husband as 'her fragile, *frileux*, diminutive, old-world, youngish but sickly, father in velvet coat and beige vest, maybe a viscount' (273). His sophistication can no longer save him from the misery of knowing that 'a North American girl-child named Dolores Haze had been deprived of her childhood by a maniac' (283). Craig Raine observes: 'It takes Humbert the length of the novel to realize what Nabokov has known all along': that is, 'the discrepancy between the dizzy desire and the dingy truth'. He concludes: there is an 'intricate surgical separation performed over the length of *Lolita*. Humbert Humbert: two people, the same person' (322). A lover and an abuser, devoted and yet utterly selfish. A criminal and an artist. He expresses his grief and his culpability in the same remarkably evocative style which he used to express his desire. After leaving Dolores's house, he writes: 'And presently I was driving through the drizzle of the dying day, with the windscreen wipers in full action but unable to cope with my tears' (Nabokov, *Lolita* 280). In these final stages of the story, the writing, the rhetoric, the sheer cleverness of Humbert's narrative are as sophisticated, as seductive as ever. Thus readers are likely to find themselves sympathising with a character guilty of the crime which the twentieth century most detested: not murder (the scene of Quilty's death is merely comic) but paedophilia.

'Swung between the old world and the new': *The Leopard*

Il Gattopardo, the only completed novel by the Sicilian nobleman Giuseppe Tomasi, Duke of Palma and Prince of Lampedusa, was posthumously published in Italy in 1958, and the English translation by Archibald Colquhoun titled *The Leopard* appeared in 1961. Luchino Visconti's much-admired film version was made in 1963. The main part of the novel's narrative is set between 1860 and 1862 during the Risorgimento, the movement for the unification of Italy. When the story opens, King Ferdinand, ruler of the Kingdom of the Two Sicilies (that is, the Bourbon state of Naples and Sicily) has recently died, and Garibaldi is about to invade and seize Sicily. The power of the Sicilian nobility is directly threatened, and this profoundly affects the novel's protagonist, Don Fabrizio, Prince of Salina.

The Prince embodies a particular kind of sophistication, defined through discourses of breeding, cultivation, manners and wisdom. (It should be remembered that the word 'wisdom', deriving from the Greek 'sophos', has the same root as 'sophistication'.) He is also represented in terms of strength, dignity and presence, and the combined effect is one of 'fascination' (Lampedusa, *Leopard* 94). The imagery of the leopard is used to convey his attraction:

> Angelica and Don Fabrizio made a magnificent couple. The Prince's huge feet moved with a surprising delicacy, and never were his partner's satin slippers in danger of being grazed. His huge paw held her waist with vigorous firmness, his chin leant on the black waves of her hair; from Angelica's bust rose a delicate scent of *bouquet Maréchale*, and above all an aroma of young smooth skin. (157)

The Prince's masculinity is reinforced by the repeated association of him with lust, sexual attractiveness, and dominance over women. Here, his desire for Angelica, the fiancée of his nephew Tancredi, is clear; elsewhere in the text he openly visits his mistress and yet also inflames his wife, whose 'diminutive body yearned vainly for loving dominion' over his (6). At the same time, the Prince's sensuality does weaken him: it blinds him to Angelica's faults and thus permits the ascendance of the low-born girl and her father, Don Calogero Sedàra, over the aristocratic Salinas; and it induces a certain laziness which prevents him from exerting himself about his estates and so hastens the erosion of his fortune. His sensuality, in combination with his 'exquisite delicacy' (7) and 'contemptuous indifference about matters he considered low' (93), leaves him vulnerable to the rapacity of the rising capitalist class. Indeed, the kind of sophistication which Lampedusa explores through his 'experienced' Prince (55) is not a facet of modernity; rather, it is threatened by modernity. The Prince represents the culmination of both a family and a class, but he has reached a pitch of sophistication which, as it cannot be sustained amidst the new social order, inevitably leads to decline.

The opening chapter of the novel is saturated with images of degeneration as the Prince walks in the garden of Villa Salina:

Enclosed between three walls and a side of the house its seclusion gave it the air of a cemetery [...]. Plants were growing in thick disorder on the reddish clay; flowers sprouted in all directions: and the myrtle hedges seemed put there to prevent movement rather than guide it. At the end a statue of Flora speckled with yellow-black lichen exhibited her centuries-old charm with an air of resignation; on each side were benches holding quilted cushions, also of grey marble; and in a corner the gold of an acacia tree introduced a sudden note of gaiety. Every sod seemed to exude a yearning for beauty too soon muted by languor.

But the garden, hemmed and almost squashed between these barriers, was exhaling scents that were cloying, fleshy and slightly putrid, like the aromatic liquids distilled from the relics of certain saints [...]. The *Paul Neyron* roses, whose cuttings he had himself bought in Paris, had degenerated; first stimulated and then enfeebled by the strong if languid pull of Sicilian earth, burnt by apocalyptic Julys, they had changed into objects like flesh-coloured cabbages, obscene and distilling a dense almost indecent scent which no French horticulturalist would have dared hope for. (8)

These suggestions of immobility, insulation from the outer world, decay and languorous sensuality have a direct application to the state of Sicilian society as the Prince perceives it, and to his own class in particular. The description of the garden is inflected by the narrator's and reader's awareness of what came after: that is, by the knowledge that these were, indeed, the last days of power for the Sicilian nobility. The existing social order is already shifting, but in this passage, as in many others in the novel, Lampedusa's lush and seductive prose fully demonstrates the allure of what is being lost. His lyrical writing has a visual counterpart in the sumptuous beauty of Visconti's film sets, costumes and set piece scenes.

Villa Salina, the Prince's main property, is in Palermo, but the family spend some months each year at their rural estate at Donnafugata. This house is based on the real palace of Filangeri-Cutò in Santa Margherita Belice where Lampedusa spent his childhood summers in the early years of the twentieth century, and which he describes lovingly in his memoir 'Places of My Infancy', written in 1955. The Prince and Princess of Salina are based on the author's great-grandparents, and his evident personal investment in the places and people of his story intensifies the nostalgic atmosphere of the novel.[30] Although the nobility no longer ruled in Sicily in Lampedusa's time, they retained their titles and continued to receive homage from the local peasants. Lampedusa's nostalgia is not for an age which is distant and detached from his own era; rather, his writing suggests strong continuities between mid-nineteenth and mid-twentieth-century Sicilian culture. (The parallels between the two periods

30 On Lampedusa's use of material from his family's history, see Colquhoun 14–15.

were reinforced in 1943, when the Allied invasion of the island recalled the arrival of the Garibaldini in 1860.) *The Leopard* certainly invests the past with glamour: as E. M. Forster observes, in comparison with its real-life model, the fictional Donnafugata 'has the lovelier name, is the more difficult to reach, has the sweeter peaches, the more dubious recesses' (Forster, Introduction 6). But it also suggests that the past is constitutive of the identity of modern Sicilian aristocrats.

For Don Fabrizio, Donnafugata is a cherished retreat from the modernity and political change which are painfully evident at Palermo; 'he loved the house, the people, the sense of feudal ownership still surviving there' (Lampedusa, *Leopard* 37). Yet on the family's arrival in August 1860, it rapidly becomes clear that social structures are altering in rural areas also. At first, everything seems as usual:

> The prince had always taken care that the first dinner at Donnafugata should bear the stamp of solemnity: children under fifteen were excluded from the table, French wines were served, there was punch *alla Romana* before the roast; and the flunkeys were in powder and knee-breeches. On just one detail did he compromise; he never wore evening dress, lest he embarrass guests who would, obviously, possess none. That evening, in the 'Leopold' drawing-room, as it was called, the Salina family were awaiting the last arrivals. From under lace-covered shades the oil-lamps spread circumscribed yellow light: the vast equestrian portraits of past Salinas were as imposing and shadowy as their memories. (52–53)

The dinner bears the stamp not only of solemnity but of sophistication. The wine signals this: it is not only the British who have long considered French-ness a mark of sophistication.[31] The aristocracy, then, shore up their position not only through open-handed hospitality but also through the display of discerning taste in matters such as clothes, wine and décor. But the taste and ancestry of the Prince, highly visible though it is on the dinner table and in the portraits, cannot protect him against the pretensions of his social inferiors, and it is no longer 'obvious' that his neighbours could not afford, nor would desire, evening dress. During the afternoon, he has learned that Don Calogero Sedàra has achieved an income and influence at Donnafugata nearly equal to the Prince's own. Now, the Prince's son bursts in to announce the astonishing fact that Don Calogero is arriving in a tailcoat. For the Prince, this lends reality and personal application to the current political crisis: 'he saw revolution in that white tie and two black tails moving at this moment up the stairs of his own home' (53).

31 Frenchness is also associated with eroticism in the text: compare the reference to a 'French horticul-turalist' in the passage quoted above. Colquhoun writes in his biographical note on Lampedusa: 'To Sicilians, the capital is still Paris, with London for clothes and accoutrements; and certainly a love of things French is reflected in nearly everything Don Giuseppe wrote' (18).

He soon takes comfort, though, in the perception that his neighbour, however wealthy, can never attain to breeding or sophistication:

When he saw him, however, his agonies were somewhat eased. Though perfectly adequate as a political demonstration it was obvious that, as tailoring, Don Caloge-ro's tail-coat was a disastrous failure. The stuff was excellent, the style modern, but the cut appalling. The Word from London had been most inadequately made flesh in a tailor from Girgenti to whom Don Calogero had gone with his tenacious avarice. The wings of his cravat pointed straight to heaven in mute supplication, his huge collar was shapeless, and, what is more, it is our painful but necessary duty to add that the mayor's feet were shod in buttoned boots. (53)

Despite his aspiration to a cosmopolitan style, Don Calogero still appears hopelessly provincial because of his too-evident economy. Yet even when he is later fitted with a more expensive evening ensemble in order to attend the Ponteleone ball, the results are only partially successful, since – as Tancredi notes – Don Calogero 'lacks *chic*' (146). Chic, an important element of sophisti-cation, thus appears as something innate, a quality which cannot be learned or purchased. Don Calogero cannot escape his origins – at the ball, he presents 'a most rustic sight' when he falls asleep in a chair with the ends of his drawers showing from beneath his trousers (162).

These passages about clothes reveal the narrator's consistent alignment with the Prince. Even when Don Fabrizio is criticised, he still appears far superior to those around him, and his irresistible appeal ensures that no reader (unless an extremely perverse and resistant one) is able to sympathise much with Don Calogero or his daughter. Angelica Sedàra's loveliness is dwelt on at length, and it is abundantly clear why Tancredi falls in love with her and throws over his cousin Concetta, whom he had previously admired. Yet the reader always sees more than Tancredi, since in every description, Angel-ica's seductiveness is compromised by some base element. At the Donnafugata dinner party, the appearance of Angelica, who has been away for some years at a college in Florence, causes a sensation: 'the Salina family all stood there with breath taken away' (53). Later, though, she repels the other young ladies with her 'strident' laughter on finding herself the object of a sexual innuendo. Angelica's 'threatening beauty' (58) is a deliberately eroticised display which, the Prince observes, puts 'the shy grace of his Concetta in the shade' (65). Discernment, careful attention and sophisticated taste are required to appre-ciate Concetta; Angelica, by contrast, represents a democratisation of desire, and she is excited 'by the obvious admiration she was arousing in every man around the table' (56). Tancredi himself admits that though Concetta 'was less beautiful, much less rich than Angelica', she 'yet had something in her which the girl from Donnafugata would never possess' (113). The old social order expresses its power through the exercise of sophisticated tastes which are mystifying to their inferiors; Angelica directly endangers this with her blatant, universal appeal.

Aware of his own breeding and culture, Tancredi feels superior to Angelica even as he desires her. (In this he recalls Winterbourne's attitude to Daisy Miller or – in a more twisted version – the Duke's attitude to Zuleika Dobson.) In yet another recurrence of the pattern of imagery identified by Litvak, in which the sophisticate-gourmet literally devours his prey, Tancredi imagines Angelica as edible: 'her skin looked as if it had the flavour of fresh cream which it resembled, her childlike mouth that of strawberries' (53). At dinner, there is a sumptuous macaroni pie which she 'devoured [...] grasping her fork half-way up the handle' (55), while her new admirer, in effect, devours her:

> Tancredi, in an attempt to link gallantry with greed, tried to imagine himself tasting, in the aromatic forkfuls, the kisses of his neighbour Angelica, but he realised at once that the experiment was disgusting and suspended it, with a mental reserve about reviving this fantasy with the pudding. (55–56)

It is not the equation of Angelica with food which seems disgusting; Tancredi only feels that it would be more suitable for him to associate her with something sweet and delicate, rather than with 'chicken and truffles in masses of piping hot, glistening macaroni' (55). Following her engagement to Tancredi, Angelica quickly learns to imitate upper-class manners, and the increasing artificiality of her behaviour is again imaged through food:

> Angelica's first visit to the Salina family as a bride-to-be was impeccably stage-managed. Her bearing was so perfect that it might have been suggested word-for-word by Tancredi [...]. Angelica arrived at six in the evening, dressed in pink and white; her soft black tresses were shadowed by a big straw hat of late summer on which bunches of artificial grapes and gilt heads of corn discreetly evoked the vineyards of Gibildolce and the granaries of Settesoli. She sloughed off her father in the entrance hall; then [...] flung herself into the arms of Don Fabrizio. (95)

Decorating herself now with *imitation* fruit and grain, Angelica is gradually becoming less digestible, and thus more dangerous. The ornaments on her hat subtly assert her power over the financially straitened Salina family, and her new 'soft' and 'shadowed' appearance is more insinuating than her earlier stridency. Under the instruction of Tancredi, who has the modern sophisticate's skill of manipulating image and appearance, Angelica leaves her father (and thus her social origins) behind, literally substituting her new relation, the Prince.

By the time of the Ponteleone ball two years later, her conduct has become still more polished, and her faults are evident only to the reader: 'Above the ordered swirl of her pink crinoline Angelica's white shoulders merged into strong soft arms; her head looked small and proud on its smooth youthful neck adorned with intentionally modest pearls' (148–49). The word 'intentionally' changes the whole tenor of the description; Angelica only simulates modesty. Similarly, her low birth seems to preclude her from ever attaining true sophistication, though she wears it as a disguise. At the end of the narrative, the narrator remarks of the seventy-year-old Angelica that four decades of living with Tancredi had been 'more than long enough to rub off the last traces of Donnafugata accent and manners; she had camouflaged herself even to the point of copying that graceful twining of the fingers which had been one of Tancredi's characteristics' (182).

The quality which Angelica really acquires is not sophistication but glamour.[32] Stephen Gundle writes that in the nineteenth century

> [g]lamour was born in a context in which the bourgeoisie was contesting many of the hereditary privileges of the aristocracy and in which society was becoming more open than ever before. However, even though it was losing power, the traditional aristocracy still defined many features of the desirable lifestyle. [...] Glamour was about the way in which the most visually striking manifestations of aristocratic privilege were taken over and reinvented by newly emergent people, groups, and institutions. (19)

This illuminates the way in which Angelica gains power in *The Leopard*; her father provides the wealth, she displays it, and her beauty and money are considered a fair exchange for the prestige of Tancredi's name and ancestry. The Salina family are contemptuous, though, when Angelica's father tries to deny their contribution to the bargain by claiming noble status in his own right. In a move which, the narrator suggests, was common among newly prosperous Sicilians, Don Calogero asserts: 'one day it will be known that your nephew has married the Baronessina Sedàra del Biscotto', adding: 'I've put the papers through; there's only one link missing'. These clichéd phrases 'gave the Prince the incomparable artistic satisfaction of seeing a type realised in all its details; and [...] he gave a depressed laugh ending in a sweetish taste of nausea' (91).[33] The Prince's fastidiousness is an important element of his role as a sophisticated artist in life. The metaphor of nausea, used repeatedly

---

32 Compare the passage in 'Places of My Infancy' about an unnamed man who is a 'vassal' of Lampedusa's mother's family, and who aspires to be a man of fashion: 'He had been one of the moths drawn by the glamorous glow of the Florios [another noble family], and who, after many a dizzy pirouette, dropped on to the tablecloth with burnt-out wings. He had been more than once to Paris with the Florios and even put up at the Ritz; and of Paris (the Paris of the boîtes, of luxurious brothels, of high-priced smartness) he had preserved a dazzled memory' (69–70).

33 In the film version, during his conversation with Father Pirrone in the observatory, the Prince remarks: 'The middle class doesn't want to destroy us but to take our place'. This line does not occur in the novel, but the novel certainly demonstrates this point.

to evoke his disgust at the mercenary basis of his interactions with his neighbour, reveals Lampedusa's naturalising of snobbery as a form of high morality. Sedàra has many admirable qualities, yet he remains, in his outward behaviour and appearance, so ridiculous, grasping and unattractive that the reader's sympathy must inevitably remain with the Prince, and we cannot help being amused by Don Fabrizio's later remark about Sedàra: 'his family I am told is an old one, or soon will be' (125).

Similarly, the sophisticated reader is invited to look down a little on the frank, trusting Cavriaghi, Tancredi's Milanese friend, who is entirely taken in by Angelica, describing her as 'clever and cultured too; and good as well' (115). Tancredi is merely amused by this over-generous assessment of his fiancée, but is greatly discomposed when Cavriaghi calls her 'the young baroness':

> For a second he did not realise who the other was referring to. Then the prince in him rebelled. 'Baroness? what d'you mean, Cavriaghi? She's a dear, sweet creature whom I love and that's quite enough.'
>
> That it really was 'quite enough' was not actually true; but Tancredi was perfectly sincere; with his atavistic habit of great possessions it seemed to him that the estates of Gibildolce and Settesoli, all those bags of gold, had been his since the time of Charles of Anjou, always. (115).

Tancredi's sincerity and noble upbringing are used to excuse his sense of entitlement, and to shield him from the suspicion that his marriage is motivated only by greed. The Prince loves Tancredi because he sees his own taste, vigour and zest for life reproduced in this nephew, much more than in his own sons. Tancredi, though, embodies a more modern form of sophistication than his uncle. His figure is 'obviously urban – slim, erect, well-dressed' (61) and his attitude is one of 'perpetual irony' (167). His father, with his 'magnificent scale of life', squandered all his fortune, ruined his family and left his house, Villa Falconeri, to decay, but the Prince proposes that his nephew's good qualities are in fact 'the result of all these disasters' (89). He says this to Don Calogero Sedàra, provocatively opposing his neighbour's thrifty, calculating approach to finance: 'maybe it is impossible to obtain the distinction, the delicacy, the fascination of a boy like him without his ancestors having romped through half a dozen fortunes' (89). Once again, sophistication can scarcely be separated from excess, yet the aristocrats' contemptuous attitude to financial affairs and insistence on liberal expenditure is one cause of their declining power.

This also leads to the question of worldliness. Joseph Litvak comments that this word

> tends in two different, even opposite, directions. On the one hand, insofar as it carries a certain taint of the 'inglorious', of the guilty or dirty secret, it means something

like 'vulgar'. On the other hand, insofar as the secret is an almost inherently sexy will to power, *worldly* more glamorously means something like 'sophisticated'. [...] *worldliness*, dirty in its glamour, glamorous in its dirt, indeed oscillates tellingly between 'sophistication' and 'vulgarity'. (82)

This has a direct bearing on the way the relationship between the Sedàra and Salina families develops over the course of Lampedusa's narrative. The Prince finds 'an odd admiration growing in him for Sedàra's qualities'. Becoming used to 'the ill-shaven cheeks, the plebeian accent, the odd clothes and the persistent odour of stale sweat', he 'began to realise the man's rare intelligence' (*Leopard* 93). Worldliness is literally presented as dirt here, and yet its direct result is the vision of glamour which is the newly stylish, grown-up Angelica. In return, Sedàra revises his opinions of the aristocracy, whom he had previously thought of as 'sheep-like creatures, who existed merely in order to give up their wool to his shears and their names and incomprehensible prestige to his daughter' (94). But on getting to know Tancredi, he finds himself

> dealing, unexpectedly, with a young noble as cynical as himself, capable of striking a sharp bargain between his own smiles and titles and the attractions and fortunes of others, while knowing how to dress up such 'Sedàra-ish' actions with a grace and fascination which he, Don Calogero, felt he did not himself possess, but which influenced him without [...] his being in any way able to discern its origins. (94)

Sedàra's is definitely not sophisticated, whereas the Salinas are, yet 'worldliness' marks both Sedàra and Tancredi. *The Leopard* illuminates the differences between worldliness and sophistication even as it blurs the boundary in the transitional figure of Tancredi, who inherits many of the attractive qualities of the declining aristocracy while also engaging with the newer structures of wealth and power in the modern united Italy.

Sedàra's is not the only outsider's perspective on the aristocracy which is offered in the text; another is presented through Father Pirrone, chaplain to the Salina family, who suggests that the nobility are difficult to understand because 'they live in a world of their own, created not directly by God but by themselves during centuries of highly specialised experiences of their own worries and joys' (133). In his account, sophistication is once again connected with excess: 'perhaps they appear so strange to us because they have reached a stage towards which all those who are not saints are moving, that of indifference to earthly goods through surfeit' (134). But aristocratic sophistication, in Father Pirrone's analysis, also has another crucial quality which takes us back to the definition, quoted at the start of this book, of sophistication as the ability to cope with a formidable menace to one's prestige. 'These nobles put a good face on their own disasters', says the priest, continuing:

To rage and mock is gentlemanly; to grumble and whine is not. [...] It's a class difficult to suppress because it's in continual renewal and because if needs be it can die
well, that is it can throw out a seed at the moment of death. Look at France; they let
themselves be massacred with elegance there and now they're back as before. I say
as before, because it is differences of attitude, not estates and feudal rights, which
make a noble. (136)

The phrase 'massacred with elegance' is particularly intriguing, because it is
ambiguous. Were the French aristocrats elegant even when being massacred,
or was their massacre in fact the result of their excessive elegance, that is, their
insistence on maintaining all their elaborate rituals of dress and manners
even in the face of crises and revolution?[34] 'Elegance' is an important value
in *The Leopard* – it stands not simply for a set of choices in lifestyle, manner
and dress, but for an attitude of mind. But the Salina elegance depends on the
maintenance of their elite status in the face of challenges, and therefore it has
disturbing undertones – even at dinner, the Prince watches his sons 'wearing
an expression of fashionable melancholy as they wielded knives and forks
with subdued violence' (14). Indeed, the imagery of violence pervades the text,
and although the battles of the Risorgimento take place offstage, they create a
threatening atmosphere in the domestic sphere. (In the film, by contrast, the
battles are shown at length, and their effects on the Sicilian villagers are also
made visible.)

In his long speech to Chevalley, the Secretary to the Prefecture, sent to invite
him to join the Piedmontese Senate, the Prince says: 'All Sicilian self-expression,
even the most violent, is really wish-fulfilment; our sensuality is a hankering
for oblivion, our shooting and knifing a hankering for death; our languor,
our exotic ices, a hankering for voluptuous immobility' (123). The Prince here
diagnoses the ills not just of the aristocracy, but of the whole kingdom. Indeed,
the imagery of decadence in the text is often entwined with discourses not
only of class, but also of race and natural selection. The family portraits in Don
Fabrizio's study juxtapose his father 'Prince Paolo, dark complexioned and
sensual lipped as a Moor' with his mother, 'Princess Carolina [...] with her fair
hair heaped into a towering dressing and severe blue eyes' (119).[35] There is a
suggestion of miscegenation in this contrasting colouring, and indeed, Prince
Fabrizio's mixed Sicilian and German ancestry proves unhealthy. The narrator

34 This phrase is a literal translation from the Italian (see Lampedusa, *Il Gattopardo* 179) but the verb
in Italian is reflexive, so that it means something like 'they went to their deaths with elegance'.
35 In his portrait, Prince Paolo wears 'the cordon of St Januarius', that is, of L'Insigne Reale Ordine di
San Gennaro, the highest order of knighthood in the kingdom, which was bestowed by the head of
the Royal House of Bourbon of the Two Sicilies. His alignment with the royal dynasty overrides his
apparently mixed-race descent (he perhaps has a North African ancestor), making him the equal of
his pale-skinned wife.

comments that, 'however attractive his fair skin and hair amid all that olive and black', his distinction of appearance is counterbalanced by 'other German strains' which do not thrive in his environment:

> an authoritarian temperament, a certain rigidity of morals, and a propensity for abstract ideas; these, in the relaxing atmosphere of Palermo society, had changed respectively into capricious arrogance, recurring moral scruples and contempt for his own relatives and friends, all of whom seemed to him mere driftwood in the languid meandering stream of Sicilian pragmatism. (7)

Blondeness and whiteness are undeniably privileged in the text, particularly in the narrator's consistent preference for fair, aristocratic Concetta over dark-haired, plebeian Angelica. Yet it is Angelica who is adapted to her environment, and who will thrive and reproduce while Concetta withers.

At the ball, the Prince disparages the 'mob of girls incredibly short, improbably dark, unbearably giggly', preferring the few 'lovely creatures such as the fair-haired Maria Palma' (151). His explanation of the girls' ugliness explicitly evokes racial decadence: 'what with the frequent marriages between cousins in recent years due to sexual lethargy and territorial calculations, with the dearth of proteins and overabundance of starch in the food', the daughters even of the best families in Palermo have come to resemble 'female monkeys' (151). Their vulgar hooting, shrieking and uncontrolled behaviour leave the Prince 'slightly nauseated' (152). This suggestion of regression is confirmed in his conversation with Don Calogero Sedàra about the décor of the ballroom: the narrator observes that golden colouring of the walls is 'not the flashy gilding which decorators slap on nowadays', but rather 'a faded gold, pale as the hair of certain nordic children, determinedly hiding its value under a muted use of precious material intended to let beauty be seen and cost forgotten' (152). While the Prince appreciates this sophisticated decoration, Don Calogero comments: 'They don't do things like this nowadays, with gold leaf at its present price!' (153). Here, the ballroom itself is evoked in racialised terms ('nordic'), and the ascendancy of the *nouveau riche* Don Calogero, who is 'insensible to its charm' but awake to its price, thus suggests a process of contamination or miscegenation (153). This is realised in the marriage of the Prince's nephew to Sedàra's daughter: this is, in some ways, a degrading union, especially since Angelica's mother turns out to be 'a kind of animal' who 'can't read or write [...]; just a beautiful mare, voluptuous and uncouth' (81).

The last two chapters of the novel move forward in long jumps of time. The penultimate one, 'Death of a Prince', takes place in 1883. Knowing he is about to die, Don Fabrizio tells his family to leave him alone to sleep, but then considers: 'to give way to drowsiness now would be as absurd as eating a slice of cake immediately before a longed-for banquet. He smiled. "I've always been a wise gourmet"' (168). In this phrase, the novel's meditation on taste, which is often explored through metaphors of food or of nausea, seems to culminate. The dying Prince reflects that although he leaves sons and a grandson behind him, he is himself 'the last Salina' (170). Admittedly, 'in Concetta's beauty and character was prolonged the true Salina strain' (172), but as she is forty and unmarried, the 'true strain' will clearly die with her. The young Fabrizietto – whose very name indicates how diminished and frivolous he seems in comparison to his grandfather – is, the Prince reflects 'so handsome, so lively, so dear … So odious. With his […] good-time instincts, with his tendency to middle-class smartness' (169). The meaning of sophistication shifts twice over the course of the novel. As Tancredi's generation replaces Don Fabrizio's, its (idealised) aristocratic form gradually gives way to a more modern, flexible and savvy version. With Fabrizietto, we have arrived at bourgeois sophistication, something which the novel rejects entirely

In the final chapter, set in 1910, Concetta and her two spinster sisters, all aged around seventy, are still living in the Villa Salina, which is haunted by traces of the past and filled with inauthentic religious relics. In contrast to their rather deadly existence is the figure of Tancredi, still vibrant in Concetta's memory and in the stories of his colleague Senator Tassoni. Tancredi's legacy is also visible in 'the sumptuous Villa Falconeri, with its flowering bougainvillaea drooping over the walls of the splendidly kept gardens' (179). This is the house which was left a wreck by his profligate father, and its newfound splendour exhibits Tancredi's rise to prosperity and contrasts markedly with the decaying garden of Villa Salina described at the start of the novel. In this last chapter, the recently widowed Angelica visits Concetta, and tells her that during the imminent celebrations of the fiftieth anniversary of Garibaldi's arrival in Sicily, Concetta's nephew Fabrizio will be bearing a placard marked 'Salina'. Angelica's enthusiasm – 'Don't you think it's a good idea? A Salina rendering homage to Garibaldi! A fusion of old and new in Sicily!' (182) – seems rather horrible in the context of the rest of the novel. Yet her words also poignantly recall a statement made by the Prince of Salina half a century earlier, one which seems to penetrate to the core of Lampedusa's nostalgic vision: 'I belong to an unlucky generation, swung between the old world and the new, and I find myself ill at ease in both' (124–25).

'The aristocracy of external appearance': *A Guide to Elegance*

By the time she published her guide to elegant dressing, the French style expert Genevieve Antoine Dariaux had many years of professional experience, both in her own couture house and as salon director at Nina Ricci. In 1964 the book must already have seemed nostalgic, since it evokes a world of upper-middle-class leisure which was rapidly vanishing and adheres to conventions of female dress which are entirely at odds with the iconic and popular styles of the sixties. In 2003, *A Guide to Elegance* was reissued by HarperCollins in a small, collectible, retro-styled hardback edition, joining a series of other lifestyle guides from earlier eras which have recently reappeared in similar formats. In 2005 and 2006, for instance, Rose Henniker Heaton's *The Perfect Hostess*, Alice Leone Moats's *No Nice Girl Swears* and Marjorie Hillis's *Live Alone and Like It* were all republished. These titles date back much further than Dariaux's guide: they appeared in 1931, 1933 and 1936 respectively, and focus on how a woman can enjoy modern freedoms and contemporary styles while also preserving her reputation and enhancing her social position. Dariaux's book, by contrast, is about how to operate in the modern world while retaining the superior elegance of earlier eras. 'Sophistication' is an important, and generally positive, term in the book, and is constructed in relation to a class-based discourse of breeding, culture and leisure. The model of sophistication which *A Guide to Elegance* purveys to twenty-first-century readers is inflected by a double nostalgia: the decision to reissue it hints at a nostalgia for the 1960s, while the text itself harks back to the interwar years.

Dariaux evidently made small revisions for the 2003 edition – such as, for instance, the addition of references to the Atkins diet (which did not begin to be popularised until the early 1970s), and to Princess Diana's chic (139, 21). In the main, though, the book is preserved in its original form: that is, as a period piece. Its subtitle, 'For every woman who wants to be well and properly dressed on all occasions',[36] is telling: the word 'properly' evokes a traditional, middle-to-upper-class model of femininity, in contrast to the postwar image of the liberated woman. The list of subheadings given on the contents page reinforces this. The text is divided into alphabetically ordered sections, and among them are 'Discretion', 'Gloves', 'Husbands', 'Knees', and even 'Veils' (v–vi). It is true that the list also includes the more modern-sounding items 'Cocktails', 'Lingerie' and 'Sex', but these sections advise women that a cocktail dress should be 'scarcely décolleté at all' (25), that women should avoid 'the seductive lingerie styles more suitable for striptease' (99), and that 'so-called "sexy" styles are never truly elegant' (164). While sexiness is rejected, the word 'sophistication' is always used with approval: to distinguish, for instance, between two kinds of perfume – 'subtle, sophisticated blends' (167) and heavier, old-fashioned scents; or between two kinds of woman – 'feminine and sophisticated' and 'the tweedy, outdoor type' (94). Dariaux's attitudes towards

36 The 1964 title was slightly different: *Elegance: A Complete Guide for Every Woman Who Wants to be Well and Properly Dressed on All Occasions.*

class and sexuality are legible in her consistent privileging of sophistication over glamour. The difference between these two terms is explored by Clive Scott in his account of fashion photography:

> 'Glamour' is youthful, dynamic, pleasure-seeking, extrovert, voluble, short-term, gregarious, uncultured, volatile, public (and thus downmarket), while 'sophistication' is mature, poised, restrained, introvert, taciturn, long-term, solitary, cultured, controlled/severe (and thus upmarket). Because of its culturedness, 'sophistication' often has a social pedigree which 'glamour' can function without. (156)

This contrast is too sharply drawn; after all, the image-sets and ideas associated with sophistication and glamour do often overlap. Also, it is questionable whether 'glamour' is necessarily youthful (ageing actresses, princesses and other celebrities often manage to retain an aura of glamour) or whether sophistication is 'taciturn' and 'solitary': one has only to think of figures such as Oscar Wilde or Noël Coward to grasp its potential affiliation with performance, display and excess. Nevertheless, Scott's analysis of the respective class coordinates of glamour and sophistication certainly accords with the findings of my own research.

The HarperCollins website describes *A Guide to Elegance* as 'a classic style bible for timeless chic, grace, and poise – every tidbit of advice today's woman could possibly need', and this slightly paradoxical appeal to a combination of timelessness and contemporaneity ('today's woman') precisely matches the later twentieth-century concept of sophistication.[37] The book itself balances between nostalgia and modernness. The author insists on 'modesty and good taste' (10), yet while she presents good taste as a constant, she encourages readers to keep up with changing fashions, pointing out how particular choices become acceptable or unacceptable in different eras. Under 'Colour', she writes: 'a shade or combination which seems impossible to us today is quite likely to enchant us tomorrow', adding that no-one would have imagined 'that, thanks to Dior, we would combine black with brown, navy with black' (25). There remains, though, a discernible conflict between, on the one hand, Dariaux's rigid rules about the maximum number of rings to be worn on each hand or which kind of handbags should be put away at 5 pm, and, on the other, her consciousness that (to return to Jessica Burstein's point, discussed in my introduction), fashion and sophistication work by defining themselves against the immediate past or against their context. 'Of course, in order to be

---

37 A similarly complex marketing strategy was used for one of Dariaux's other books, *The Men in Your Life* (1968), republished by HarperCollins in 2004. The cover, with its flowing script and picture of a top hat, presents the book as a period piece, while the newly added subtitle, 'Timeless Advice and Wisdom on Managing the Opposite Sex', plays on the enduring value of Dariaux's book, and the jacket blurb, in comparing it to a recent bestseller ('Men are from Mars, women are from Venus, but Madame Dariaux has always known that') capitalises on its contemporary relevance.

elegant, you must be in fashion' (47), she says, but a few pages later comes the instruction: 'when the fashion of the moment happens to be one which doesn't suit you at all [...] you should remain absolutely firm and remind yourself that elegance is not necessarily synonymous with fashion' (53).

The section on knees contains only these words: 'The proverb: *Pour vivre heureux, vivons cachés* was invented for them!' (97). There is a stark incompatibility between this injunction and the fashion innovation for which the sixties are particularly remembered, the miniskirt. But we should bear demographics in mind: while the miniskirt may be central to our remembered image of sixties' fashion, it was favoured mainly by younger women. Dariaux was fifty when she wrote her *Guide to Elegance*, and while she ostensibly addresses women of all ages, her comments rarely seem particularly relevant to teenagers and young women. Nevertheless, her clear (though never explicit) rejection of the miniskirt is an indication that she conceives sophistication and elegance as rather incompatible with modern youth or with provocative dressing. Sophistication is for grown-ups, and is injurious to the appeal of girls: 'since they have at last been given fashions of their own, today's teenagers are more satisfied to dress their age and less tempted by over-sophisticated styles' (189).

Dariaux refers regretfully to certain extinct practices which were conducive to elegance: 'Years ago, every well-bred young girl was given posture lessons', she remarks (137), going on to emphasise the continuing importance of a graceful carriage. She also laments that veils are 'somewhat out of fashion at the moment' (196), but explains how to wear them anyway, in the hope that 'designers will revive the mode of veils worn over the entire face' (197). In the case of gloves, she is more determined, and insists that they are still compulsory for city wear:

> gloves should always be worn on the street but never indoors, except at the theatre, at a formal reception, or a ball. They should always be removed when eating [...]. But a lady never takes off her gloves in order to shake hands. (64–65)

The term 'lady' clearly signals the class inflection of Dariaux's nostalgia. She is primarily interested in the styles appropriate to the lifestyle of a wealthy, leisured woman with a full calendar of social engagements, no housework to perform, and time to change her clothes several times a day:

> In the morning, most smart women live in suits, and the afternoon dress has disappeared from our wardrobes to be replaced by the more youthful and less ceremonious two-piece ensemble. From 6 P.M. on, the dress comes into its own again, in the form of a cocktail or dinner dress. (39)

The snob appeal of Dariaux's book is further emphasised by her advice on what to wear for a weekend party in a country house, on board a yacht, or for a public appearance – such as might arise from one's 'civic or philan-thropic activities' (141). The instructions given for such occasions must, for most readers in 1964, have been largely superfluous; by 2003, they have a distinctly period charm. For audiences in both eras, these parts of *A Guide to Elegance* surely evoke an unreachable social world. Nevertheless, Dariaux does not move wholly in these rarefied circles, and is often ready with sugges-tions which would be useful to middle-class women. She advises, for example, about achieving elegance on a small budget, choosing office-wear, coping with extremes of weather and matching colours attractively. The book's ideal reader in 1964, then, may have been a rich, leisured wife, but the women who really bought the book were probably attracted (as are readers of magazines such as *Vogue*) by the mixture of practical advice and access to a fantasy world of wealth and high style.

The nostalgic structuring of *A Guide to Elegance* is also visible in its commentary on conformity, distinction and eccentricity. Under 'Uniformity', Dariaux observes that high living standards in the West, together with the vast expansion in mass-produced fashion, have resulted in a society in which 'all women [...] want to resemble one another – even though at the same time they are spending more and more on their clothes, cosmetics, and hairdressers!' (194). Her account of modern culture suggests that sophisti-cation diminishes as mass production and consumerism increase. Drawing on the established authority of the French in matters of style and sophisti-cation, she observes that the women of Paris buy a small number of outfits, all of excellent quality, whereas the American woman 'has been told that her role in the national economy is to continually buy and consume' (148). Under 'Comfort', Dariaux remarks that 'many of the details which were considered to be a mark of elegance some years ago are condemned today for reasons of comfort' (31), adding disparagingly, 'if women continue to seek comfort above all [...] they may eventually find that they have allowed themselves to become slaves to the trainer, Lycra from head to toe, ready meals, organized travel, functional uniformity, and general stultification' (32). Her resistance to mass production leads to a celebration of its two alternatives: hand-crafted fashions and custom-made couture. She recalls the sweaters she used to knit at school, which she designed herself so that 'nobody else would appear in the classroom in the same outfit as mine' (viii). Unsurprisingly, she also praises creativity and individuality in the world of fashion, though always balancing this with a dislike of extremes and attention-seeking styles. In her chapter on 'Individuality', she remarks: 'when originality lacks taste and moderation, it can indeed lead to comic effects', and then adds: 'However, fashion can only be renewed by a continual stream of original experiments, which cease to shock as soon as they have been adopted by a certain number of people' (125). In general, *A Guide to Elegance* is about balancing: achieving distinction without eccentricity; following conventions of dress without appearing dowdy and unimaginative; following fashions without being enslaved by them. Indeed, in one form or another, this quality of balance marks all the texts about sophistication discussed in the present study.

Dariaux seems fully aware that clothes are not simply expressive of identity but also constitutive of it. That is, an outfit does not project a pre-formed 'self'; rather, the wearer's behaviour may be influenced by her attempt to inhabit her clothes fully – to live up to the image which they suggest. This relates to the question of whether sophistication itself is innate or whether it can be simulated by strategic clothing choices and carefully modulated behaviours. This issue is indirectly explored in Dariaux's section on 'chic', which is perhaps the most interesting in the book. It seems to me that her conception of chic is very close to the conception of sophistication which I have been outlining in this study. She writes:

> The essence of casual refinement, chic is a little less studied than elegance and a little more intellectual. It is an inborn quality of certain individuals, who are sometimes unaware that they possess it. Chic is only perceptible to those who have already acquired a certain degree of civilization and culture and who have in addition both the leisure time to devote to improving their appearance and the desire to be part of a particular kind of elite, which might be called the 'aristocracy of external appearance'. It is a gift of the gods and has no relationship to beauty nor to wealth. (20)

This tension between the idea of chic/sophistication as an innate quality and the possibility that it can be learned marks many of the literary texts I have been examining, and is especially evident in smart magazines. Dariaux's book has many continuities with such magazines. Though *A Guide to Elegance* was published in a later age, in some ways it belongs to the era of the last years of *Vanity Fair* and the early years of *The New Yorker* – the 1930s of Dariaux's youth. Just as the magazines did, Dariaux presents sophistication and chic as signs of an advanced culture, and she reinforces this by the inclusion of quotations on the subjects of elegance, fashion and taste from writers such as Fielding, Molière and Rousseau. Chic, then, has dimensions of intellect and civilisation; elsewhere, Dariaux mentions that 'to be elegant is first of all to know oneself, and to know oneself well requires a certain amount of reflection and intelligence' (129).[38]

38 This point is strongly reinforced in Linda Grant's recent book *The Thoughtful Dresser* (2009): 'For people have written and thought about clothes ever since they could write and think' (17). The book grew out of Linda Grant's blog, the readers of which were 'always intelligent, thoughtful and extremely funny' (20).

The elitist (though not necessarily class-based) value system which Dariaux draws on here is, as in the smart magazines, countered by her attempt to coach women in how to acquire at least the semblance of chic:

> In order to increase your chances of acquiring chic when it is lacking, the first requirement is to be aware of the fact that you do not possess it. You can then entrust to experienced specialists the responsibility of changing your silhouette, coiffure, make-up, gestures, and wardrobe. (21)

This distinction between the innate quality of chic and the learned practice of elegance relates very directly to modern conceptions of sophistication. To some extent, to seem sophisticated is to be so, but there is no chance of even seeming sophisticated unless you first recognise what sophistication is, and to do this, you must have some inborn intelligence and sense of style. Dariaux, then, seems to split the concept of sophistication into two elements: the underlying chic and the surface elegance. The former, she suggests, has no relation to wealth, but the latter can be purchased by means of the expensive services of a range of professionals. Again, this aligns her with the fashionable magazines, since readers of *Vanity Fair* or *Vogue* were (and are) encouraged to buy particular kinds of cars, books, designer originals or other items with cachet in order to display their sophistication, but at the same time, to avoid vulgar excess and showiness. To quote Clive Scott again: 'The sophisticated [...] oscillates between the truly luxurious and the undemonstrative, in a noticeably educated language' (156).

Dariaux includes a section headed 'Rich' in which she explains that in the modern era, 'opulent' has become synonymous with 'vulgar' and 'ostentatious'. She retains, though, an appreciation for luxury and good quality, which is evident throughout her book and particularly in this section:

> True opulence, like true luxury, should be practically imperceptible – except to the eyes of the initiated few who can recognize at a glance that a simple little navy blue reefer is a Balenciaga original which probably cost as much as a fur coat. (155)

Once again, she appeals to the discernment of an elite, the aristocrats of style, who overlap with, but do not precisely coincide with, the wealthy upper class of France, Britain or America (the three countries she uses as reference points). These sophisticates are always able to distinguish an imitation from an 'original', and at several points in her text, Dariaux fiercely disparages imitations: 'Nothing is less chic, more unattractive and comparatively ruinous, than an imitation jewel attempting to pass itself off for the real thing [sic]' (93). She also describes rhinestones masquerading as diamonds as 'like all kinds of imitations, the height of inelegance' (117). And yet, the aim of her book is to create a generation of imitations: women who lack chic but achieve an appearance of elegance. She is therefore caught up in the paradox of sophistication: it is a performative quality which claims to be innate.

This tension emerges straight away in Dariaux's basic definition of elegance, given in her foreword: 'It is a sort of harmony that rather resembles beauty, with the difference that the latter is more often a gift of nature and the former the result of art' (vii). She also advises women to give serious thought to their appearance, but to avoid the appearance of effort, giving the instructive example of Princess Margaret who, 'by trying too hard to be chic, succeeded in being neither regal nor elegant but only conspicuous' (158). Dariaux's vision of elegance, then, depends on the use of the artificial in order to conform to norms which she attempts to *naturalise* by presenting them as correct and consensual. Those who do not conform to her rules are categorised as wrong: a woman who wears a bathing suit anywhere but on the beach, for instance, is 'incorrect' (14), and those who dye their hair an aggressive red or unnatural platinum blond are 'very vulgar' (70). Like most of the texts discussed in this book, *A Guide to Elegance* recalls Bourdieu's maxim that 'tastes are perhaps first and foremost distastes' (*Distinction* 56); Dariaux notes that the word 'elegance' comes from the Latin *eligere*, which means 'to select' (vii). This, perhaps, inspired HarperCollins to advertise their new edition of the book as 'the original *What Not To Wear*'.[39] Dariaux's rules are often highly complicated, which suggests that they are designed to mark off an elite who are 'in the know' from a mass of undistinguished women. For example, she writes: 'Jet necklaces are smart only when they are worn with white ensembles. White beads are elegant only in the summer' (118), and she also distinguishes between those necklaces which may be worn from early in the morning – 'pearls or a gold necklace' – and those which may be worn only from lunchtime onwards, such as 'outfit jewellery or semi-precious stones' (117). The rules also change according to setting, and certain things which are forbidden on the street may be acceptable at the seaside.

Stephen Gundle argues in *Glamour: A History* that glamour emerged in the nineteenth century at the same time that the modern city became the primary site of social display, and that it gained in importance with the developing twentieth-century culture of spectacle and consumption. While Dariaux's book aligns itself much more with sophistication than with glamour, nevertheless she too privileges the city as the setting for the most effective displays of elegance. Though she has sections on what to wear on the beach or in the

---

39 <http://www.harpercollins.com/books/9780060757342/A_Guide_to_Elegance/index.aspx> [accessed 21 July 2008]. *What Not to Wear* is a makeover reality TV show which started on BBC 2 in 2001. It was hosted for five seasons by Trinny Woodall and Susannah Constantine, and subsequently by Lisa Butcher and Mica Paris. There is also an American version.

country, they are very brief and sketchy: 'in the country it is good taste to wear no jewellery at all' (91), she says. Evincing a dislike of leather clothes, she admits that a leather coat might just about do 'on weekends, in convertible cars, and during country hikes' (98). Rural and coastal places, then, are presented as temporary retreats from the main business of life, and as places where elegance is not likely to be so rigorously maintained. The women whom her text addresses spend much of their time at dinner parties, cocktail parties and the theatre, and, despite their high heels, they are also often out on the street. The book is full of glimpses of urban environments: she says that the fashion stylists who create matching sets of accessories 'have contributed a great deal to improving the aspect of our city street scene' (108), and in another chapter writes that brightly coloured coats: 'add a note of gaiety to a city scene and bring a flush of pleasure to your face when you catch a glimpse of your reflection as you pass in front of a shop window' (24). The emphasis on the woman's reflection here is quite telling: though Dariaux advises her readers not to spend time admiring themselves in mirrors (58), she clearly envisages that the elegant woman will be continually aware of how she appears to others. The more ominous implications of this emerge in her attempted consolation to short women: 'you should realize that there are many men who simply adore doll-like women, and you ought to accentuate your appealing air.' She advises them to '[be] delicate [...] scatter-brained, tender-hearted, and helpless' (75). Worse still is her assertion: 'The modern woman may be a breadwinner, but her number one objective is still to win a man' (164). This statement, in combination with the possible note of homophobia in her remark 'a man who looks like a fashionplate is unbearable. Elegant, yes. Foppish, no!' (112), reveals that this text has a little too much of intolerance to be wholly modern. It defines the sophisticated in terms of style and the art of living, but not in terms of the open-mindedness and refusal to be shocked which characterises many other texts of later twentieth-century sophistication.

Conclusion
'The problem of leisure':
millennial sophistication

In 1995, BBC Radio 4 broadcast a winter series of dramas titled 'Season of Romance', and the play featured on Christmas Day was Coward's *Private Lives*, starring Stephen Fry and Imogen Stubbs. Sheridan Morley introduced it, and began by recalling 1969, when he was writing the first biography of Coward. He had asked him 'how often he now thought back to the great defining success of his career, *Private Lives*', and to Gertrude Lawrence, who had been dead for nearly twenty years:

> 'How often do I remember her?' Noël echoed, looking as though I had asked him if he was really English. 'Every night when I go to sleep, and every morning when I wake up, I see her in that white Molyneux dress on that *Private Lives* balcony, and she never goes away.'[1]

The original 'moment of sophistication', Coward and Lawrence's performance, is irrecoverable. (Indeed, it was deliberately ephemeral: Coward would not allow the plays he starred in to run for more than a few months so that he would not get bored acting them.[2]) But the attempt to recover the sophistication of 1930 results in a complex layering of nostalgia. First, there is Coward's endlessly reiterated nostalgia for the first performance and for his lost Gertie and his lost youth. Second, there is Morley's nostalgia for the late 1960s, when Coward was alive and he could share in his memories. Third, there is the nostalgia of the Radio 4 producers, reviving the play and choosing it for the centrepiece of the 'Season of Romance'. I could even add my own nostalgia for 1995, when I taped the play from the radio so that I could listen to it repeatedly. I still play my tape, although I now have a copy on DVD as part of the newly

---

1   This recording, including Morley's introduction, is on disc 2 of *The Coward Collection* (BBC DVD, 2008).
2   Morley mentions this in his introduction to the radio play.

issued set, *The Coward Collection*. Sophistication, though forever appearing to identify itself with the modern, often turns out to be a nostalgic structure which takes a clear, definable shape only in retrospect.

Nostalgia for earlier technologies, or for pre-technological eras, is very relevant here, because the word 'sophistication' is now most often used in relation to technology. In the field of marketing, nostalgic product styling is used most often for hi-tech and electrical goods. Stephen Brown writes in *Marketing: The Retro Revolution* (2001):

> Retro, indeed, seems to be everywhere these days. Old-style styling is *de rigeur* in numerous product categories: motorcycles, coffee makers, cameras, radios, refrigerators, telephones, toasters, perfumes and promos for Pentium processors. Retro is apparent across the various components of the marketing mix, from pseudo-antique packaging and repro retail stores to on-line auctions, which represent a hi-tech throwback to pre-modern pricing practices. (v–vi).

As well as electronics and domestic gadgets, other products and services frequently advertised using the word 'sophisticated' include alcoholic drinks, fine dining and holidays. Hotel adverts often explicitly define sophistication as an effective combination of modernness and nostalgic styling. In a recent travel supplement to *Vanity Fair* magazine, an advertising feature entitled 'It's Nice to be Niche' described the Colony Club Hotel in Barbados as combining 'timeless sophistication with up-to-the-minute standards of quality and comfort', while the Premier Palace in Kiev 'retains the elegance and sophistication of the past' but also 'offers the best of 21st-century comfort and service' ('It's Nice' 65, 69). Advertisers who choose magazines such as *Vanity Fair* are seeking to appeal to a self-consciously sophisticated audience: the 'niche' theme of the *Vanity Fair* advertising feature appeals to travellers who conceive of themselves in terms of discernment and distinction. Editorial copy in some sections of smart magazines such as *Vanity Fair* or *The New Yorker* often complements the advertisements: for instance, both periodicals regularly run features celebrating the most stylish American cities, with guides to the fashionable bars and gourmet cuisine of Chicago, Boston and, of course, New York itself.

In reviews and comic pieces, on the other hand, *The New Yorker* often adopts a different posture, lamenting over a perceived cultural decline in America and constructing sophistication in a nostalgic idiom. For example, in a 2005 film round-up, David Denby observes wearily: 'Gentility, not to mention sophistication and indirection, has departed from our raucous culture forever' (102). Feature writers often adopt a highly self-conscious attitude towards the supposed urbanity of *New Yorker* readers. A 1999 piece titled 'How to Act Local' offers advice to an imaginary gay couple taking a summer let in the country-side and trying to fit in:

> A Visit to a Farm: Try not to compliment the fresh-picked vegetables by describing them as 'camera-ready'. Do not refer to the pigpen as 'the little prosciutto area'. Curb your impulse to suggest that, pictorially speaking, the stable would work better if the farmer were to 'lose the goat shed'. [...] Say that you find fresh corn 'humbling'. Cultivate disdain for 'summer people.' (Alford)

In another paragraph, though, the article pokes fun simultaneously at the pretentiousness of the visitors and the limited horizons of the country dwellers, instructing: 'Understand that the introduction "This is my personal assistant, Eduardo" will meet with less indulgence than it has heretofore'. Like many narratives of sophistication, this cuts both ways.[3]

Turning from magazines to the internet, textual and visual manifestations of sophistication proliferate. The photo-sharing site Flickr invites users to label the pictures they upload so that searches on particular themes are possible. A search in January 2009 revealed no fewer than 3,563 images tagged 'sophistication'.[4] A majority of these show elegantly dressed women (and occasionally men), often photographed in black and white, some wearing vintage fashions. Other pictures feature high-heeled shoes, coffee cups, candles or cocktail glasses; a few show machinery or skyscrapers. Several are ironic, depicting tacky souvenirs or badly dressed tourists. Many of the pictures are actually images of simplicity, and are labelled with the comment attributed to Leonardo da Vinci, 'simplicity is the ultimate sophistication'. (This apocryphal remark, which simultaneously affirms and disavows sophistication, recurs endlessly through twenty-first-century self-help books and business manuals.)

The website Dandyism.net combines an extensive 'library' of classic literary accounts of the dandy with columns on contemporary dandyism. The front page presents the site as follows:

> Like the dandy, Dandyism.net aims to be effortlessly elegant, caustically witty, coldly superior and dryly amusing. Its editorial policy is caprice. It turns its diabolical monocle on the past and present to dispassionately decree who's a dandy and who's not, who is innovative and who is eccentric, who is classic and who is bland, who is dashing and who is ostentatious, who sets styles and who is a slave to fashion.[5]

---

3   Irony as a strategy of sophistication is also important to the new generation of men's magazines: the slogan for *Loaded*, for instance, is 'for men who should know better'. Such magazines use irony, as Jancovich notes, 'to indulge in the "uneducated" or "politically incorrect", while simultaneously asserting a knowing distance from both these indulgences. [...] They simultaneously reject the seriousness of educated taste and the naiveté of uneducated taste, and assert their superiority to both' (11).

4   <http://www.flickr.com> [accessed 25 January 2009].

5   <http://www.dandyism.net> [accessed 28 December 2008].

Parading their own distinction and disdaining popular opinion, the editors gleefully quote from feedback received:

Readers have called the site:
  'Infuriatingly snooty'
  'Fusty, philistine claptrap'
  'Vitriolic, caustic and without humor'
  'Cocksure'
  'Rather pathetic'

The front page also introduces the editors and contributors; among them is the author of a column titled 'The Sophistocrat', who describes himself as follows:

Michael Mattis lives his values – fortunately these are few. In fact, if he can be said to revere anything at all it would be, as with the dedicated Episcopal churchgoer, a really well cut navy blazer. In addition, Mattis values a good glass of claret, a dry martini, and an evening of light and convivial conversation.

This revival of dandyism is of course playful and self-conscious, though the amount of work which must have gone into this beautifully presented, content-rich site suggests that the project is not quite 'effortless' and that the editors, for all their self-mockery, take their dandyism rather seriously. Dandyism.net also runs adverts from London tailoring firms, wine merchants, and retailers of nostalgic fashion prints, revealing the niche commercial appeal of this supposedly specialised, recherché cultural phenomenon.

In film, Sofia Coppola's *Marie Antoinette* (2006), starring Kirsten Dunst, provides an intriguing example of postmodern sophistication. The film unashamedly reads pre-Revolutionary France in modern terms, revelling in the anachronisms of a soundtrack which combines eighteenth-century opera (Rameau) and keyboard pieces (Scarlatti, Couperin) with 1970s' and 1980s' New Wave (The Cure, Siouxsie and the Banshees, Gang of Four, New Order). The lyrics of Gang of Four's 'Natural's Not In It' (from their 1979 album *Entertainment*) perfectly match Coppola's reflection on the connections between the luxury of Versailles and modern consumerism:

The problem of leisure
What to do for pleasure
Ideal love a new purchase
A market of the senses[6]

Coppola's Marie Antoinette is simultaneously a childlike figure, bewildered in a highly sophisticated court world that she does not fully understand, and an embodiment of self-indulgent excess. Early scenes in the film dramatise her

6 <http://www.notgreatmen.com/gof_l1.html#2> [accessed 20 January 2009]. This is Gang of Four's official site and lyrics are reproduced here with permission of the band.

arrival, at the age of fourteen, in the French court, with an understanding of her own value as a commodity, but no grasp of the elaborate, highly restricting protocol of Versailles; the middle part of the film focuses on her failure to persuade her husband to consummate the marriage; later episodes show her seeking consolation for the aridity of her marriage and public role by ordering hundreds of dresses and pairs of shoes, consuming a great many chocolates and glasses of champagne, and playing with her friends at Le Petit Trianon. In this postmodern screen figure, one element of the tradition of pastoral outlined by Empson strangely culminates:

> the joke from comic primness about the innocent young girl [...] runs on through Sheridan, Thackeray, Dodgson, and Wilde – that it is only proper for her to be worldly, because she, like the world, should know the value of her condition, and that there must be no question of whether she is conscious or not of being worldly, so that she is safe (much too safe) from our calling the bluff of her irony, because she deserves either not to be told of the cold judgements of the world or not to be reminded of them. (*Pastoral* 193)

The Marie Antoinette of the film, unlike the protagonist of Antonia Fraser's biography, on which the film is based, is protected from the full knowledge of the cold judgements of the world: the film ends with her last sight of Versailles, and does not go on to show her time in the Tuileries or her execution.

Marie Antoinette exemplifies the complex interplay between innocence and sophistication which I have identified in many of the literary texts discussed in this book. Pretending and imitating, in Coppola's film, are shown as equally necessary to child's play, pastoral fantasy and sophisticated social behaviour. *Marie Antoinette* also exhibits sophistication's delicate balancing between excess and restraint, pleasure and discrimination, self-awareness and self-absorption. Sophistication is about distinction from context. And it is about doubleness, performance, artifice. Finally, it is about class, taste, pleasure and consumption. All these elements are present in the film, and they are surrounded by an aura of fantasy which is often crucial to the purveying of sophistication in literature and the media. Sophistication's fantastical dimension, in combination with its irony and artifice, can make it resistant to analysis, but it is precisely for this reason that more rigorous reading is necessary, since sophistication remains a very under-theorised term.

The word 'sophistication' has undergone a major transformation in meaning in the period between the real life of Marie Antoinette and its most recent mythologisation in Sofia Coppola's film. I will end by proposing some reasons for this shift. Etymologically, 'sophistication' developed from a derogatory term referring to falsification or adulteration to a term of praise suggesting distinction and discriminating taste; and my close readings in the preceding chapters have uncovered some of the cultural shifts underlying this change. In the nineteenth century, the decline of Romanticism, with its idealisation of sentiment and sensibility, innocence and naturalness, opened the way for the elaboration of the alternative set of values associated with sophistication. In addition, the rise of the middle class, with its insistent appropriation of aristocratic markers of distinction, made sophistication increasingly desirable as a social strategy. As the power of the aristocracy diminished, its function as an arbiter of taste was assumed by various other groups, including dandies, aesthetes, homosexuals, and others who embraced, rather than avoiding, the label 'sophisticate'. The idea of 'natural' aristocracy – that is, of an elite quality which is legible on the body, through clothing, and audible in manners and conversation – gradually assumed ascendance over the traditional idea of nobility as encoded in the blood. In the twentieth century, changing ideals of femininity reduced the emphasis on modesty and gentleness, allowed women more access to the public sphere, re-evaluated their intellectual contribution and capacities, and – in short – allowed women to become openly sophisticated. While the sophisticated women of nineteenth-century fiction are never permitted happy endings, those of twentieth-century fiction are often victorious. Sophistication has played a crucial role in the ongoing project of dismantling traditional categories of gender, sexuality and class. The two World Wars also had their effect; postwar disillusionment is compatible with a distrust of consensual morality and a pose of sophisticated weariness.

None of this necessarily implies, though, that the politics of sophistication have become more contestatory over time. Indeed, sophistication was most oppositional in the contexts of Romanticism and Victorian earnestness, even though it was, at a deeper level, implicated in both. In the twentieth century, it became quite mainstream; by the millennium, even banal. The very uncertainty about the meaning of the word 'sophistication' in earlier periods – the doubt as to whether it was a term of praise or censure – led to its being deployed with great care: it occurs once in the whole of Jane Austen, once or twice in some of Dickens's lengthy novels. In the later twentieth century, though, 'sophistication' began to be applied rather indiscriminately to everything stylish, luxurious, clever or technically complex, and became far more the preserve of advertisers than of writers or critics.

The allegiances of 'sophistication' in the twentieth century are multiple. In earlier decades, its potential alignment with dominant cultural paradigms such as modernism was balanced by an apparently contrary affiliation with middlebrow strategies of imitation and appropriation; indeed, sophistication often functioned to break down boundaries between modernist and middlebrow cultural production. In contemporary commercial discourse, the more widely the word 'sophisticated' is used to advertise everything from exclusive hotels to technologically advanced consumer goods, the closer the spectre of mass sophistication seems to approach. At the same time, the underlying dynamic of sophistication still requires distinction from context; this longing for distinction seems, increasingly, to be focused on past ideals of elegance whose attraction derives largely from their unattainability in the present. The National Portrait Gallery in London recently ran retrospectives of the work of several photographers whose black-and-white images unfailingly evoke the inaccessible sophistication of an earlier age – Cecil Beaton (2005), Lee Miller (2005), Angus McBean (2006) – and followed these up with the *Vanity Fair Portraits* exhibition of 2008, which devoted most of its space to the Jazz Age incarnation of the magazine. Similarly, the 2009 BBC 4 television series *Style on Trial* focused on the fashions of successive decades, beginning with the 1940s. The first episode played on the almost impossible glamour of the New Look, and the surprising elegance of make-do-and-mend austerity fashion, showing images from forties' magazines and advertisements. Guests on the show repeatedly expressed envy of, and longing for, this lost sophistication. The idea behind this programme is quite distinct from that of retro fashion shows, which attempt to explain to viewers how to 'get the forties look' (or the twenties, sixties, or even nineties look) through the purchase of currently available goods from high street stores. This returns us to the question of nostalgia, and so, once more, to that defining figure of modern sophistication, Noël Coward. Kenneth Tynan wrote of Coward in 1953: 'I have heard him accused of having enervated English comedy by making it languid and blasé. The truth, of course, is the opposite: Coward took sophistication out of the refrigerator and set it bubbling on the hob' (287). This has been exactly my ambition in this book.

Bibliography

'A Child's Humorous Venture in Fiction.' *New York Times Review of Books* (27 July 1919): 386.

Adams, James Eli. *Dandies and Desert Saints: Styles of Victorian Masculinity*. Ithaca: Cornell UP, 1995.

Albright, Daniel. *Modernism and Music: An Anthology of Sources*. Chicago: U of Chicago P, 2004.

Alford, Henry. 'How to Act Local.' *The New Yorker* (16 August 1999): 35.

'Americana.' *The American Mercury* 1.1 (January 1924): 46–49.

Amory, Cleveland and Frederic Bradlee, eds. *Vanity Fair: A Cavalcade of the 1920s and 1930s*. New York: Viking, 1960.

Anderson, Amanda. *The Powers of Distance: Cosmopolitanism and the Cultivation of Detachment*. Princeton, NJ: Princeton UP, 2001.

Anderson, Sherwood. *Winesburg, Ohio*. 1919. New York: Penguin, 1976.

Ardis, Ann. *Modernism and Cultural Conflict, 1880–1922*. Cambridge: Cambridge UP, 2002.

Ashford, Daisy. *Daisy Ashford: Her Book*. London: Chatto and Windus, 1920.

Ashford, Daisy. *The Young Visiters; Or, Mr Salteena's Plan*. Ed. Juliet McMaster et al. Edmonton, AB: Juvenilia P, 1997.

Auburn, Mark S. *Sheridan's Comedies: Their Contexts and Achievements*. Lincoln and London: U of Nebraska P, 1977.

Austen, Jane. *Emma*. 1816. London: Folio Society, 1975.

Austen, Jane. 'Love and Freindship.' In *Shorter Works*. By Jane Austen. London: Folio Society, 1975. 70–96.

Austen, Jane. *Mansfield Park*. 1814. London: Folio Society, 1975.

Austen, Jane. *Northanger Abbey*. 1818. London: Folio Society, 1975.

Backman, Mark. *Sophistication: Rhetoric and the Rise of Self-Consciousness*. Woodbridge, CT: Ox Bow Press, 1991.

Balliett, Whitney. 'Books: Moses in the Old Brit'n.' *The New Yorker* (18 January 1958): 99–101.

Barker-Benfield, G. J. *The Culture of Sensibility: Sex and Society in Eighteenth-Century Britain.* Chicago: U of Chicago P, 1992.

Barrie, J. M. Preface to *The Young Visiters* by Daisy Ashford. 1919. Rpt in *The Young Visiters.* By Daisy Ashford. Ed. McMaster. 63-67.

Baudelaire, Charles. 'The Painter of Modern Life.' 1863. Trans. Jonathan Mayne. Extract rpt in *Art in Theory, 1815–1900: An Anthology of Changing Ideas.* By Charles Harrison, Paul Wood and Jason Gaiger. Oxford: Blackwell, 1998. 493–506.

Beauman, Nicola. 'Persephone Books.' In Hammill, Miskimmin and Sponenberg. 185–86.

Beerbohm, Max. *The Illustrated Zuleika Dobson.* New Haven and London: Yale UP, 2002.

Berman, Jessica. *Modernist Fiction, Cosmopolitanism and the Politics of Community.* Cambridge: Cambridge UP, 2001.

Bishop, Edward. 'Re:Covering Modernism: Format and Function in the Little Magazines'. *Modernist Writers and the Marketplace.* Ed. Ian Willison, Warwick Gould, and Warren Chernaik. Basingstoke: Macmillan, 1996. 287–319.

Blackman, Cally. *100 Years of Fashion Illustration.* London: Laurence King Publishing, 2007.

Bluemel, Kristin. *George Orwell and the Radical Eccentrics: Intermodernism in Literary London.* Basingstoke: Palgrave Macmillan, 2004.

Bohls, Elizabeth A. *Women Travel Writers and the Language of Aesthetics 1716–1818.* Cambridge: Cambridge UP, 1995.

Bonaparte, Felicia. 'Reading the Deadly Text of Modernism: Vico's Philosophy of History and Max Beerbohm's *Zuleika Dobson.*' *Clio* 27.3 (Spring 1998): 335–62. Online version: 11 printed pages.

Botshon, Lisa and Meredith Goldsmith, eds. *Middlebrow Moderns: Popular American Women Writers of the 1920s.* Boston, MA: Northeastern UP, 2003.

Bourdieu, Pierre. *Distinction: A Social Critique of the Judgement of Taste.* 1979. Trans. Richard Nice. London and New York: Routledge and Kegan Paul, 1986.

Bowlby, Rachel. *Shopping With Freud.* London: Routledge, 1993.

Boym, Svetlana. *The Future of Nostalgia.* New York: Basic Books, 2002.

Bradbury, Malcolm and James McFarlane, eds. *Modernism, 1890–1930.* 1976. Brighton: Harvester, 1978.

Bradlee, Frederic. 'Frank Crowninshield: Editor, Man, and Uncle.' Amory and Bradlee 11–12.

Brennan, Maeve. 'Books: Brief Affair.' *The New Yorker* (24 December 1966). 66–67.

Brown, Erica, ed. *Investigating the Middlebrow. Working Papers on the Web* 11 (July 2008). <http://research.shu.ac.uk/middlebrow-network/Publications.php>

Brown, Stephen. *Marketing: The Retro Revolution.* London: Sage, 2001.

Burney, Frances. *Evelina; or, The History of a Young Lady's Entrance into the World.* 1778. London: Macmillan, 1903.

Burstein, Jessica. 'A Few Words About Dubuque: Modernism, Sentimentalism, and the Blasé.' *American Literary History* 14.2 (2002): 227–54.

Bushman, Richard L. *The Refinement of America: Persons, Houses, Cities.* New York: Knopf, 1992.

Byrne, Sandie. *The Unbearable Saki: The Work of H. H. Munro.* Oxford: Oxford UP, 2007.

Carey, John. *The Intellectuals and the Masses: Pride and Prejudice among the Literary Intelligentsia, 1880–1930.* London: Faber and Faber, 1992.

Carpenter, Mary Wilson. '"Eat Me, Drink Me, Love Me": The Consumable Female Body in Christina Rossetti's *Goblin Market.*' *Victorian Poetry* 29.4 (Winter 1991): 415–34.

Carroll, Lewis. *Alice's Adventures in Wonderland.* 1865. Rpt with *Through the Looking-Glass.* Ed. Roger Lancelyn Green. Oxford: Oxford UP, 1982. 1–111.

Carroll, Lewis. *Through the Looking-Glass and What Alice Found There.* Rpt with *Alice's Adventures in Wonderland.* Ed. Roger Lancelyn Green. Oxford: Oxford UP, 1982. 113–245.

Chandler, James K. and Kevin Gilmartin, eds. *Romantic Metropolis: The Urban Scene of British Culture, 1780–1840.* Cambridge: Cambridge UP, 2005.

Ciancio, Ralph. 'Unity of Vision in *Winesburg, Ohio.*' *PMLA* 87 (1972): 994–1006.

Citron, Stephen. *Noël and Cole: The Sophisticates.* London: Sinclair Stevenson, 1992.

Clark, Suzanne. *Sentimental Modernism: Women Writers and the Revolution of the Word.* Bloomington, IN: Indiana UP, 1991.

Colette. *Le Blé en Herbe.* 1923. Paris: Flammarion, 1974.

Colquhoun, Archibald. 'Giuseppe di Lampedusa. A Note by the Translator.' In *Two Stories and a Memory.* By Giuseppe di Lampedusa. First published as *Racconti.* 1961. Trans. Archibald Colquhoun. London: Collins and Harvill, 1962. 13–26.

Coppola, Sofia, dir. *Marie Antoinette.* Sony, 2006.

Coward, Noël. *The Essential Noël Coward Songbook.* 1953. London: Omnibus P, 1980.

Coward, Noël. *The Letters of Noël Coward.* Ed. Barry Day. London: Methuen, 2007.

Coward, Noël. Introduction. *The Penguin Complete Saki.* By Saki [H. H. Munro]. 1967. Harmondsworth: Penguin, 1982. xi–xiv.

Coward, Noël. Introduction. *Play Parade: The Collected Plays of Noël Coward.* Volume I. London: Heinemann, 1934. vii–xviii.

Coward, Noël. *Private Lives.* 1930. Rpt in Coward, *Play Parade: The Collected Plays of Noël Coward.* Volume I. London: Heinemann, 1934. 465–554.

Cowart, Georgia J. *The Triumph of Pleasure: Louis XIV and the Politics of Spectacle.* Chicago: U of Chicago P, 2008.

Craik, Jennifer. *The Face of Fashion: Cultural Studies in Fashion.* London: Routledge, 1994.

Danson, Lawrence. *Max Beerbohm and the Act of Writing.* New York: Oxford UP, 1989.

Dariaux, Genevieve Antoine. *A Guide to Elegance.* 1964. London: HarperCollins, 2003.

Dariaux, Genevieve Antoine. *The Men in Your Life.* 1968. London: HarperCollins, 2004.

Davis, Fred. *Yearning for Yesterday: A Sociology of Nostalgia.* New York: The Free Press, 1979.

Deen, Stella, ed. *Challenging Modernism: New Readings in Literature and Culture, 1914–45* Aldershot: Ashgate, 2002.

DeJean, Joan. *The Essence of Style: How the French Invented High Fashion, Fine Food, Chic Cafés, Style, Sophistication, and Glamour.* New York: The Free Press, 2005.

Denby, David. 'The Current Cinema: Partners.' *The New Yorker* (12 September 2005): 102–103.

Dickens, Charles. *Nicholas Nickleby.* 1839. Ed. Michael Slater. London: Penguin, 1978.

Dickens, Monica. *Mariana.* 1940. London: Persephone, 1999.

Dimock, George. 'Childhood's End: Lewis Carroll and the Image of the Rat.' *Word & Image: A Journal of Verbal/Visual Enquiry* 8.3 (July–Sept. 1992): 183–205.

Disraeli, Benjamin. *Vivian Grey*. 1826-7. Bradenham Edition. London: Peter Davies, 1926.

Douglas, George H. *The Smart Magazines: Fifty Years of Literary Revelry and High Jinks at Vanity Fair, The New Yorker, Life, Esquire,* and *The Smart Set*. North Haven, CT: Archon, 1991.

D. P. [Dorothy Parker]. 'So This Is New York! The Story of a Warrior's Return.' *Vanity Fair* 12.3 (May 1919): 21.

Earle, David M. *Re-Covering Modernism: Pulps, Paperbacks and the Prejudice of Form*. Farnham: Ashgate, 2009.

Earnshaw, Steven, ed. *Literature and Value. Working Papers on the Web* 2 (November 2001). <http://www.shu.ac.uk/wpw/previousissues.html>

Eatwell, Ann. 'Tea à la Mode: The Fashion for Tea and the Tea Equipage in London and Paris.' In *Boucher and Chardin: Masters of Modern Manners*. Ed. Anne Dulau. Glasgow and London: University of Glasgow and Paul Holberton Publishing, 2008. 50–76.

Eliot, T. S. *The Family Reunion*. 1939. Rpt in *The Complete Poems and Plays*. By T. S. Eliot. London: Faber and Faber, 2004. 283–350.

Empson, William. *Some Versions of Pastoral*. 1935. London: Penguin, 1995.

Empson, William. *The Structure of Complex Words*. 1951. London: Chatto and Windus, 1964.

Everett, Barbara. 'The New Style of *Sweeney Agonistes*.' *Yearbook of English Studies* 14 (1984): 243–63.

Fass, Paula. *The Damned and the Beautiful: American Youth in the 1920s*. New York: Oxford UP, 1977.

Faulks, Sebastian. 'Life and Letters: Forever a Mistress.' *The New Yorker* (27 April and 4 May 1998): 146–50.

Fitzgerald, F. Scott. *The Beautiful and Damned*. 1922. Harmondsworth: Penguin, 2001.

Flanner, Janet. 'Letter From Paris.' *The New Yorker* (24 July 1954): 47–48.

Flowerdew, Lynne. 'Corpora and Context in Professional Writing.' In *Advances in Discourse Studies*. By Vijay K. Bhatia, John Flowerdew and Rodney H. Jones. London: Routledge, 2007. 115–27.

Forster, E. M. *Aspects of the Novel*. New York: Harcourt Brace, 1927.

Forster, E. M. Introduction to *Two Stories and a Memory*. By Giuseppe di Lampedusa. First published as *Racconti*. 1961. Trans. Archibald Colquhoun. London: Collins and Harvill, 1962. 5–8.

Fraser, Antonia. *Marie Antoinette: The Journey*. London: Phoenix, 2001.

Friedman, Susan Stanford. 'Periodizing Modernism: Postcolonial Modernities and the Space/Time Borders of Modernist Studies.' *Modernism/Modernity* 13.3 (September 2006): 425–43.

Frosch, Thomas R. 'Parody and Authenticity in *Lolita*.' 1982. Rpt in *Vladimir Nabokov's Lolita: A Casebook*. Ed. Ellen Pifer. New York: Oxford UP, 2003. 39–56.

Gagnier, Regenia. *Idylls of the Marketplace: Oscar Wilde and the Victorian Public*. Aldershot: Scolar P, 1986.

Garrick, David. Prologue to *The School for Scandal*. By Richard Brinsley Sheridan. In

Sheridan 5–6.

Gibbons, Stella. *Cold Comfort Farm*. 1931. Harmondsworth: Penguin, 2006.

Gibbons, Stella. 'Genesis of a Novel.' *Punch* (20 April 1966): 578–79.

Gifford, Terry. *Pastoral*. New Critical Idiom series. London: Routledge, 1999.

Gigante, Denise. 'Romanticism and Taste.' *Literature Compass* 4.2 (2007): 407–19.

Gigante, Denise. *Taste: A Literary History*. New Haven and London: Yale UP, 2005.

Giles, Judy. *The Parlour and the Suburb: Domestic Identities, Class, Femininity and Modernity*. Basingstoke: Palgrave Macmillan, 2004.

Gill, Brendan. 'Books: The Uses of Love.' *The New Yorker* (5 March 1955): 114–15.

Goldman, Jonathan. 'The Parrotic Voice of the Frivolous: Fiction by Ronald Firbank, I. Compton-Burnett, and Max Beerbohm.' *Narrative* 7.3 (October 1999): 289–306.

Grant, Linda. *The Thoughtful Dresser*. London: Virago, 2009.

Green, Roger Lancelyn. Introduction to *Alice's Adventures in Wonderland* and *Through the Looking Glass* by Lewis Carroll. 1971. Oxford: OUP, 1982. ix–xxv.

Grover, Mary. *Cultural Embarrassment in Interwar Britain: The Ordeal of Warwick Deeping*. Cranbury, NJ: Associated University Presses, 2009.

Gundle, Stephen. *Glamour: A History*. Oxford: Oxford UP, 2008.

Gundle, Stephen and Clino Trini Castelli. *The Glamour System*. Basingstoke: Palgrave Macmillan, 2006.

Hall, N. John. Introduction to *The Illustrated Zuleika Dobson*. By Max Beerbohm. New Haven and London: Yale UP, 2002. N.p.

Hamilton, Sharon. 'Mencken and Nathan's *Smart Set* and the Story behind Fitzgerald's Early Success', *The F. Scott Fitzgerald Review* 4 (2005): 20–48.

Hammill, Faye. '*Cold Comfort Farm*, D. H. Lawrence, and Literary Culture Between the Wars.' *Modern Fiction Studies* 47.4 (Fall 2001): 831–54.

Hammill, Faye. 'Sophistication, Modernism and Celebrity in *Vanity Fair*', Forthcoming in *Modernist Star Maps: Celebrity, Modernity, Culture*, Ed. Jonathan E. Goldman and Aaron Jaffe. Farnham: Ashgate, 2010.

Hammill, Faye. 'Stella Gibbons, Ex-centricity and the Suburb.' In *Intermodernism*. Ed. Kristin Bluemel. Edinburgh: Edinburgh UP, 2009. 75–92.

Hammill, Faye. *Women, Celebrity and Literary Culture Between the Wars*. Austin, TX: U of Texas P, 2007.

Hammill, Faye, Esme Miskimmin and Ashlie Sponenberg, eds. *Encyclopedia of British Women's Writing 1900–1950*. Basingstoke: Palgrave Macmillan, 2006.

Hampton, Christopher, dir. *Dangerous Liaisons*. Warner, 1988.

Hapgood, Lynne. *Margins of Desire: The Suburbs in Fiction and Culture, 1880–1925*. Manchester: Manchester University Press, 2005.

Hazlitt, William. 'Brummelliana.' [1820 version] *The Literary Pocket-Book; or, Companion for the Lover of Nature and Art* (1820). Rpt in *New Writings of William Hazlitt*. Ed. Duncan Wu. Oxford: Oxford UP, 2007. 329–33.

Hazlitt, William. 'Brummelliana.' [1828 version] *London Weekly Review* (2 Feburary 1828). Rpt in *The Complete Works of William Hazlitt*. Ed. Percival Presland Howe et al. London: J. M. Dent, 1934. 20: 152–54.

Hazlitt, William. 'The Dandy School.' *The Examiner* (18 November 1827). Rpt in *The*

Complete Works of William Hazlitt. Ed. Percival Presland Howe et al. London: J. M. Dent, 1934. 20: 143–48.

Hazlitt, William. 'On Gusto.' *The Examiner* (26 May 1816). Rpt in *Romanticism: An Anthology.* Second edn. Ed. Duncan Wu. Oxford: Blackwell, 2000. 597–99.

Hedley, Joe. *François Boucher: Seductive Visions.* London: The Wallace Collection, 2004.

Hegeman, Susan. 'Taking *Blondes* Seriously.' *American Literary History* 7.3 (1995): 525–54.

Hillier, Bevis. *Art Deco of the 20s and 30s.* London: Studio Vista, 1968.

Hilton, Matthew. *Smoking in British Popular Culture.* Manchester: Manchester UP, 2000.

Homberger, Eric. *Mrs Astor's New York: Money and Social Power in a Gilded Age.* New Haven, CT: Yale UP, 2002.

Horne, Charles F., ed. *The Sacred Books and Early Literature of the East.* Vol. VIII: *Medieval Persia.* New York: Parke, Austin, and Lipscomb, 1917.

Horner, Avril and Sue Zlosnik. 'Agriculture, Body Sculpture, Gothic Culture: Gothic Parody in Gibbons, Atwood and Weldon.' *Gothic Studies* 4.2 (Nov. 2002): 167–77.

Howells, William Dean. *Selected Letters.* Ed. George Arms and et al. Vol. 2: 1873–1881. Boston: Twayne, 1979.

Howland, John. *Ellington Uptown: Duke Ellington, James P. Johnson, and the Birth of Concert Jazz.* Ann Arbor: U of Michigan P, 2009.

Humble, Nicola. *The Feminine Middlebrow Novel, 1920s to 1950s: Class, Domesticity, and Bohemianism.* Oxford: Oxford UP, 2004.

Hunston, Susan. *Corpora in Applied Linguistics.* Cambridge: Cambridge UP, 2002.

Hunt, Leigh. *The Autobiography of Leigh Hunt, With Reminiscences of Friends and Contemporaries.* Vol. 2. New York: Harper and Brothers, 1850.

Hunt, Leigh. 'The Late Mr Sheridan.' *The Examiner* 446 (14 July 1816): 433–36.

Hutcheon, Linda. *Methods for the Study of Literature as Cultural Memory.* Vol. 6 of *Proceedings of the XVth Congress of the International Comparative Literature Association.* Ed. Annemarie Estor and Raymond Vervliet. Amsterdam and Atlanta, GA: Rodopi, 2000. 189–208.

Hutchinson, George. *The Harlem Renaissance in Black and White.* Second edn. Boston, MA: Harvard UP, 1995.

'It's Nice to be Niche.' *Vanity Fair: On Travel* (April 2008): 65–69.

Jaffe, Aaron. *Modernism and the Culture of Celebrity.* Cambridge: Cambridge UP, 2005.

James, Henry. *The American Scene.* 1907. Ed. Leon Edel. London: Hart-Davis, 1968.

James, Henry. *Collected Travel Writings: The Continent.* New York: Library of America, 1993.

James, Henry. *Daisy Miller.* 1878. Harmondsworth: Penguin, 1995.

James, Henry. *Henry James: A Life in Letters.* Ed. Philip Horne. London: Penguin, 2001.

James, Henry. *The Portrait of a Lady.* 1881. Ed. Nicola Bradbury. Oxford: Oxford UP, 1981.

James, Henry. Preface to the New York Edition of *Daisy Miller.* 1907. Rpt in *Daisy Miller.* Ed. Geoffrey Moore and Patricia Crick. Harmondsworth: Penguin, 1986. 40–43.

Jameson, Robert. 'Purity and Power at the Victorian Dinner Party.' In *The Archaeology of Contextual Meanings.* Ed. Ian Hodder. Cambridge: Cambridge UP, 2009: 55–65.

Jancovich, Mark. 'Placing Sex: Sexuality, Taste and Middlebrow Culture in the Reception of *Playboy* Magazine.' *Intensities: A Journal of Cultural Media* 2 (Autumn/Winter 2001). <http://www.intensities.org.> 14 pages.

Johnson, Samuel. *A Dictionary of the English Language.* 11th edn. Volume 2. London, 1799.

Kaye-Smith, Sheila and G. B. Stern. *Talking of Jane Austen*. London: Cassell, 1943.

Kiernan, Robert F. *Frivolity Unbound: Six Masters of the Camp Novel*. New York: Continuum, 1990.

Kolb, David. *Postmodern Sophistications: Philosophy, Architecture, and Tradition*. Chicago: U of Chicago P, 1990.

Kucich, John. *The Power of Lies: Transgression in Victorian Fiction*. Ithaca, NY: Cornell UP, 1994.

Lamb, Charles. 'On the Artificial Comedy of the Last Century.' 1822. Rpt in *The Essays of Elia*. By Charles Lamb. 1823. Philadelphia: Willis P. Hazard, 1856. 183–90.

Lambert, Constant. *Music Ho!* 1934. Harmondsworth: Penguin, 1948.

Lampedusa, Giuseppe Tomasi di. *Il Gattopardo*. 1958. Milan: Feltrinelli, 1969.

Lampedusa, Giuseppe Tomasi di. *The Leopard*. First published as *Il Gattopardo*. 1958. Trans. Archibald Colquhoun. 1961. London: Harvill, 1996.

Lampedusa, Giuseppe Tomasi di. 'Places of My Infancy.' 1955. In Lampedusa, *Two Stories and a Memory*. First published as *Racconti*. 1961. Trans. Archibald Colquhoun. London: Collins and Harvill, 1962. 27–74.

Latham, Sean. *'Am I a Snob?' Modernism and the Novel*. Ithaca, NY: Cornell UP, 2003.

Lawrence, Margaret. *The School of Femininity: A Book For and About Women As They Are Interpreted Through Feminine Writers of Yesterday and Today*. New York: Frederick A. Stokes, 1936.

Leick, Karen. 'Popular Modernism: Little Magazines and the American Daily Press.' *PMLA* 123.1 (January 2008): 125–39.

Lewis, Wyndham. *Time and Western Man*. 1927. Ed. Paul Edwards. Santa Rosa: Black Sparrow P, 1993.

Light, Alison. *Forever England: Femininity, Literature and Conservatism Between the Wars*. London: Routledge, 1991.

Lippmann, Walter. *Public Opinion*. 1922. New York: Free Press, 1997.

Litvak, Joseph. *Strange Gourmets: Sophistication, Theory and the Novel*. Durham, NC: Duke UP, 1997.

Long, Helen C. *The Edwardian House: The Middle-Class Home in Britain, 1880–1914*. Manchester: Manchester UP, 1993.

Loos, Anita. *A Girl Like I*. 1966. London: Hamish Hamilton, 1967.

Macdonell, A. G. *England, their England*. 1933. London: Picador, 1983.

Mackenzie, Henry. *The Man of Feeling*. 1771. Paris, 1807.

Malcomson, R. M. *Daisy Ashford: Her Life*. London: Chatto and Windus, 1984.

Mansfield, Katherine. 'A Child and her Note Book.' Review of *The Young Visiters* by Daisy Ashford. *The Athenaeum* (30 May 1919): 400.

Mather, Jeffrey. Introduction to *The Young Visiters*. By Daisy Ashford. Edmonton, AB: Juvenilia P, 1997. ix–xvii.

McEnery, Tony and Andrew Wilson. *Corpus Linguistics*. Second edn. Edinburgh: Edinburgh UP, 2001.

McMaster, Juliet. 'Virginal Representations of Sexuality: The Child Author and the Adult Reader.' *English Studies in Canada* 24 (1998): 299–308.

McMaster, Juliet. 'What Daisy Knew: The Epistemology of the Child Writer.' In *The Child*

Writer From Austen to Woolf. Ed. Christine Alexander and Juliet McMaster. Cambridge: Cambridge UP, 2005. 51–69.

Mencken, H. L. Editor's introduction to *Americana 1925*. New York: Knopf, 1925. v–vi.

Mencken, H. L. and George Jean Nathan. Editorial. *The American Mercury* 1.1 (January 1924): 30.

Meyer, Moe. 'Reclaiming the Discourse of Camp.' In *The Politics and Poetics of Camp*. Ed. Moe Meyer. New York: Routledge, 1994. 1–22.

Miller, D. A. 'Sontag's Urbanity.' *October* 49 (Summer 1989): 91–101.

Miller, Nina. *Making Love Modern: The Intimate Public Worlds of New York's Literary Women*. New York: Oxford UP, 1999.

Moers, Ellen. *The Dandy: Brummell to Beerbohm*. New York: Viking, 1960.

Mole, Tom. *Byron's Romantic Celebrity: Industrial Culture and the Hermeneutic of Intimacy*. Basingstoke: Palgrave Macmillan, 2007.

Monk, Leland. 'Glycerine. Yes, Hot, Excellent.' Review of *Strange Gourmets* by Joseph Litvak. *NOVEL: A Forum on Fiction* 31.2 (Spring 1998): 257–59.

Montgomery, Maureen E. *Displaying Women: Spectacles of Leisure in Edith Wharton's New York*. London: Routledge, 1998.

Morley, Sheridan. *A Talent to Amuse: A Biography of Noël Coward*. Garden City, NY: Doubleday, 1969.

Morrisson, Mark S. *The Public Face of Modernism: Little Magazines, Audiences and Reception, 1905–1920*. Madison, WI: U of Wisconsin P, 2001.

Morton, Timothy, ed. *Cultures of Taste/Theories of Appetite: Eating Romanticism*. New York: Palgrave Macmillan, 2004.

Mullen, Richard. Editor's introduction to *Domestic Manners of the Americans*. By Fanny Trollope. Oxford: OUP, 1984. ix–xxxi.

Murphy, Michael. 'Medieval Max and *Zuleika Dobson*.' *English Literature in Transition* 30.3 (1987): 303–307.

Murphy, Michael. 'One Hundred Per Cent Bohemia: Pop Decadence and the Aestheticization of the Commodity in the Rise of the Slicks.' In *Marketing Modernisms: Self-Promotion, Canonization, Rereading*. Ed. Kevin J. H. Dettmar and Steven Watt. Ann Arbor: U of Michigan P, 1996. 61–89.

Nabokov, Vladimir. *Lolita*. 1955. London: Penguin, 1995.

Nabokov, Vladimir. 'On a Book Entitled *Lolita*.' 1956. Rpt in *Lolita*. By Vladimir Nabokov. London: Penguin, 1995. 311–17.

Napper, Lawrence. *British Cinema and Middlebrow Culture in the Interwar Years*. Exeter: U of Exeter P, 2009.

Nardini, Robert F. 'Mencken and the "Cult of Smartness"'. *Menckeniana* 84 (Winter 1982): 1–12.

Newton, Esther. *Mother Camp: Female Impersonators in America*. Englewood Cliffs, NJ: Prentice-Hall, 1972.

Ohmann, Richard. *Selling Culture: Magazines, Markets, and Class at the Turn of the Century*. London: Verso, 1996.

Pace, Eric. 'Françoise Sagan, Who Had a Best Seller at 19 with "Bonjour Tristesse", Dies at 69.' Obituary. *The New York Times* (25 September 2004). <http://www.nytimes.com>

[accessed 10 November 2008].

Pack, Robert and Marjorie Lelash. Introduction to *Così fan tutte*. In *Three Mozart Libretti*. By Wolfgang Amadeus Mozart and Lorenzo Da Ponte. Trans. Pack and Lelash. New York: Dover, 1993. 222–23.

Parkins, Wendy. 'Moving Dangerously: Mobility and the Modern Woman.' *Tulsa Studies in Women's Literature* 20.1 (2001): 77–92.

Parsons, Deborah. *Streetwalking the Metropolis: Women, the City and Modernity*. Oxford: Oxford UP, 2000.

Pepper, Terence. 'The Portrait Photograph in the Modern Age.' In *Vanity Fair Portraits: Photographs 1913–2008*. By David Friend, Christopher Hitchens and Terence Pepper. London: National Portrait Gallery, 2008. 18–37.

Peterson, Theodore. *Magazines in the Twentieth Century*. Urbana: U of Illinois P, 1964.

Pick, Daniel. *Faces of Degeneration: A European Disorder, c. 1848–1918*. Cambridge: Cambridge UP, 1993.

Professor, The. 'Limitations of Intellectuals.' *The New Yorker* (11 April 1925): 19–20.

Proust, Marcel. *Remembrance of Things Past*. Trans. C. K. Scott Moncrieff, Terence Kilmartin, and Andreas Mayor. New York: Vintage, 1982. Volume 3.

Radcliffe, Ann. *The Romance of the Forest*. 1791. Oxford: Oxford UP, 1986.

Radway, Janice. *A Feeling for Books: Book-of-the-Month Club, Literary Taste and Middle-Class Desire*. Chapel Hill: U of North Carolina P, 1997.

Raine, Craig. Afterword to *Lolita*. By Vladimir Nabokov. London: Penguin, 1995. 319–31.

Rainey, Lawrence. *Institutions of Modernism: Literary Elites and Public Culture*. New Haven, CT: Yale UP, 1999.

Roberts, Lewis C. 'Children's Fiction.' In *A Companion to the Victorian Novel*. Ed. Patrick Brantlinger and William B. Thesing. Oxford: Blackwell, 2002. 353–69.

Ross, Claire J. 'Putting Over a Prima Donna: Some Reflections on the Gentle Art of Press Agenting.' *Vanity Fair* 12.1 (Mar. 1919): 100, 102.

Rubin, Joan Shelley. *The Making of Middlebrow Culture*. Chapel Hill: U of North Carolina P, 1992.

Sagan, Françoise. *Bonjour Tristesse*. 1954. Paris: Juillard Poche, 1985.

Sagan, Françoise. *Bonjour Tristesse*. 1954. Trans. Irene Ash. 1955. Harmondsworth: Penguin, 1958.

Saki [H. H. Munro]. *The Penguin Complete Saki*. 1967. Harmondsworth: Penguin, 1982.

Sawallis, Pamela. 'Daisy Ashford: A Preliminary Checklist.' *Bulletin of Bibliography* 50 (1993): 255–62.

Scholes, Robert. *Paradoxy of Modernism*. New Haven, CT: Yale UP, 2005.

Scott, Clive. *The Spoken Image: Photography and Language*. London: Reaktion, 1999.

S. D. Letter to the *Saturday Review* (6 September 1919): 250.

Sedgwick, Eve Kosofsky. *The Epistemology of the Closet*. Berkeley, CA: U of California P, 1990.

Sheridan, Richard Brinsley. *The Critic*. 1779. London: Heinemann, 1905.

Sheridan, Richard Brinsley. *The School for Scandal*. 1777. Ed. F. W. Bateson. London: Ernest Benn, 1979.

Simmel, Georg. 'The Metropolis and Mental Life.' 1903. Trans. Edward Shils. 1948. Rpt in *The Blackwell City Reader*. Ed. Gary Bridge and Sophie Watson. 2002. 11–17.

Smollett, Tobias. *Travels Through France and Italy*. 1766. Ed. Frank Felsenstein. Oxford: World's Classics, 1981.

Sontag, Susan. 'Notes on Camp.' *Partisan Review* (Fall 1964): 515–30. Rpt in *Against Interpretation and Other Essays*. By Susan Sontag. London: Eyre and Spottiswoode, 1967. 275–92.

Spooner, Catherine. *Fashioning Gothic Bodies*. Manchester: Manchester UP, 2004.

St Clair, William. *The Reading Nation in the Romantic Period*. Cambridge: Cambridge UP, 2004.

Steele, Valerie. 'The Social and Political Significance of Macaroni Fashion.' *Costume: The Journal of the Costume Society* 19 (1985): 94–109.

Steiner, George. *Nostalgia for the Absolute*. 1974. Toronto: Anansi, 1997.

Stevenson, Randall. *The Last of England: The Oxford English Literary History Volume 12: 1960–2000*. Oxford: Oxford UP, 2005.

Stewart, Susan. *On Longing: Narratives of the Miniature, the Gigantic, the Souvenir, the Collection*. 1984. Durham, NC: Duke UP, 1996.

Stubbs, Michael. *Words and Phrases: Corpus Studies of Lexical Semantics*. Oxford: Blackwell, 2001.

Swartz, Omar. Review of *Sophistication: Rhetoric and the Rise of Self-Consciousness* by Mark Backman. *Rhetoric Review* 12.1 (Autumn 1993): 214–18.

Sweeney, Kevin W. 'Alice's Discriminating Palate.' *Philosophy and Literature* 23.1 (1999): 17–31.

Swinnerton, Frank. *The Georgian Literary Scene, 1910–1935*. 1935. Rev. edn. London: Hutchison, 1969.

Tinkler, Penny. *Smoke Signals: Women, Smoking and Visual Culture in Britain*. Oxford: Berg, 2006.

Todd, Janet. *Sensibility: An Introduction*. London: Methuen, 1986.

Tratner, Michael. *Modernism and Mass Politics: Joyce, Woolf, Eliot, Yeats*. Palo Alto, CA: Stanford UP, 1995.

Trollope, Fanny. *Domestic Manners of the Americans*. 1832; rev. edn 1839. Ed. Richard Mullen. Oxford: Oxford UP, 1984.

Truss, Lynne. Introduction to *Cold Comfort Farm*. By Stella Gibbons. Harmondsworth: Penguin, 2006. vii–xix.

Twycross-Martin, Henrietta. Introduction to *Miss Pettigrew Lives for a Day* by Winifred Watson. London: Persephone, 2000. v–xii.

Twycross-Martin, Henrietta. 'Watson, Winifred 1906–2002.' In Hammill, Miskimmin and Sponenberg. 267–68.

Tynan, Kenneth. 'A Tribute to Mr Coward.' 1953. Rpt in *Tynan on Theatre*. Harmondsworth: Penguin, 1964. 286–87.

Urmson, J. O. 'Sophists.' In *The Concise Encyclopedia of Western Philosophy*. Ed. J. O. Urmson and Jonathan Rée. Third edn. London: Routledge, 2005. 361–62.

Veblen, Thorstein. *The Theory of the Leisure Class*. 1899. Ed. Martha Banta. Oxford: Oxford UP, 2007.

Vermilye, Wayne Van R. [James Thurber]. 'Answers-to-Hard-Questions Department.'

The New Yorker 6.24 (2 August 1930): 17–18.

Vicinus, Martha. *Independent Women: Work and Community for Single Women 1850–1920*. London: Virago, 1985.

Visconti, Luchino, dir. *Il Gattopardo (The Leopard)*. 1963. Twentieth Century Fox Home Entertainment, 2004.

Vogtherr, Christoph Martin. 'New Beginnings in French Genre Painting: de Troy, Chardin, Boucher.' In *Boucher and Chardin: Masters of Modern Manners*. Ed. Anne Dulau. Glasgow and London: University of Glasgow and Paul Holberton Publishing, 2008. 26–49.

Watson, Winifred. *Miss Pettigrew Lives for a Day*. 1938. London: Persephone, 2000.

Waugh, Evelyn. *Put Out More Flags*. 1942. Harmondsworth: Penguin, 1943.

Weisbuch, Robert. 'Winterbourne and the Doom of Manhood in *Daisy Miller*'. In *New Essays on Daisy Miller and The Turn of the Screw*. Ed. Vivian R. Pollak. Cambridge: Cambridge UP, 1993. 65–89.

Wells, Helen [Dorothy Parker]. 'The Autobiography of Any Movie Actress, Set Down in the Regulation Manner.' *Vanity Fair* 13.6 (Sept. 1919): 33, 110.

Whalen, Mark. *Race, Manhood, and Modernism in America: The Short Story Cycles of Sherwood Anderson and Jean Toomer*. Knoxville: U of Tennessee P, 2007.

Wharton, Edith. *The Age of Innocence*. 1920. Ed. Michael Nowlin. Peterborough, ON: Broadview, 2002.

Wharton, Edith. *A Backward Glance*. New York: D. Appleton-Century, 1934.

White, T. H. *The Age of Scandal: An Excursion Through a Minor Period*. 1950. Penguin, 1962.

Wilde, Dorian. *The Picture of Dorian Gray*. Ed. Isobel Murray. London: Oxford UP, 1974.

Wilde, Oscar. *A Woman of No Importance*. 1894. In *The Importance of Being Earnest and Other Plays*. Ed. Peter Raby. Oxford: Oxford UP, 1998. 93–158.

Williams, Raymond. *The Country and the City*. 1973. London: Hogarth, 1975.

Williams, Raymond. *Keywords. A Vocabulary of Culture and Society*. 1976. Second edn. New York: Oxford UP, 1983.

Woolf, Virginia. *The Moment, and Other Essays*. 1947. New York: Harcourt Brace, 1948.

Wordsworth, William. Preface to the 1800 edition of *Lyrical Ballads*. Rpt in *Lyrical Ballads*. By William Wordsworth. Ed. R. L. Brett and A. R. Jones. Second edn. London: Routledge, 1991. 241–72.

Wu, Duncan, ed. *New Writings of William Hazlitt*. Oxford: Oxford UP, 2007.

Yagoda, Ben. *About Town: The New Yorker and the World It Made*. Duckworth, 2000.

Index

Page references for illustrations are in italics; those for notes are followed by n

Index

Index

Index

Index